The Barakah Effect

MORE WITH LESS

The Barakah Effect

MORE WITH LESS

Mohammed Faris

CLARITAS BOOKS

1 2 3 4 5 6 7 8 9 10

CLARITAS BOOKS

Bernard Street, Swansea, United Kingdom
Milpitas, California, United States

CLARITAS
BOOKS

First Published in January 2024

Typeset in Whitney 16/12
Illustrations by Aneesah Satriya
Barakah Logo by Soraya Syed of Inspiral Design
Barakah Logo is a trademark of the Productive Muslim Company

The Barakah Effect: More With Less
by Mohammed A. Faris

Series Editor
Sharif H. Banna

A CIP catalogue record for this book is available from the British Library

ISBN: 978-1-80011-006-9

بسم الله الرحمن الرحيم

Bismillah.
Start every action with **sincere intention,** and ask Allah for help. Life is not about you, it's about **serving your Lord** with excellence. **Thank Allah** for what you have, and seek His sustenance beautifully. Be like a **gardener**: focused, hardworking, gentle, and trust Allah with the results. **Cherish your parents**, and treat them with mercy and compassion. **Plant seeds** whose harvest will benefit generations to come. **Pray and persist** for your goals, until you achieve them or are guided to what's better. **Remember death often** to stay focused on what matters. Send abundant salawat upon **Prophet Muhammad** ﷺ.
Alhamdulillah.

Opening Supplication

In the name of Allah, Most Gracious, Most Merciful

Praise be to Allah, and Peace and Blessings
Be Upon Prophet Muhammad

I started writing this book the morning of Arafat in the year 1441 Hijri, asking Allah to infuse the Barakah of this blessed day on this book and whoever reads it and acts upon it until the Day of Judgement.

Ameen.

Author Bio

Mohammed Faris is a globally recognised executive coach, author, and speaker, known for his unique approach to intertwining spirituality with personal and professional development. Born in Tanzania and of Yemeni descent, his multicultural experiences fuel his insight into the global issues confronting the *ummah*.

As the founder of The Productive Muslim Company, Mohammed has committed his life to empowering individuals and teams to achieve their best - spiritually, physically, and socially. His best-selling book, *The Productive Muslim: Where Faith Meets Productivity*, remains a cornerstone in Muslim self-help.

Mohammed has shared his insights at seminars and workshops across 15 countries, on the TEDx stage, and at Fortune 500 companies & major Islamic organisations, including Google, American Airlines, Salesforce, Texas Instruments, Accenture, and the Islamic Development Bank.

Recognised among the World's 500 Most Influential Muslims in 2014, he received the Dubai Government's Islamic Economy Award in 2016 for his contribution to the Global Islamic Economy in the media category.

When he's not revolutionising the way professionals operate, Mohammed enjoys running, cycling, baking, and cherishing moments with his family. His latest book, *The Barakah Effect*, is a testament to his dynamic career and personal journey, and promises to provide further insight into his unique perspective on faith, productivity, and personal development.

Contents

Introduction

In 1974, Shakour AbuGhazalah had a dream: to open a restaurant in the city of Jeddah, Saudi Arabia that offers high-quality, affordable meals in a clean, inviting environment. Putting all his hard-earned savings into this venture, he opened a high-quality deep-fried chicken restaurant called 'Broast' at a prominent location in the city. Unfortunately, his restaurant struggled during its first two years of operation, and in 1976, Shakour lost a battle with cancer and died at the age of 48.

His two sons, Ihsaan and Rami, took over the business and were determined to make their father's dream a reality. This was no easy task. As Ihsaan put it, "With the demise of our father, we lost the agency rights and had to start from scratch. We had to liquidate assets, pay off debts, streamline the business and reduce costs". Moreover, the competition was growing fast. "By the time I took over the business, over 400 copycat restaurants were serving 'broast' chicken in Jeddah alone. We had to find something that would set us apart," said Ihsaan. With sincerity and hard work, they turned this fledgling restaurant into one of the most beloved fried-chicken chains in Saudi Arabia, known as Al-Baik.

If you've been to *umrah* or *hajj*, you will have fond memories of Al-Baik: the spicy crispy chicken nuggets, the secret garlic sauce, and you'll also remember the long lines you had to wait in to get your order. You might have wondered: what is the secret to Al-Baik's success? No matter what time of day it is, Al-Baik restaurants are busy.

If you ask a management consultant to analyse Al-Baik's success, they might attribute this to the chain's winning recipes, branding strategy, or choice of locations. Yet all these factors do not add up, especially since much larger competitors with multi-million-dollar budgets located right next to Al-Baik branches don't enjoy similar levels of success (sorry KFC!).

When researching this story, I discovered what I believe is the secret of Al-Baik's success. A secret that goes beyond the recipes, branding, and business model. A spiritual secret to success linked to a small act started by its founder.

When Shakour Abu Ghazalah opened his restaurant, he set one simple rule: for every fried chicken he sells, he'll donate one riyal to charity. And he never broke that rule, even when his restaurant performed poorly in its early years. When he passed away and his sons took over the business, they honoured their father's legacy and continued with this tradition, making charitable donations part of Al-Baik's business model.

Why would a restaurant owner give money to charity when the business is struggling? It may not have made sense on paper, but Shakour and his sons knew that a business is a means to a greater purpose. Owning a business is not a selfish endeavour; for a business to be truly successful, it needs to tap into something beyond a 'common-sense' business strategy. It needs to tap into the Barakah Effect.

As a young East African boy with Yemeni roots, I often heard the word 'Barakah' from my elders, but I never quite understood its meaning. Like many Muslims, my basic understanding of Barakah is that it's a good thing, and you should pray for it. Yet I needed to figure out how it worked or how to tap into it.

When I got my first job, people prayed for Barakah in my new job. People prayed for Barakah in my car when I bought my first one. When I got married, people repeated a Prophetic *dua* (supplication): "*Barak Allahu laka wa baraka alaik, wa jama'a bainakuma fi khair*". May Allah place Barakah for you, place Barakah upon you, and bring goodness between you and your spouse (TIRMIDHI). And with every newborn I was blessed with, family and friends would make *dua* for Barakah in my children.

In 2007, while studying at the University of Bristol, UK, I started a blog called 'The Productive Muslim'. The purpose of the blog was to connect Islamic concepts to productivity science. It was around this time that I stumbled across the following *hadith* (saying) of Prophet Muhammad ﷺ: "O Allah, put Barakah for my nation in the early hours" (ABU DAWUD). Three things excited me about this *hadith*, which led to my obsession with Barakah:

1. **The Prophet Muhammad ﷺ specifically asked God for Barakah for his nation** – so Barakah must be important

for the *ummah*.

2. **The Prophet ﷺ requested Barakah to be attached to a specific time** - the early hours - which many productivity experts recommend as the best time to get things done.
3. The narrator of this *hadith* – Sakhr Bin Wada'ah – started sending his merchandise to the market early in the morning and **became wealthy as a result,** thereby making a spiritually intelligent business decision to experience Barakah in his business.

I started digging into the Quran, Prophetic sayings, and our Islamic history to learn more about Barakah and how one can attract Barakah in their life. Whenever I came across a talk or class on Barakah, I took careful notes and added them to my research. A friend who knew about my obsession with Barakah recommended a book written 700 years ago by Imam Al-Hubaishi on the concept.

Slowly but surely, I started piecing together a body of knowledge on Barakah and connecting it to our modern lives.

Some of my early articles on this topic, such as the '18 Sources of Barakah' and 'Barakah Culture vs Hustle Culture', became a reference on the subject of Barakah in the English language, quoted by scholars and imams during Friday sermons and taught in Islamic schools worldwide. Other works, such as the Barakah Journal (see BarakahJournal.com), which we launched in Rajab 1442 (Feb 2021), were met with such enthusiasm that I knew this was a concept that many were seeking to understand and were trying to figure out how to attract.

After migrating to the US, I started conducting workshops on 'The Barakah Effect' with Muslim professional associations and faith-based employee resource groups at Fortune 500 companies, including Google, American Airlines, Salesforce, American Express, Texas Instruments, Accenture, and PWC. The feedback was loud and clear: we need Barakah in our personal and professional lives.

In 2017, I gave a keynote address on the concept of Barakah at the World Domination Summit in Portland, Oregon, in front of 1500 non-Muslim entrepreneurs, authors, and artists. I was overwhelmed by the positive response I received and how the topic of Barakah resonated with Muslim and non-Muslim audiences alike.

This book is the culmination of my years of research and teaching on Barakah. It's divided into two parts:

- **Part one** aims to understand what Barakah is, what it isn't, and how to measure it. It'll also address why most of us feel like we have lost Barakah in our volatile, uncertain, and fast changing world.
- **Part two** will delve into the Barakah Culture Manifesto, each chapter exploring an element of the manifesto and how it brings Barakah to our lives.

Throughout the book, I'll combine traditional Islamic knowledge with modern-day research, practical tips, and stories to make Barakah an actionable and tangible concept for you to live by *inshaAllah*.

I HAVE SEVEN INTENTIONS FOR WRITING THIS BOOK

1. To write a book about Barakah that pleases God and calls people to a spiritual way of living.
2. To fight the Hustle Culture approach to productivity that distracts people from their true purpose in life.
3. To reconnect the Muslim world to their forgotten heritage of Barakah Culture.
4. To make the concept of Barakah easy to understand and accessible with practical examples and frameworks.
5. To encourage professionals and organisations to adopt Barakah Culture in their personal and professional settings.
6. To popularise the concept of Barakah to Muslims and non-Muslims.
7. To be a form of beneficial knowledge accepted as *sadaqa jariya* (ongoing charity) after I die.

I ask Allah to make the above intentions sincere for Him and accept this book from me despite its shortcomings.

Finally, Barakah is a deep and infinite concept since it's connected to the Divine, and no human book can fully comprehend its whole meaning and impact. This is a small attempt to share what I have discovered about Barakah over the years. It'll spark your interest to seek Barakah more intentionally and find practical ways to integrate it into your personal and professional life.

BY READING THIS BOOK, YOU WILL BE ABLE TO

1. Understand the concept of Barakah and its vast application in life and business.
2. Apply the Barakah Culture Manifesto and framework to your personal and professional life.
3. Develop practical routines and processes to embed Barakah Culture in your daily life.

Let's get started. *Bismillah ala Barakatillah (In the name of God, and with His Barakah).*

PART

01

Understanding Barakah

CHAPTER ONE

What is Barakah?

Once, a righteous poor man had a dream in which two men asked if he wanted the hidden treasure of 1,000 dinars beneath a tree. He inquired, "Is there Barakah in them?" When they said no, he declined the offer, saying he didn't need them. The next evening, the two men reappeared in his dream, now offering the remaining 500 dinars under the tree. Again, he asked about Barakah, and when they told him there was none, he turned down their offer.

This pattern continued for several nights, with the treasure's amount decreasing each time. Finally, the two men asked if he wanted the last two dinars left under the tree. As before, he questioned: "Is there Barakah in them?" This time, they said yes. Eagerly, he asked for the treasure's location. The next morning, he went to the spot shown in his dream and discovered the two dinars.

With the two blessed dinars in hand, he went to the market and bought a fish to take home. Upon cutting it open, he found a precious jewel inside the fish's belly, worth thousands of dinars.

Barakah is often translated as blessing, yet the term fails to encapsulate the entirety of its profound meaning.

Barakah is an enigmatic concept - it's like trying to describe the taste of honey to someone who has never tried it.

To attempt and define Barakah, we must construct a web of meaning that illustrates its essence. Over the years, I've collected various definitions of Barakah from scholars, experts, books and interviews, each of which offered unique insights that helped me construct a comprehensible definition.

BELOW ARE THE DEFINITIONS I'VE COME ACROSS

1. Imam Al-Raghib Al-Asfahani, an 11th-century scholar, saw Barakah as "the attachment of Divine Goodness to a thing".
2. The 13th-century scholar Ibn Al-Qayyim defined Barakah as the "abundance and permanence of goodness".
3. Dr. Samir Mahmoud, the Academic Director of Usul Academy, described it as "a spiritual energy or force emanating from Allah that enters people, places, and objects, transforming them into conduits or vehicles for this divine energy".

4. Dr. Tamara Gray, founder of Rabata.org, referred to Barakah as a "spiritual force that brings increase to a person's life without a defined input".
5. Dr. Abdallah Rothman, a professor in Islamic Psychology, characterised Barakah as "an abundant flowing positive energy resulting from alignment with Allah".
6. Dr. Khalil Abdur-Rashid, a lecturer at Harvard Divinity School and the first Muslim Chaplain at Harvard University, identified Barakah as "a mystical experience - a form of communication from Allah".

From these definitions, we can synthesise a broader understanding of Barakah that can be divided into **four parts:**

1. The Divine Nature of Barakah

Barakah is from Allah. It is a gift from the Divine to whomever and whatever He wills. When we say to someone "*Barakah Allah feek*" we are expressing our desire for Allah to infuse Barakah in that person.

Allah described himself as the source of Barakah in the Quran: "Blessed is the One in Whose Hands rests all authority. And He is Most Capable of everything" (QURAN 67:1). Imam Ibn Al-Qayyim, commenting on this verse, said:

> "All Barakah belongs to Him, the Most High, and from Him since He is the *Mubarak* (Blessed). Whoever Allah bestows His Barakah on is blessed. That is why His Book is blessed, His House is blessed, and the times

and places that He honoured and distinguished from others are blessed."

This understanding that Barakah is from Allah and He can place it in whomever and whatever He wants, inspires hope that we too can be recipients of Barakah. By seeking His Grace and Mercy, and purifying ourselves to become sincere vessels of Barakah, we can have Barakah in our lives too.

2. The Divine Placement of Barakah

Allah infuses His Barakah within various aspects of our world, creating a spiritual connection to our physical existence. Think of Barakah as the spiritual attachment to our physical realm. And it can attach itself to anything - tangible or non-tangible - your time, wealth, children, devices, home, relationships, career etc. These things become conduits or vehicles of Barakah, whether or not we recognise their presence. Here are some examples from the Quran illustrating where Allah places His Barakah:

	Evidence from Quran and Sunnah
Barakah in Places	*The Barakah of Masjid Al-Aqsa and its surroundings* Glory to Him who made His servant travel by night from the sacred place of worship to the furthest place of worship, **whose surroundings We have blessed,** to show him some of Our signs: He alone is the All Hearing, the All Seeing. (QURAN 17:1)

Barakah in People	**Barakah of Prophets** ▪ *Prophet Ibrahim and his son Ishaq* And blessed him and Isaac too: some of their offspring were good, but some clearly wronged themselves. (QURAN 37:113) ▪ *Prophet Eesa* Made me blessed wherever I may be. He commanded me to pray, to give alms as long as I live. (QURAN 19:31)
Barakah in Having Faith and God-consciousness	If the people of those towns had believed and been mindful of God, We would have showered them with blessings from the heavens and earth, but they rejected the truth and so We punished them for their misdeeds. (QURAN 7:96)
Barakah in Time	It was narrated from Ibn Umar that the Messenger of Allah ﷺ said: "O Allah, bless my nation early in the morning". (IBN MAJAH)
Barakah in the Quran	This, too, is a blessed Scripture which We have sent down- follow it and be conscious of your Lord, so that you may receive mercy. (QURAN 6:155)

Barakah can be placed in very specific places or things. You might find Barakah in one aspect of your life and not in others. This explains the statement of Umar Bin Al-Khattab: "Whoever sees Barakah in something, let him stick to it". For example, you might find Barakah in a specific trade, career, house or even a car. And if you do, stick to it, and don't turn away and lose it.

"A sign that it is God who has put you in a certain state is that He keeps you in it while its fruits mature."

IBN ATA'ILLAH

3. The Barakah Effect

In the words of Sh. Mutwalli Al-Sha'rawi, a famous 20th century Quran scholar: "Barakah is a divine soldier of the soldiers of Allah. He sends it to support whomever He wills. When it enters wealth, it increases it. When it enters children, it nurtures them. When it enters the body, it strengthens it. When it enters time, it fills it with what is beneficial. When it enters the heart, it makes it happy."

When Barakah enters a thing, a spiritual multiplier effect takes place that brings superabundance, prosperity, positivity, happiness, permanence, and continuity that touches all who encounter it. For example, if you've ever been to the Prophet's Mosque in Medina, you'll experience a special feeling of tranquillity in that place - a consequence of the Prophet's supplication that said: "O Allah! Bestow on Medina twice the Barakah You bestowed on Mecca." (BUKHARI)

This is the toughest part to wrap our heads around because Barakah transcends logical explanation, as it exists beyond the cause-and-effect realm we inhabit.

We often struggle to accept that Allah, the Creator of the laws governing cause and effect, can alter these very laws as He pleases. For example, we may donate to charity, believing our money to be lost, yet the Barakah in our remaining funds amplifies its value beyond what was given away. As it's often said, "We believe in God, but we don't believe God".

Have you ever found yourself hosting more guests than anticipated and fearing that the food won't be enough? Miraculously, not only is there enough food, but there are leftovers too! That is the power of Barakah. Or perhaps you have experienced heightened productivity in the early morning hours, accomplishing in mere minutes what would take hours at the office. Again, this is Barakah.

WHEN BARAKAH INFUSES YOUR LIFE, YOU'LL START EXPERIENCING THE FOLLOWING

1. Time seems to expand, allowing you to achieve more.
2. Even small amounts of food leave you feeling sated.
3. Your money and wealth stretch further than anticipated and benefit many.
4. Small efforts and projects you start lead to big lasting results.
5. You thrive despite difficulties and challenges in your life.

CONVERSELY, WHEN BARAKAH IS ABSENT, ONE EXPERIENCES

1. A constant state of hurry, stress and dwindling time.
2. A spacious home that feels cramped and tense.
3. Fruitless endeavours despite abundant resources.
4. A successful career or business that brings emptiness and discontent.

Barakah flips the script on material gain in life: something little with Barakah is better than something abundant without Barakah. Prophet Yusuf had 11 brothers, yet they all turned against him and tried to kill him. On the other hand, Musa had one brother who became a Prophet and supported him in his mission.

Barakah can also enter something that is already abundant and further increase the benefit and impact. For example, Prophet Suleiman was a wealthy Prophet and he prayed to Allah to give him all the Kingdom of the Earth. Allah granted that Kingdom along with the Barakah to use that Power to serve His message on earth.

In essence, Barakah is more with less.

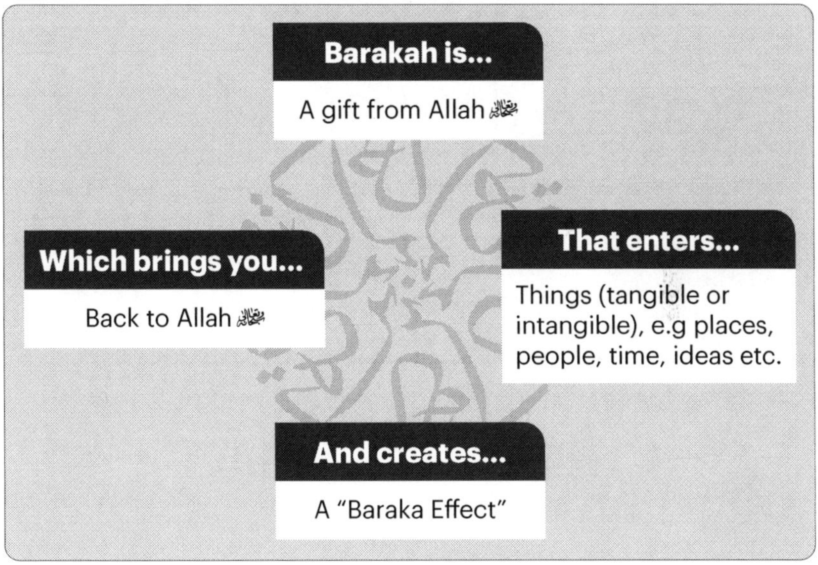

"He who has been blessed in life attains, in a short time, to such gifts from God that no expression or symbolic allusion could describe."

IBN ATA'ILLAH

4. Barakah Leads You Back to Allah

In the end, the Barakah you encounter in life should bring you back to the Bestower of Barakah, Allah. Recognising that the abundance, prosperity, and happiness you experience are gifts from Allah and not from yourself, you use these blessings to draw closer to Him. If the blessings you enjoy take you away from Allah, then there is no Barakah in them. Imagine someone who purchases a new car and uses it to regularly visit the mosque and serve their community – that car possesses Barakah, and its Barakah increases as it is used in service to Allah. Contrast this with someone who buys a car but uses it to disobey Allah and visit places He dislikes – in this case, the car has no Barakah or may lose any Barakah it had due to the person's actions.

Therefore, even though sometimes you may see people who outwardly seem to enjoy a lot of Barakah yet the real test for them is whether those blessings help bring them closer to Allah. For instance, Pharaoh and Qarun were 'blessed' with power and wealth in a worldly sense. However, since these blessings lacked Barakah and were used to spread corruption on earth and harm Prophet Musa and his people, they eventually became a source of calamity and self-destruction for Pharaoh and his followers.

The Barakah Effect is the culmination of the above four steps taking place in various aspects in our lives. In summary: It's a **1) gift from Allah, 2) that enters something, 3) that leads to a special effect or abundance 4) and brings you closer to Allah.** It is the hidden and subtle element of success that boosts the impact, benefit, and longevity of something beyond your expectations.

What would life look like if you were to tap into Barakah more intentionally? What would happen if you experienced Barakah in your work, family, time, food, and even your smartphone?

In a world that constantly insists we need more and more to be happy, perhaps there is a way for us to experience life more fully with less through the power of Barakah[1].

The B Coefficient - A Mathematical Illustration of Barakah

Allow me to explain Barakah using an equation I developed as part of my work at The Productive Muslim Company.

To be productive and achieve anything in life, you need three components:

Energy x Focus x Time = Outcome

As humans, our energy, focus and time are finite. Therefore, our outcomes are inherently limited.

For example, imagine you want to write a book. Between your various roles and responsibilities, you have only 30 minutes a day for writing. Using the formula above, your time constraint is defined. Your challenge is to manage your limited energy and focus to complete the book within a reasonable time frame.

Now, let's add the Barakah element to the equation:

β(Energy) x β(Focus) x β(Time) = β(Outcome)

Here, Barakah is represented by the β coefficient, which is the gift from Allah that enhances your energy, focus, and time. It creates a spiritual multiplier effect that impacts your physical reality.

Returning to our example, let's say you decide to attract Barakah to your book project by waking up early – a practice known to bring Barakah to your time. You'll likely notice a few things:

1. You'll have <u>more energy and motivation</u> to write during the early hours.
2. You're more likely to <u>enter the 'zone,'</u> engage in deep thinking, and develop original insights.
3. The <u>output of your 30-minute</u> writing session in the early morning might produce the equivalent of 2-3 hours of writing during other parts of the day.

This is Barakah. Some of these benefits can be attributed to less distraction and increased willpower in the morning. However, some elements go beyond logical comprehension, such as having remarkably clear insights that set your book apart or the feeling that time 'expands' so you can accomplish more with less in those early hours.

Can you see the power of Barakah and its potential impact on your daily life?

If we maintain a narrow view of the world, understanding it only through the limited cause-and-effect physical realm, our achievements in life will be restricted. However, when we perceive the world through our spiritual hearts and genuinely believe in the concept of Barakah, life's possibilities become limitless, as we connect with the Source of Barakah: Allah, who can grant us outcomes beyond our wildest dreams.

How Do You Experience Barakah?

Abu Hurairah, a close companion of Prophet Muhammad ﷺ, once brought some dates to the Prophet, asking him to bless the dates with Barakah.

The Prophet prayed for Barakah and advised Abu Hurairah to store the dates in his bag without scattering them.

Astonishingly, Abu Hurairah was able to eat from the dates and share them with others for years, until the day Uthman was martyred – more than 35 years after the Prophet's passing (TIRMIDHI).

Such stories can be challenging to comprehend, as they encompass unseen elements. Additionally, we might assume that we lack Barakah in our lives if we don't encounter similar miraculous experiences.

However, I'm here to share that we all experience Barakah in one way or another. We just need to learn how to recognise and appreciate the Barakah in our lives.

Let's explore the question: "how do I know if I have Barakah in my life, and how do I experience it?" We can categorise Barakah into two primary forms:

1. Physical manifestations of Barakah
2. Unseen manifestations of Barakah

Let's examine these categories in greater detail.

1. Physical Manifestations of Barakah

A common perception of Barakah is observing material expansion or growth in areas such as business, family, wealth or time that surpasses expectations and defies logical explanation. This notion of Barakah stems from its linguistic meaning, which encompasses growth, increase and happiness.

The story of Al-Baik I shared earlier is a great example of Barakah in the physical realm. When Shakour AbuGhazalah founded his eatery and committed to donating one riyal to charity for each fried chicken sold, he never imagined that 20 years later, his restaurant would secure an exclusive contract to open a restaurant in Mina, serving fried chicken to millions of pilgrims, during the days of *hajj*.

But not all material manifestations of Barakah appear in the form of increase or growth. Sometimes the material manifestation appears in the form of stability or continuity like owning a house for a long period of time or being in a successful, lasting and stable marriage or career. As Ibn Al-Qayyim says, "The reality of Barakah is steadfastness, constancy, and stability". To understand this, we need to refer to two others linguistic meanings of Barakah.

a. Stability: Arabs would say "*Barakal Jamal,*" meaning the camel has knelt and stayed in a specific spot, symbolising stability and steadfastness.

In our volatile, uncertain, complex, and ambiguous (VUCA) world, finding stability and rootedness is an invaluable source of Barakah. Instead of being perpetually adrift, Barakah helps ground us in our wealth, relationships, and life, enabling us to concentrate on our primary purpose: being a true servant of Allah.

In Surah Fussilat, Allah says in the Quran:

> *He placed solid mountains on it, blessed it, measured out its varied provisions for all who seek them––all in four Days.* (QURAN 41:10)

Allah links the stability of a mountain with Barakah since stability fosters growth and progress in life. Imagine if you and your family changed cities every six months, how difficult it'd be for you to grow in your career or establish long lasting friendships.

b. Continuity: Another interpretation for Barakah is continuity. Arabs would say "*Barakat Al-Sama,*" meaning rain has fallen continuously without interruption. The metaphor conveys that sometimes Barakah can come in small drops of blessing, but when it's continuous, these small drops can lead to vegetation and blessing beyond one's expectation.

In the mosque near my home in Jeddah where I grew up, there were four neighbours who met every day after *fajr* prayer to read a *tafsir* (exegesis) of the Quran. They would spend no more than 10 minutes each morning reading and sharing reflections, and they've continued to do so for at least 10 years. I once heard one of them remark that through this continuous small effort, they completed countless books of *tafsir* they probably would never have found time to read on their own.

IN CONCLUSION, THERE ARE THREE WAYS TO GAUGE THE PHYSICAL MANIFESTATION OF BARAKAH IN YOUR LIFE

1. Witnessing material growth and increase beyond your expectations and efforts, and/or;
2. observing stability in your affairs, such as marriage, income, career and children and/or;
3. experiencing continuity in your activities, like an on-going project that might not be growing exponentially but continues consistently without stopping.

People will sometimes interpret these physical manifestations of Barakah as luck, especially by highly successful people. As Muslims, we must recognise this luck as divine gifts from the Most Merciful, or Barakah.

"So which of the favours of your Lord would you deny?"

QURAN 55:13

2. Unseen Manifestation of Barakah

Barakah may reveal itself in intangible, psychological and spiritual ways. For instance:

1. You **maintain energy and focus** on a project or task, even when faced with challenges.
2. You experience **a deep sense of inner peace,** calmness and tranquillity in your heart despite significant shocks or traumas (e.g., death, divorce, or serious illness).
3. You find **ease and facilitation in your affairs,** even when you believe the situation is difficult (e.g., a client unexpectedly selects your business proposal despite more qualified competitors).
4. You make decisions that appear insignificant initially but lead to **long-term positive outcomes** (e.g., attending a university that may not have been your top choice but ultimately meets your academic and career needs).
5. You receive **non-material *rizq*** (sustenance) in the form of ideas, supportive words, and creative inspiration from unexpected sources.

Recognising unseen manifestations of Barakah is crucial because someone may not display physical signs of Barakah—perhaps due to poverty or unfortunate circumstances—yet still experience intangible manifestations that make their life feel blessed compared to others. They may have inner peace, contentment, and a restful sleep at night.

> A king once passed by a poor servant sweeping the floors of his palace but he looked happy and content, singing whilst doing his job. The king told his vizier, "Look at this servant. He's poor, destitute, probably doesn't have enough to feed his family, yet he's so happy! And look at me - I'm a powerful, rich king, yet I'm so unhappy". The vizier said: "Your majesty - this poor servant never faced the ninety-nine problem". "What's the ninety-nine problem?" asked the king. "Your majesty, this evening, allow me to put a bag of coins in front of this servant's house. I'll label the bag '100 Gold Coins' but I will only put 99 gold coins inside it. And tomorrow you'll understand the 99 problem." The king agreed to the plan and the vizier placed the bag of coins at night. When the servant woke up and opened his door, he was ecstatic to see the bag of coins. He couldn't believe his eyes when he read the label '100 Gold Coins'. He quickly went inside his home and started counting, only to find 99 coins inside, instead of 100. At first, he thought it was a counting error – surely, with all his excitement, he must have forgotten one. He counted again - it was 99. He counted a third time - still 99. The poor servant became distressed and appeared sad and depressed throughout the day, asking himself: where is the last gold coin?

This story serves as a reminder that what we perceive as Barakah, such as a sudden increase in material wealth, can sometimes negatively affect our spiritual well-being and cause us to lose the peace and tranquillity we once enjoyed. It's not that the servant shouldn't have received the gold coins; rather, if he had been content with the 99 coins, and shared his newfound wealth, it could have become a source of even greater Barakah and blessings from Allah.

Experiencing Barakah in physical or unseen ways signifies a connection with Allah. Our lives are touched by the Divine, resulting in growth, continuity, stability, and tranquillity that cannot be explained in human terms.

CAN NON-MUSLIMS EXPERIENCE BARAKAH?

A common question that arises when discussing Barakah is whether non-Muslims can experience it. Based on research and consultation with various scholars, the answer appears to be yes, non-Muslims can experience Barakah. However, they may not fully experience the complete effect of Barakah, as it might not lead them back to the Bestower of Barakah, Allah (unless Allah guides them).

For instance, during the time of Prophet Muhammad ﷺ, the people of Mecca lived in one of the most blessed places on Earth and enjoyed abundant safety and provisions. They also had the most blessed man to ever live among them - Prophet Muhammad ﷺ. However, some disbelieved in the Prophet and even attacked him. While they benefited from the Barakah of safety and abundance in Mecca, this Barakah did not lead them back to Allah, and as a result, they didn't fully experience the Barakah of Mecca or the Prophet ﷺ.

Nevertheless, if a non-Muslim adopts the Barakah mindset, values, and rituals described in this book, they will experience some form of Barakah, regardless of their faith. For example, people from all backgrounds can experience the Barakah of waking up early, being honest in business, or giving to charity.

Personally, I find the concept of Barakah to be an excellent conversation starter with non-Muslim friends and colleagues, especially with People of the Book (Jews and Christians) who believe in God and the Hereafter. This could be a great topic for an inter-faith dialogue and a wonderful way to introduce people who are atheists or agnostic to the reality of a spiritual life and help them recognise the Bestower of Barakah in their lives: Allah.

CHAPTER SUMMARY

- Barakah is a gift from Allah and can be placed in any aspect of our lives, tangible or intangible, such as time, wealth, relationships, and more.
- The Barakah Effect is a spiritual multiplier effect, leading to increased abundance, prosperity, and happiness in one's life. It goes beyond logic and cause-effect relationships, showing Allah's ability to alter these laws as He pleases.
- When Barakah is present in one's life, it leads to positive outcomes such as expanded time, increased satisfaction with limited resources, and thriving in the face of challenges. Conversely, when Barakah is absent, one experiences stress, emptiness, and discontent.
- Physical manifestations of Barakah can include material growth, stability in various aspects of life, or continuity in activities, while unseen manifestations can involve inner peace, ease, and non-material support.

CHAPTER TWO

How We Lost Barakah

"The Hour will not be established until time passes rapidly, such that a year is like a month, a month is like a week, a week is like a day, a day is like an hour, and an hour is like the flicker of a flame."

PROPHET MUHAMMAD ﷺ

It is a common complaint among many people that Barakah is missing from various aspects of their lives, including time, wealth, children, and work.

It seems that despite the tremendous technological progress we have made as a society, we are lacking in Barakah.

Even something as seemingly simple as writing highlights this issue. Despite our modern conveniences such as fast typing speeds, the most prolific modern authors cannot compare to the Islamic predecessors who were able to handwrite 50-150 pages a day!

In this chapter, I will explore the question of how we have lost Barakah from two perspectives: a macro (societal) perspective and a micro/individual perspective. By doing so, we can gain better understanding of why Barakah is missing in our world today.

The Macro Perspective: How Materialism Sapped Barakah from Our Lives

Three friends decided to invest in a date farm together. Two of them had day jobs while the third was a freelancer, which gave him more time to take care of the farm. The farm was located in an area with many poor and needy people who would often visit it and ask for dates.

The friend who was tending to the farm felt a sense of empathy for the needy visitors and started giving away some of the dates. However, his two working friends were not pleased when they noticed that the production of dates seemed to decrease. They asked him about it, and he explained that he had been giving charity to the needy visitors.

The two friends were furious and told him to stop giving away any dates from the farm until harvest season came. This was a difficult request for the friend tending to the farm as he saw the desperate condition of his neighbours, so the three friends decided to divide the farm into thirds, with each of them respon-

sible for one-third of the farm. They agreed that the friend who was tending to the farm could give away dates only from his portion of the farm.

A year passed, and it was time for the harvest season. The friends gathered to weigh the dates from all the palm trees, and they were surprised to find that the harvest from the one-third of the land belonging to the friend who was giving charity was twice as much as the dates coming from the other two-thirds. It was clear that Barakah entered the portion of the generous friend but was lost from the portion of the others who withheld their dates.

Spirituality today is largely divorced from daily life and cornered into private spaces and houses of worship.

The modern lifestyle with its myopic view of the world - only focusing on the material realm and ignoring the spiritual realm - has left no space for us to observe or experience Barakah in our daily lives.

Many of us who grew up in contemporary societies with globalised economies become so dazzled by the technological advancement of our modern times that we actively turn a blind eye to the spiritual, psychological, and moral decay happening in society.

It's hard to believe, but we live in an unprecedented time where the roots of spirituality and faith have been upended from society. Life has become devoid of Barakah because we've stopped believing in the potentiality of the unseen and its impact on our physical world.

The question is: how did we get here?

For centuries, spirituality and faith played an active and central role in people's lives, organising how they think, what they believe, and their lifestyle choices. Concepts such as Barakah were common knowledge across Muslim societies and actively sought in someone's business, marriage, and lifestyle.

The shift towards materialism and the disregard for spirituality started in the Western world in the early modern era. During the Industrial Revolution, powerful technological advancements gave rise to a culture that values the material realm above all else. This shift towards materialism coincided with the Enlightenment, a period when philosophers sought to free man from the 'shackles' of religion and tradition.

When Europeans started traveling to the Islamic world (first as traders and technical or military advisors, then as colonists), Muslims were bedazzled by the machine-made advancements that Europeans brought with them. Muslim societies wanted to play catchup.

In her fascinating book, *Inventing Laziness: The Culture of Productivity in Late Ottoman Society*, Dr. Melis Hafez traces how moralists and religious leaders in 19th century Ottoman society, engaged in a concerted effort to convince the public to let go of old ideals of life such as self-sustainability, contentment, and *tawakkul* (reliance on Allah) to adopt far more aggressive ideas of wealth and profit that were needed to advance the Ottoman economy and help it "catch up" with the growing material and military power of Europe.

Unfortunately, in the process of "catching up" with the Europeans, we restructured our lives from the Barakah lifestyle we enjoyed for centuries and drastically changed the way we live our lives:

- We have become **estranged from rural life** and instead have confined ourselves within concrete cities, causing us to lose our connection with nature and the profound knowledge that comes with understanding the natural life cycle of plants, trees, animals, as well as celestial bodies such as the stars, moon, and the sun - all of which are essential elements that help us appreciate the Barakah in Allah's creation.
- We organised our time **around the mechanical clock and the 9-5 job, instead of prayer times,** hence we have become less connected with sacred times. This shift has resulted in a disconnection from the spiritual rhythm of daily life and a decrease in the importance of the five daily prayers as an organising force in Muslim societies.
- We organised our months and years **according to the Gregorian calendar** and have forsaken the Islamic lunar calendar (a divinely inspired calendar) as a secondary calendar, even though for 15 centuries, the Islamic calendar was the primary calendar used across the Muslim world.[2]
- **We turned our backs on the Barakah** that comes from living

in multigenerational homes with our parents and grandparents, and instead chased economic opportunities in distant lands. This shift in societal norms was paired with a hefty dose of individualism, leading us to prefer living in nuclear families consisting of a father, mother, two children, and a pet over living with extended relatives.

- We restructured our **education system to follow the model of the ex-colonisers** like the Americans, British, and the French which are heavily materially driven. Sadly, this shift in focus came at a great cost as we began to undervalue the significance of seeking spiritual knowledge. Rather than cultivating the spiritual growth of our youth, we prioritised academic success, believing that the pursuit of spiritual knowledge was a hindrance to academic success.
- We've been conditioned to believe that **our worth and success are solely defined by our job titles and salary figures.** We've been taught to prioritise our careers over everything else in life and to view spiritual development as a pursuit for after retirement. We've been tricked into believing that true success lies in the corner office and that spirituality is an obstacle to our ambitions.
- We have **forgotten the value of resourcefulness and conservation.** We have embraced a wasteful, 'throw-away' culture, discarding food, goods, and products as quickly as we acquire them, disregarding the divine blessings that Allah has bestowed upon us.

We changed much in our lives - do you now wonder why we

lost Barakah?

> *Corruption has spread on land and sea as a result of what people's hands have done, so that Allah may cause them to taste 'the consequences of' some of their deeds and perhaps they might return 'to the Right Path'.* (QURAN 30:41)

Is Barakah Even Possible in Our Modern Lives?

As we reflect on the modern world and how it distracts us from the unseen world, it's easy to feel overwhelmed and ask: is seeking Barakah even possible in our modern society? The answer is a resounding yes and this book will help explain how.

BUT FIRST, WE NEED TWO THINGS TO START THIS JOURNEY

- **An abundance of hope:** No matter how desperate the situation may seem, and how distant we are from a spiritually aligned life, we must constantly hold onto hope in Allah's forgiveness and mercy. As He says in the Quran: "O My servants who have gone to extremes against themselves: despair not of Allah's mercy, for indeed Allah forgives all misdeeds; indeed, He is the Oft-Forgiving, the Bestower of mercy." (QURAN: 39:53)

- **An abundance of confidence:** Hope alone is not enough. We must also have an abundance of confidence in our faith and in our ability to re-engineer modern life in line with the teachings of Prophet Muhammad ﷺ. We need to firmly believe that Islam has more to offer the world than to take, and we need to find the confidence to breathe spirituality back into the modern world and not feel ashamed or embarrassed of our faith.

It may seem daunting, but as Allah says in the Quran: "...God will not change the state of a people until they change the state of their own souls" (QURAN, 13:11). We can't change society overnight, but we can change ourselves. And that is always the starting point. Let us have hope and confidence and let us bring Barakah back into our lives and the lives of those around us.

I want to share here a conversation that took place in 1897 between an Italian ambassador and a Moroccan merchant that captures the essence of the above changes. It was written from the perspective of the Italian ambassador who was trying to understand why the Moroccan merchant wasn't impressed with all of Europe's advancement:

> *Today I had a lively discussion with a merchant in Fez with a view to finding out about what the Moors think of European civilisation... He was a fine man, about forty years old, with an honest and serious face, who had made business visits to the most important cities in Western Europe and had lived a long time in Tang-*

ier, where he learnt Spanish...I asked him therefore what kind of impression the large cities of Europe had made on him...He looked hard at me and answered coldly: "Large streets, fine shops, beautiful palaces, good workshops, everything clean". He gave the impression that with these words, he had mentioned everything in our countries that was worthy of praise. "Have you not found anything else in Europe that is beautiful and good?" I asked. "Is it possible," I went on, 'that an intelligent man like you, who has visited several countries so marvelously superior to your own, can speak about them without astonishment, or at least without the emotion of a country boy who has seen the pasha's palace? What can you possibly admire in the world? What sort of people are you? Who can possibly understand you?" "Perdone Usted," he answered coldly, "it is for me to say that I cannot understand you. I have told you all the things which I consider to be better in Europe. What more can I say? Have I to say something that I do not believe to be true? I repeat that your streets are larger than ours, your shops finer, that you have workshops such as we do not have, and also rich palaces. That is all. I can only add one thing: that you know more than we do, because you have many books, and read more..."

I changed the subject, and referred to the comforts of European civilisation... "That is true," he replied. "A bit of sun? A sunshade! Rain? An umbrella! Dust? A pair of gloves! Walking? A walking-stick! Looking around? Eyeglasses! An excursion? A coach! Sitting down? A chair! Eating? Knives and forks! A scratch? A doctor! Death? A statue! You want for nothing! Are you really men? Por Dios, you are infants!" He even made fun of our architecture, when I spoke to him about the comfort of our houses. "What? Three hundred of you live in a single building, all on top of one another! You have to climb, climb, climb... There is no air, no light, and no garden!"... He changed the subject of the conversation, and suddenly said with a smile, looking me up and down from head to foot: "Mal vestidos (badly dressed)". I replied that dress was of no importance, but added that in this domain too he would surely acknowledge our superiority, for instead of idly sitting cross-legged for hours, we employed our time in thousands of useful or entertaining pursuits. To this he gave a more subtle answer than I had expected: it did not seem a good sign to him, he said, that we felt the need to do so many things in order to pass the time. Life itself must be torture for if we were unable to sit still for a single hour, without being killed by boredom and having to seek relief in some distraction or conversation. Were we afraid of ourselves? What was it that tormented us?...

I now spoke of the European industries, the railways,

> *the telegraph and all the great public works. He let me speak without interruption, and even nodded his head from time to time. But when I finished, he sighed and said: "All very well, but what use are these things when we all must die?" "In brief," I said, "you would not exchange your situation for ours?" He thought a little and then replied: "No, for you do not live longer than we do, you are not healthier, nor better, nor more pious, nor happier. Leave us then in peace. Do not wish that everyone should live as you do and be happy according to your lights".*
>
> *"So you believe", I said, "that you will always remain as you are, that we shall not gradually succeed in compelling you to change?" "I do not know," he replied, "you have the power; you will do what you will. But everything that has to happen is already written by God. And whatever it is that must happen, God will not forsake those who remain faithful to Him". With these words, he took my right hand, pressed it to his heart, and walked away majestically...*[3]

What I love about the above story is how the merchant from Fez - although acknowledges European technological and civilisation superiority at that time - has the dignity, contentment, and confidence of the Barakah lifestyle he was living. He understood that more doesn't necessarily mean better - and if Allah opens His gifts on a society, it doesn't mean that it's full of Barakah. He understood that what's important to seek in life is God's acceptance and His Barakah. We need this same confidence today.

The Micro Perspective: Hustle Culture – When Work Becomes Religion

"I wake up 5 o'clock in the morning to attend a conference call, but I can't wake up 5 o'clock to pray fajr". Fighting back tears, Hanna[4] revealed how work has completely absorbed her and is slowly killing her soul.

Like many young professional Muslims, Hanna grew up in a family that valued education and hard work. She was the model child who followed the script of life - the script that we all grew up with: study hard, work hard, get a good job, and enjoy life.

Yet at the height of her career, Hanna felt empty, lacking Barakah. Her body is tired, her mind in a fog, and her soul has been reduced to a tiny voice that every now and then tries to remind her that there's more to life than just work.

Hanna's story is not an anomaly. It's the story of many Muslim professionals who feel they've sold their soul to the 'corporate devil' in exchange for material comfort and success.

In the modern era, there has been a significant shift in society's priorities from valuing one's inner self and spiritual development to placing excessive importance on one's career and professional identity. As a consequence, concepts such as Barakah, which promote spiritual growth and connection with the divine, have been relegated to the sidelines, and the 'religion of work' has taken centre stage, promising wealth and status as the ultimate measures of success.

As columnist Derek Thompson points out in his article 'Workism is Making Americans Miserable' for The Atlantic, work has become more than just a means to economic production; it has become a new religion that promises identity, community, and purpose beyond the daily grind of life. This 'workism' culture has become so pervasive in our society that 95% of teens in a 2019 Pew Research study said that having a job or career they enjoy is extremely or very important to them as an adult, ranking higher than helping others in need or getting married.

To succeed in this new religion, followers are urged to adopt the 'Hustle Culture' narrative that glorifies constant work and busyness. This toxic productivity culture is celebrated on social media platforms with the hashtags #hustle and #hustleculture. Those who do not subscribe to this culture are often labelled as lazy or lacking ambition.

Unfortunately, this Hustle Culture hits women the hardest. Women are often forced to choose between their family responsibilities and the unrelenting demands of work. Many women have been taught from a young age that having a successful career is the ultimate measure of success. This can create an impossible choice, as Sylvia Ann Hewlett explains in her article for the Harvard Business Review, "At midlife, between a third and a half of all successful career women in the United States do not have children...for many women, the brutal demands of ambitious careers, the asymmetries of male-female relationships, and the difficulties of bearing children late in life conspire to crowd out the possibility of having children".

Muslim defenders of Hustle Culture would be quick to remind me that although work does occupy a big chunk of their time, they are still able to pray at work and wear the hijab and be good practicing Muslims. To that point, I'd counter with these questions:

- How many prayers did you miss because you're in the middle of a meeting or "doing important work?"
- How many times have you had to 'check-out' your faith at the entrance of work because it's "unprofessional" to talk about religion at work?
- How many times have you compromised your Islamic values - whether sitting at a gathering that's serving alcohol, agreeing to interest-bearing contracts, or interacting inappropriately with the opposite gender - all in the name of work?

To be clear, there's nothing wrong with work. Islam encourages work and being self-sufficient to provide for your family and support your community. However, when work becomes a religion on its own, competing with spirituality, family, health, and mental well-being, we need to pause and reflect.

Why Are We Addicted to Hustle Culture?

The Five Pillars of Hustle Culture

When the Covid-19 pandemic swept across the globe in 2020, it served as a wake-up call for many to re-evaluate the all-consuming nature of Hustle Culture. In the aftermath, numerous individuals chose not to return to pre-pandemic levels of toxic productivity, placing greater emphasis on family, mental, and physical well-being.

However, this shift was short-lived. As we now find ourselves facing a potential global recession and the disruptive impact of AI on white-collar jobs, people have reverted to the relentless hustle mentality.

Our addiction to Hustle Culture stems from five key pillars that underpin the modern world

1. Materialism
2. Individualism
3. Consumerism
4. Capitalism
5. Fear of Death

Let's explore these pillars briefly below:

PILLAR ONE: MATERIALISM

Materialism revolves around the belief that wealth and possessions hold the utmost importance in life, often resulting in an excessive focus on acquiring material goods and basing one's self-worth on financial success.

This mindset shifts our attention away from spirituality and Barakah, making us more fixated on material accomplishments and perpetuating our addiction to Hustle Culture.

Materialism has permeated every aspect of our lives, shaping decisions about our careers, living situations, and even who we marry.

Unfortunately, this outlook has also seeped into our spirituality as well. The Islamic counterpart of the "prosperity gospel," often preached among evangelical Christians, has infiltrated our belief system. Instead of praying, donating, and fasting solely for the sake of Allah, we engage in these acts with the expectation of tangible rewards. As a result, our relationship with Allah has become predominantly materialistic, as described in the Quran:

> *[The nature of] man is that, when his Lord tries him through honour and blessings, he says, 'My Lord has honoured me,' but when He tries him through the restriction of his provision, he says, 'My Lord has humiliated me.'*
>
> (QURAN 89:15-16)

The relentless pursuit of materialism can ultimately harm us by promoting selfishness, eroding moral values, and diminishing the significance of authentic connections and empathy—all of which contribute to the loss of Barakah in our lives.

Islam does not prohibit the enjoyment of material wealth. However, when materialism dictates how we assess ourselves, our relationships, and our spirituality, we lose sight of our true selves, and our true purpose in life: to worship Allah.

> *Neither wealth nor children will bring you nearer to Us, but those who believe and do good deeds will have multiple rewards for what they have done, and will live safely in the lofty dwellings of Paradise.* (QURAN 34:37)

PILLAR TWO: INDIVIDUALISM

As human beings, we each possess unique traits and needs, and a modest degree of individualism can be healthy as it fosters creativity and innovation. However, Hustle Culture capitalises on extreme individualism, celebrating the notion of the 'self-made' individual who, through sheer determination and personal effort, ascends from rags to riches. It glorifies those who work 80+ hour weeks and achieve great success.

We idolise stories of CEOs who dropped out of college, started companies in garages, and became billionaires before turning 30. Our aspirations revolve around becoming someone who 'changes the world' and leaves an indelible mark—even if it comes at the cost of broken family relationships and/or our relationship with God.

In Hustle Culture, individual dreams and passions eclipse the importance of spirituality, family, and community, which are often dismissed as mere distractions. This mindset breeds narcissism, with individuals expecting the universe to fulfil their material desires. When things don't go as planned, people either fall into depression, feeling like failures, or grow resentful, blaming society—or even God.

PILLAR THREE: CAPITALISM

There is a classic story of an American investment banker encountering a humble Mexican fisherman in a small coastal village. The fisherman led a content and fulfilling life, spending time with his family, friends, and pursuing leisurely activities. The banker, however, tried to convince him to invest his time and resources in expanding his fishing business, with the goal of selling the company and making millions:

> The Mexican fisherman asked: "But, how long will this all take?"
>
> To which the American replied" "15 – 20 years".
>
> "But what then?" asked the Mexican.
>
> The American laughed and said, "That's the best part. When the time is right you would announce an IPO and sell your company stock to the public and become very rich. You would make millions!"
>
> "Millions – then what?"
>
> The American said, "Then you would retire. Move to a small coastal fishing village where you would sleep late, fish a little, play with your kids, take siestas with your wife, stroll to the village in the evenings where you could sip wine and play your guitar with your amigos."

This story encapsulates the absurdity of the third pillar of Hustle Culture: capitalism. While it has driven considerable economic growth, capitalism has perpetuated the Hustle Culture's relentless pursuit of 'more' even when it may not align with our values or contribute to a fulfilling life.

In 1930, economist John Maynard Keynes predicted that within a century, people would work no more than 15 hours per week if economic growth continued. However, as we approach the 100-year mark, we find ourselves working harder than ever before. It seems that Keynes underestimated the insatiable desire for more money and success once our basic needs were met.

The intention here is not to undermine your ambitions or discourage you from striving for global success or becoming the next influential Muslim CEO. Rather, it is to encourage critical thinking about the narratives that pervade our lives, and to recognise the pitfalls of capitalism, which often tries to convince us that more is always better.

By reflecting on our true priorities and focusing on cultivating Barakah in our lives, we can resist the harmful influences of Hustle Culture and live a more meaningful and fulfilling life.

PILLAR FOUR: CONSUMERISM

Some people may not be seduced by the endless desire to grow in their business or careers, and they can be quite content with their day job and small shop. Yet, such people can still fall for the trap of Hustle Culture in one of its most prevalent forms: consumerism.

You buy a house and just about finish paying it off, and you think of buying a bigger house. You buy a car, and now your kids are older and you need to buy a second car. You buy a phone and within a year or two it becomes obsolete, and you need to upgrade. It never stops. Every time you reach a new income level and think that you have enough for yourself and your family, new expenses pop up that make you feel as poor and cash strapped as before, leaving you feeling like there's no Barakah in your life.

The trend to spend and 'shop 'til we drop' began after World War II. Malls are main centres of congregation and window-shopping a favourite pastime. Our holidays are organised around consumer-driven events starting with New Year's Eve, Valentine's Day, Mother's Day, Father's Day, Summer BBQ, Back-to-School, Halloween, Thanksgiving, and Christmas. Even Ramadan, Eid, and *hajj* didn't escape consumerism culture. Commercialisation of these Islamic months is at an all-time high across Muslim society. Add credit cards and easy payment plans to the mix, and the tentacles of consumer culture constantly strangle our wallets, keeping us in debt and submissive to Hustle Culture.

The impact of a consumer-driven society goes beyond just 'having more stuff'; many families cannot afford to live on a single-income anymore and both parents must work to simply keep up with the pace of spending (and for single-parents, this means taking two or three jobs just to pay the bills). Some of this is driven by necessity and need, but for many middle-income and upper-middle income families, it's driven by the constant drive to consume and 'keep up with the Joneses'. As one scholar noted, one of the anomalies of modern life is that the rich are choosing to work more instead of working less, an unprecedented phenomenon that's worth thinking about.

The stress of losing one's job is multiplied tenfold for families accustomed to a certain level of comfort. Young graduates take jobs they might not like, simply because it affords them a certain lifestyle. Senior professionals feel 'stuck' in their day job because of "golden handcuffs". Moreover, 'survival of the fittest' mindsets motivate someone to do whatever it takes (ethical or unethical) to hold their job.

What drives this consumer behaviour, even though we know intuitively that material possessions don't genuinely bring happiness? It's because Hustle Culture doesn't give us the time to truly live and fulfil our purpose in life. We attempt to buy our happiness with material items, even if only for a brief period. Additionally, we try to compensate for time spent away from our families by purchasing things for them. As a result, we feel stuck in a never-ending cycle, thinking that committing to Hustle Culture is the only way to maintain happiness and avoid being considered failures in life.

PILLAR FIVE: FEAR OF DEATH

At the core of materialism, consumerism, capitalism, and individualism lies a fundamental driving force: the fear of death.

When we feel that we have only one life to live, we try to pack it with as much tangible accomplishment and individual success as possible, hoping to avoid feeling empty at the end of our lives.

To cope with the natural fear of death, many of us rely on what psychologists call Terror Management Theory. In essence, we make irrational decisions that we may regret later in life. We believe that by working more, buying more, and chasing the mirage of success, we will feel more accomplished on our deathbeds. However, this is far from the truth.

When you ask people nearing the end of their lives about their biggest regrets, they seldom mention wishing they had spent more time in the office or bought more material possessions. Instead, they usually express regret for not preparing for death, performing more good deeds, and spending quality time with their family and friends.

As Allah says in the Quran: "Competition in [worldly] increase diverts you, until you go into your graves." (QURAN 102:1-2)

If consumerism and capitalism are the carrots that Hustle Culture dangles in front of us, then death is the stick used to keep us trapped in the rat race.

The Five Pillars of Islam – An Antidote to the Five Pillars of Hustle Culture

As Muslims, we must confront the reality that we have adopted Hustle Culture and allowed it to become the dominant force in our lives. We have failed to recognise how this lifestyle contributes to the loss of Barakah in our lives and the social and moral decay we experience in our communities.

If we genuinely believe that Islam is a complete way of life, always modern and relevant, we need to regain our confidence in its applicability to modern life and free our souls from Hustle Culture. To achieve this, we must first acknowledge that the five pillars of Islam serve as the most powerful antidotes to Hustle Culture:

The antidote to materialism lies in the first pillar of Islam: the *shahadah*. When we testify that there is no god worthy of worship except Allah and that Muhammad ﷺ is His messenger, we acknowledge that there is more to this world than the physical realm. We assert our belief in the Creator, Angels, Books of Revelations, the Prophets, and the Hereafter. We declare that a person's worth is not measured by their wealth, but by their relationship with Allah.

The antidote to individualism is found in the second pillar of Islam: *salah*. In our prayers, whether alone or in congregation, we recite Surah Al-Fatiha, the first chapter of the Quran, which begins with a communal prayer: "Guide us to the straight path". This connection with a spiritual community through prayer reminds us that we are first and foremost part of the *ummah* of Prophet Muhammad ﷺ, and our strength lies in our unity to serve our Lord.

To counter capitalism, we must remember the rights of the poor as we seek God's bounty. The third pillar of Islam, *zakat*, teaches us that the poor have a rightful share of at least 2.5% of our wealth, ensuring that wealth doesn't only circulate among the rich in society.

The antidote to consumerism lies in training ourselves to

say no to insatiable desires. The fourth pillar of Islam, *sawm* (fasting) during Ramadan, teaches us to curb our basic instincts and practice self-restraint from dawn until dusk for 29 or 30 days. Fasting in a consumer society that thrives on instant gratification is a blessing, as it cultivates discipline and the ability to embrace discomfort for a higher purpose.

The fifth pillar of Islam, *hajj*, addresses the fear of death by preparing us for the journey of death. *Hajj* serves as a dress rehearsal for Judgement Day and a reminder that instead of running away from death, we should face it with our good deeds and a sincere turning towards God.

The above discussion might seem philosophical, but understanding the worldview we are immersed in and recognising that combating Hustle Culture begins with internalising the five pillars of Islam in our lives is crucial.

In the next chapter, we will present an alternative lifestyle to Hustle Culture – one based on Barakah, called Barakah Culture.

CHAPTER SUMMARY

- Barakah is perceived to be missing in various aspects of modern life due to a shift towards materialism and a focus on the material realm at the expense of spiritual growth and connection with Allah.
- Societal changes in the Muslim world, including moving away from a fitrah (natural disposition) life, restructuring our education systems according to Western values, and prioritising career and material success, have contributed to the loss of Barakah.
- The Hustle Culture and workism promote constant work and busyness, often resulting in spiritual disconnection.
- Hustle Culture addiction arises from five pillars: materialism, individualism, consumerism, capitalism, and fear of death.
- The five pillars of Islam are the perfect antidote to the five pillars of Hustle Culture.

CHAPTER THREE

Barakah Culture: An Alternative to Hustle Culture

The life of this world is nothing but a game and a distraction; the Home in the Hereafter is best for those who are aware of God. Why will you [people] not understand? (QURAN 6:32)

For many years, alarm bells have been sounding against the pervasive Hustle Culture and its detrimental effect on our spiritual and mental health. This dark reality has ensnared us in our daily lives, causing us to trudge through each day like zombies in a video game, blindly seeking the next level up without considering where this lifestyle might lead us.

We often feel trapped in Hustle Culture, as though we can't escape it. However, Hustle Culture is much like a spider's web: intricate but ultimately fragile.

The parable of those who take protectors other than Allah is that of a spider spinning a shelter. And the flimsiest of all shelters is certainly that of a spider, if only they knew. (QURAN 29:41)

It's time for us to break free from the webs of Hustle Culture and recognise that there's more to life than relentless striving in pursuit of worldly gains.

While it's tempting to believe that the antidote to Hustle Culture is simply to 'un-hustle'—slow down, meditate, attend a retreat, downsize our homes, or embrace minimalism—these solutions, although helpful, only address the symptoms rather than the root cause. To truly dismantle Hustle Culture from our lives and organisations, we must adopt an entirely new worldview rooted in faith: Barakah Culture.

At its core, Barakah Culture posits that true increase or benefit comes from Allah and can be attained by aligning our body, mind, and soul with His intentions for our lives on Earth. This worldview encourages us to achieve more with less through Allah's blessings, rather than through sheer grit and an exhausting pursuit of material gain.

Barakah Culture is also about striking a balance—*mizan*—in our lives. This means harmonising our inner and outer worlds, balancing the material and spiritual, and reconciling human needs with divine expectations. Embracing Barakah Culture ultimately leads to greater success, fulfilment, and happiness than Hustle Culture ever could. In the next section, we'll delve into the benefits of Barakah Culture versus Hustle Culture and provide thought exercises to help you implement Barakah Culture in your life, as well as within your professional teams.

11 Ways Barakah Culture Outperforms Hustle Culture

1. God-Centric vs Ego-Centric

> *"But only seeking the countenance of his Lord, Most High. And he is going to be satisfied."* (QURAN 92: 20-21)

> *"...those who desire the countenance of Allah, and it is they who will be successful."* (QURAN 30: 38)

At its heart, Barakah Culture is about knowing and connecting with Allah through not just formal acts of worship, but in every word, action, and decision we make. It stems from the Islamic philosophy of *ubudiyyah* (submitting oneself fully to God), which emphasises our need to make conscious choices that submit to the will of our Creator. *Ubudiyyah* involves recognising Allah and His commands, and aligning our personal and professional lives with what He loves.

In contrast, Hustle Culture revolves around serving oneself, one's ego, or what the Islamic tradition refers to as the *nafs*. This subtle substance develops as the soul enters the body and grows alongside the individual. If not spiritually nurtured or disciplined, the *nafs* remains immature. We all know an adult with an underdeveloped *nafs*—self-centred and moody even though they should know better. In the business world, the ego manifests in a relentless pursuit of personal success and accolades, sometimes at the expense of being a true servant of God.

When your life revolves solely around your ego, you'll find yourself on a rollercoaster of inconsistency – some days are good, while others are not – all dictated by your mood and the state of your *nafs*. On the other hand, when your life centres around Allah, it helps smooth out life's ups and downs, and ultimately leads to increased Barakah and blessings in all aspects of your life and true success and happiness in the next.

THOUGHT EXPERIMENTS FOR INDIVIDUALS

- Examine your daily schedule and ask yourself: how much of what you do is about you? How much of it is about serving Allah or others?
- If Allah were your ultimate concern from the moment you wake up until you go to sleep, how might that change things? How would you arrange your life differently?
- How could you plan your life around your prayers rather than prioritising your own comfort or the demands of your lifestyle?

THOUGHT EXPERIMENTS FOR TEAMS

- Consider what it means to operate as a God-centred team. Are we focused on pleasing Him? If so, how does that impact the way we work?
- Would a new team member, visitor or customer notice our God-centred approach?
- How can we ensure that our team's actions align with this core value?

2. Purpose & Impact-Driven vs Personal Success-Driven

> *"And that there is not for man except that [good] for which he strives. And that his effort is going to be seen."*
> (QURAN 53:39-40)

Barakah Culture is about having a mission that extends beyond yourself. It stems from recognising that your ultimate purpose is to worship Allah and act as His *khalifah* (representative) on earth.

> *"And [mention, O Muhammad], when your Lord said to the angels, "Indeed, I will make upon the earth [khalifah] a successive authority...."* (QURAN 2:30)

This role entails trust and responsibility, requiring individuals and teams to consider their impact beyond their financial assets or profit margins. It calls for living our lives, both individually and collectively, in a manner that honours our position as God's *khalifah* on earth, protecting the planet and our environment, rather than serving ourselves and humanity's insatiable desires, knowing we will be held accountable for our choices.

In contrast, Hustle Culture focuses on personal success, gauged by money, power, and fame. Although sometimes disguised as financial freedom or 'leaving a legacy', at its core, it's about the individual and catering to their ego, or *nafs*, as discussed earlier.

THOUGHT EXPERIMENTS FOR INDIVIDUALS

- What do you consider indicators of success? How much of your perceived success is tied to personal achievement?
- How can you redefine success to concentrate on your broader purpose and the impact you have on your community?

THOUGHT EXPERIMENTS FOR TEAMS

- If you weren't paid to be on the team, which tasks would you still undertake? Are you genuinely invested in the team's objectives, beyond your material success? If not, what would you like to see different at your company that will make you feel you're serving a greater purpose.

3. Hereafter Focus vs Worldly Focus

> *"Whoever desires the harvest of the Hereafter – We increase for him in his harvest. And whoever desires the harvest of this world – We give him thereof, but there is not for him in the Hereafter any share."* (QURAN 42:20)

Barakah Culture is about taking a (very) long-term view of life and recognising that there's life after death, and a day will come when our words and deeds will be held to account. The result is either an eternal abode in heaven or hellfire. Operating with this belief makes you consciously focus your life on the three investments that Prophet Muhammad ﷺ taught us would continue to exist after our death: our children and their prayers for us after we die; an ongoing charity that's genuinely sustainable and beneficial to people; and developing and spreading a useful body of knowledge that's timeless.

Hustle Culture takes a myopic, short-term view of life. It's about the next quarterly report, the following annual review, and the next carrot in the never-ending game of corporate snakes and ladders. It's fed by a YOLO (You Only Live Once) mentality and compels you to maximise pleasure for pleasure's sake, while pushing you to get it all as quickly as possible—ideally yesterday.

An author adopting Barakah Culture will write their book to last a thousand years, so it benefits society long after they have gone. An author adopting Hustle Culture, on the other hand, will focus only on hitting the bestseller lists within the first weeks of launch and rush through his book project because he or she is trying to catch a new trend before it's too late.

THOUGHT EXPERIMENTS FOR INDIVIDUALS

- How much of your time, energy, and focus goes towards the three investments that will outlive you and your children? Are you actively developing beneficial knowledge? Do you have plans to establish or support an ongoing charity?
- What small project could you initiate now and consistently work on for the rest of your life?

THOUGHT EXPERIMENTS FOR TEAMS

- What does it mean for our team to believe in the Hereafter, heaven, hell, and the Day of Judgement? How can we build a company or product that lasts for a thousand years and benefits humanity?

4. Focus on Acceptance from Allah vs Focus on Results

"And say, "Do [as you will], for Allah will see your deeds, and [so, will] His Messenger and the believers. And you will be returned to the Knower of the unseen and the witnessed, and He will inform you of what you used to do." (QURAN 9: 105)

Narrated by Umar Ibn Al-Khattab: Allah's Messenger said ﷺ, "The reward of deeds depends upon the intention and every person will get the reward according to what he has intended. So, whoever emigrated for Allah and His Apostle, then his emigration was for Allah and His Apostle. And whoever emigrated for worldly benefits or for a woman to marry, his emigration was for what he emigrated for." (BUKHARI)

Barakah Culture emphasises focusing on delivering work that pleases Allah. It centres on the two conditions required for Allah to accept our actions: sincere, good intentions and sincere effort and action. In contrast, Hustle Culture emphasises material results, where the ends justify the means.

Some readers might ask, "Surely focusing on material results is better than intentions and actions? What's the point of having good intentions and working hard, if there are no results to show for it?"

The philosophical difference stems from recognising who is in control. Individuals operating within Hustle Culture believe that we are in control of our own lives and the material results we achieve. Barakah focused individuals acknowledge that Allah is ultimately in charge and that our hard work is never wasted, as long as our intentions are pure and we sincerely put our best efforts forward, regardless of the material results we achieve. This mindset provides numerous mental health benefits and even material benefits, though material gain is not the primary focus.

A metaphor that we will explore in greater detail in a later chapter is the difference between a gardener and a carpenter: A gardener plants seeds, waters the land, and works hard on the garden. If the garden doesn't bear fruit as expected, they accept it as Allah's decree, renew their intentions, and work harder and smarter for the next season. They understand they can only control their intentions and actions, and leave the outcome to Allah. They fully understand and appreciate the meaning of this verse:

> *"And have you seen that [seed] which you sow? Is it you who makes it grow, or are We the grower?"*
>
> (QURAN 56:63-64)

A carpenter, on the other hand, has a fixed image of what their product should look like and may feel frustrated or even depressed when they fail to achieve that perfect result. They try to control the uncontrollable and experience significant stress as a result.

In other words, Barakah Culture is about focusing on what you can control—your intentions and your actions—and leaving what's not within your control to Allah. Hustle Culture is living the daily stress of trying to control the uncontrollable, under the false impression that expectations always meet reality.

THOUGHT EXPERIMENTS FOR INDIVIDUALS

- Do you have a gardener mindset or carpenter mindset? Ask your family for their opinion.
- When things don't go according to your plan, how do you react? If you find yourself stressed, how can you shift your outlook?

THOUGHT EXPERIMENTS FOR TEAMS

- What failures have occurred in the past that were beyond your control? How did you react to those failures as a team? How did things turn out after the failure?
- How can you shift your thinking from a focus on material results to focusing on intentions and quality work?

5. Abundance Mindset vs Scarcity Mindset

> *Satan threatens you with poverty and orders you to immorality, while Allah promises you forgiveness from Him and bounty. And Allah is all-Encompassing and Knowing.* (QURAN 2:268)

Barakah is all about having an abundance mindset. A follower of this culture recognises that blessings and bounty are from Allah, He is Eternal, His Kingdom and Blessings are infinite and limitless. The Vastness of Allah eliminates the fear of loss and limitedness.

> *Abu Dharr reported Allah's Messenger ﷺ as saying that Allah, the Exalted and Glorious, said: "[...] O My servants, even if the first amongst you and the last amongst you and the whole human race of yours and that of jinns also all stand in one plain ground and you ask Me and I confer upon every person what he asks for, it would not in any way, cause any loss to Me (even less) than that which is caused to the ocean by dipping the needle in it."* (MUSLIM)

Hustle Culture, on the other hand, is cutthroat. It's a dog-eat-dog world out there, and you need to be the earliest bird to catch all the worms. It's about capitalism – "limited resources," "tough global competition," and "you need to get what's yours before everyone else does." It's turning human beings into beasts fighting over the crumbs of life, turning away refugees fleeing war or extreme poverty because they are scared "they'll take over our jobs."

> *"[...] And whoever is protected from the stinginess of his soul – it is those who will be successful."* (QURAN 59:9)

Walk through any souk in Medina, Jerusalem, Cairo, Fez or Istanbul, and you'll see rows and rows of shopkeepers selling the exact same items for the exact same price. You might even catch one of them telling you not to buy from their store but to go to their friend's shop because their friend didn't sell enough today. That's an abundance mindset in action.

If corporations and businesses adopted an abundance mindset and focused on collaboration and helping one another, there would likely be less waste, better job security, and an overall improvement in societal living standards. This cooperative spirit often emerges during major calamities, when people realise the importance of working together to lift each other up and overcome challenges.

Embracing an abundance mindset in our daily lives and businesses can lead to a more compassionate, supportive, and sustainable society. By recognising that Allah's blessings are limitless, we can foster an environment of cooperation and generosity, promoting success and well-being for everyone involved.

THOUGHT EXPERIMENTS FOR INDIVIDUALS

- What are you afraid to lose if you give some of your resources away? What do you think will happen if you do share these resources with an abundance mindset?

THOUGHT EXPERIMENTS FOR TEAMS

- Who are your top competitors? What if you reached out to them and asked to help them solve a problem they face? What if you sent some of your clients to your competitors?

6. Content vs Never Satisfied

It was narrated from Salamah bin Ubaidullah bin Mihsan Al-Ansari that his father said: "The Messenger of Allah ﷺ said: 'Whoever among you wakes up physically healthy, feeling safe and secure within himself, with food for the day, it is as if he acquired the whole world.'" (IBN MAJAH)

Barakah Culture emphasises contentment with one's current situation and blessings. This approach encourages gratitude and appreciation for what we have, rather than constantly striving for more without taking the time to be present and satisfied with our lives.

In contrast, Hustle Culture is centred around the idea of never being satisfied, constantly pushing for more, and never accepting one's current reality. This relentless pursuit of growth and achievement can lead to stress, burnout, and a sense of never truly enjoying the fruits of one's labour.

When considering the role of ambition within Barakah Culture, it's important to distinguish between different types of ambition:

- If your ambition is centred on God, focused on the Hereafter, and driven by purpose and impact, then pursuing that ambition while remaining content with your current situation is in alignment with Barakah Culture.
- However, if your ambition is fuelled by ego, focused on worldly gains, and primarily tied to personal success at any cost, then it may be more harmful than beneficial in the long run.

The power of contentment lies in the ability to enjoy the Barakah of life, even amidst challenges and setbacks. When one cultivates a sense of contentment, they can navigate trials and tribulations with grace and resilience. On the other hand, a lack of contentment can make life more difficult to bear, particularly when faced with unexpected adversity.

Prophet Muhammad ﷺ said, "Be content with what Allah has given you, and you will be the richest of people." (TIRMIDHI)

THOUGHT EXPERIMENTS FOR INDIVIDUALS

- The next time you feel discontent with your life and annoyed at the smallest things, pause and ask yourself: how can I be more content? What am I grateful for?
- What are your ambitions in life? How many of them are God-centred, Hereafter-focused, and purpose and impact driven?
- What would your life look like if you were more content and stopped being stressed with 'what if' and 'if only' and 'I wish I had…'?

THOUGHT EXPERIMENTS FOR TEAMS

- What do you appreciate about your team and the work you do? What makes you content?
- How can you manage your team or company's ambitions while remaining content with the journey you have taken together so far?

7. Focused vs Distracted

The Messenger of Allah ﷺ said: "Whoever is focused only on this world, Allah will confound his affairs and make him fear poverty constantly, and he will not get anything of this world except that which has been decreed for him. Whoever is focused on the Hereafter, Allah will settle his affairs for him and make him feel content with his lot, and his provision and worldly gains will undoubtedly come to him." (IBN MAJAH)

Barakah Culture is focused. It's focused on Allah; focused

on the Hereafter, on living a life of purpose and impact. It comes with a clear direction in life, and its followers are actively encouraged to pursue this direction.

Hustle Culture is distracted. It has a million projects to do at once. Its followers are scattered. They are pulled in so many different directions and on a never-ending emotional rollercoaster of ups and downs.

Once you start looking, it is easy to notice the difference between Hustle Culture and Barakah Culture. Take, for example, the following morning routines:

- An adherent to Hustle Culture wakes up, and the first thing they do is check emails, respond to messages, and get on with their to-do list.
- An adherent to Barakah Culture wakes up, and the first thing they do is remember God, pray, recite the Quran, and then tackle the day ahead of them.

You might say 'yeah, but the Hustle Culture guy gets SO much done by the time your Barakah Culture guy finishes praying'. Here's where understanding the true meaning of Barakah becomes crucial: Barakah is not about running like a hamster on a wheel and knocking out as many things as possible from your to-do list. Instead, Barakah is about getting the right things done, at the right time, leading to long-term meaningful success.

THOUGHT EXPERIMENTS FOR INDIVIDUALS

- When you wake up in the morning, what's the first thing you do? If you said that you check your phone, then try this tomorrow morning: get a basic analogue alarm for your room and charge your phone in another place on silent or plane mode. When you get up, remember Allah, pray, read, and resist the temptation to check your phone for at least two to three hours. Notice the difference in your mornings and how much important work you get done that day.

THOUGHT EXPERIMENTS FOR TEAMS

- If your team feels overwhelmed and pulled in different directions, consider what might be causing these distractions. Reflect on how to refocus and ground the team. Identify the essential tasks that will move the company forward, and work together to eliminate or minimise distractions. By cultivating a more focused approach, your team can achieve greater progress and alignment with your long-term goals.

8. Being Grateful vs Seeking Credit

"And [remember] when your Lord proclaimed, 'If you are grateful, I will surely increase you [in favour]; but if you deny, indeed, My punishment is severe.'"

(QURAN 14: 7)

Abu Hurairah narrated that the Messenger of Allah ﷺ said: "Whoever is not grateful to the people, he is not grateful to Allah." (TIRMIDHI)

Barakah Culture encourages you to acknowledge that any success you achieve is ultimately a blessing from Allah. By embracing this perspective, followers of Barakah Culture experience a constant state of *shukr* (gratefulness) for every accomplishment, big or small. They even find gratitude in failures and obstacles, recognising the blessings that come from facing and overcoming difficulties. This mindset also fosters a sense of appreciation for the people who have supported them along their journey.

Understanding that success comes from Allah not only cultivates gratitude but also reminds you to seek success from Allah through prayer. The brilliance of this approach lies in the fact that asking for success from Allah helps to purify and renew your intentions. Your aspirations become less ego-centric and more focused on purpose and impact, as you seek to use the success Allah provides in a meaningful way.

THOUGHT EXPERIMENTS FOR INDIVIDUALS

- Write down your blessings. Don't stop until you feel overwhelmed with gratitude, maybe even to tears. Trust me, it's a humbling experience.

THOUGHT EXPERIMENTS FOR TEAMS

- When celebrating success, make a conscious effort to recognise the people and factors that facilitated that achievement. Instead of indulging in self-congratulatory gestures or lavish celebrations, turn to Allah in thanks, contribute to charity, or support a local project in an underprivileged community. This approach encourages a team culture rooted in gratitude and meaningful impact.

9. Tranquillity and Presence vs Rushed and Busy

"And the servants of the Most Merciful are those who walk upon the earth easily, and when the ignorant address them [harshly], they say [words of] peace..."

(QURAN 25:63)

Abdullah bin Umar reported: the Messenger of Allah ﷺ took hold of my shoulders and said, "Be in the world like a stranger or a wayfarer". Ibn Umar used to say: "When you survive till the evening do not expect to live until the morning, and when you survive till the morning do not expect to live until the evening. While in good health (do good deeds) before you fall sick; and while you are alive (do good deeds) before death strikes." (BUKHARI)

Barakah Culture fosters tranquillity and presence, teaching you to be in tune with your emotions and embrace the importance of living in the present while preparing for the Hereafter. It encourages you not to dwell on the past or worry excessively about the future, but instead to focus on pleasing Allah in the present moment.

> *"In order that you not despair over what has eluded you and not exult [in pride] over what He has given you. And Allah does not like everyone self-deluded and boastful."* (QURAN 57:23)

In contrast, Hustle Culture often leaves you feeling rushed and perpetually in 'urgent' mode. This mindset can make it difficult to concentrate on what truly matters or to enjoy the present moment, as you're constantly thinking about what's coming next: the next client, the next problem, the next financial crisis around the corner. At its worst, Hustle Culture can lead to neglecting personal relationships and the needs of those around you.

One might argue: isn't it healthy to be worried about the future, so you can prepare for it? Barakah Culture promotes preparing for the future in a balanced way. Continuously stressing about the future, especially after taking all reasonable precautions, is unproductive and detrimental to your wellbeing.

By adopting a Barakah Culture mindset, you become more present and mindful, allowing you to recognise when someone needs help and understand that Allah may have sent them as a test of your willingness to offer support or learn from them.

THOUGHT EXPERIMENTS FOR INDIVIDUALS

- The next time you pray, try praying as if it's your first time, experiencing each supplication as if it's new to you. Observe the positive impact that the tranquillity and presence from this prayer has on the following hours of your day.

THOUGHT EXPERIMENTS FOR TEAMS

- The next time your team finds itself rushing or firefighting to complete a task, allow any team member to call for a time-out. Develop a habit of discussing what could be done differently and how you can prevent future crises. Encourage a sense of mindful purpose and presence in the workplace.

10. A Sense of Responsibility vs Sense of Entitlement

It was narrated that Abdullah said: "The Messenger of Allah ﷺ entered my apartment and said: "I have been told that you stand all night (in prayer) and fast all day.' I said: 'Yes (I do).' He said: 'Do not do that. Sleep and stand (in prayer); fast and break your fast. For your eyes have a right over you, your body has a right over you, your wife has a right

> *over you, your guest has a right over you, and your friend has a right over you. I hope that you will have a long life and that it will be sufficient for you to fast three days of each month. That is fasting for a lifetime because a good deed is equal to ten like it.' I said: 'I feel able to do more.' I was strict, so I was dealt with strictly. He said: 'Fast three days each week.' I said: 'I am able to do more than that; I was strict, so I was dealt with strictly. He said: 'Observe the fast of the Prophet of Allah, Dawud, peace be upon him. I said: 'What was the fast of Dawud?' he said: 'Half of a lifetime. Ata said: "someone who heard him told me that Ibn Umar (said) that the Prophet said: 'Whoever fasts every day of his life, then he has not fasted."*
>
> (AN NASA'I)

Within Barakah Culture, there is an understanding that each person is a single organism within a larger ecosystem, with rights and responsibilities extending to various aspects of life. This begins with our relationship with Allah and our responsibilities as His followers. From there, it extends to the rights and responsibilities we have towards our families, neighbours, fellow Muslims, and the broader community.

In contrast, Hustle Culture often breeds a sense of entitlement and self-centeredness. After a hard day at work, it is all about 'me-time'. It is a deserving mentality. The hustlers want to tap on an app and get their next meal, watch some Netflix, and go to bed early so they can wake up at 4:00am and repeat the cycle. Family, neighbours, parents, and other people in their community are afterthoughts. The hustler's idea of work-life balance is that work is life.

Barakah Culture promotes life balance. You recognise that you're a shepherd responsible for your flock and that, as such, your obligations go beyond work and serving your own desires.

THOUGHT EXPERIMENTS FOR INDIVIDUALS

- Take a piece of paper and draw a bar graph:
  - On the x-axis write down all the roles you have in life (e.g., father/mother, spouse, parent, son/daughter, etc.).
  - On the y-axis, write 'performance', which you'll measure from 0 – 100%.
- For each of your roles, give yourself a personal score based on the question, 'how well am I performing as a [fill in the role]? 50%? 70%?'
- Repeat for all your roles. What do you notice?
- After adopting Barakah Culture, perform the same experiment three months later and see if anything has changed.

THOUGHT EXPERIMENTS FOR TEAMS

- As a team, are you helping each other achieve life balance? If yes, how so and how can you be sure? What rituals, HR policies, or ideas, etc. can you implement as a team that make total life balance possible?

11. Small But Consistent Efforts vs Big Moves and Constant Pivoting

"Have you not considered how Allah presents an example, [making] a good word like a good tree, whose root is firmly fixed and its branches [high] in the sky? It produces its fruit all the time, by permission of its Lord. And Allah presents examples for the people that perhaps they will be reminded.
And the example of a bad word is like a bad tree, uprooted from the surface of the earth, not having any stability." (QURAN 14: 24-26)

The Messenger of Allah ﷺ was asked about the act most pleasing to Allah. He replied:
'That which is done continuously, even if it is small."
(MUSLIM)

Barakah Culture can be likened to a date palm tree. It takes time and patience to grow, but once it matures, it stands strong, deeply rooted, and consistently bears sweet fruit.

Hustle Culture, on the other hand, revolves around the idea of "fail fast, fail forward, and constant pivoting. It celebrates grand launches and dramatic shifts, often without establishing long-term foundations.

The interesting observation is that true, impactful success requires dedication, time, and consistency. By maintaining focus, presence, sincerity, and striving for excellence daily, you can achieve success beyond your wildest dreams over a lifetime. However, if you're constantly pivoting and changing directions, you may never develop deep roots and may ultimately end up like a withered, uprooted tree.

This is not to say that change is always negative. There are circumstances where adapting and shifting direction may be necessary, but only after exhausting all other possibilities. The Prophet Muhammad ﷺ, for example, only migrated to Medina after thirteen years of preaching in Mecca when his life and those of his followers were at stake.

THOUGHT EXPERIMENTS FOR INDIVIDUALS

- Reflect on your habits and routines – spiritual, physical, social, and work-related – and determine which ones benefit you in the long-term and which ones hinder your success.
- Identify a small habit or routine you can adopt and maintain so that over the course of a year (or a lifetime), it yields positive outcomes (e.g. reading or running)

THOUGHT EXPERIMENTS FOR TEAMS

- What common goals or objectives are you willing to work towards together for the next five to 10 years?
- Consider when your team tends to pivot. Is it due to external factors or is it when you become overwhelmed and struggle to engage in meaningful, purpose-driven work?

Whenever I present the above characteristics of Barakah Culture vs Hustle Culture in a corporate setting, I get a lot of push-back from the audience. They vehemently try to defend Hustle Culture and how it's necessary for survival in our modern world. I agree that subscribing to Hustle Culture has become an evil necessity due to the systems and structures of modern society, but this does not mean we should accept it as the de-facto way of living. Rather, we should do everything in our power to fight the culture, if not for our generation, then, at least for our children's generation. The Messenger of Allah ﷺ said:

> *"Whosoever of you sees an evil action, let him change it with his hand; and if he is not able to do so, then with his tongue; and if he is not able to do so, then with his heart—and that is the weakest of faith."* (MUSLIM)

If you've reached this point in the book, I hope by now you're thinking: yes, I see how Barakah Culture makes more sense. But how do I start? In the next part of the book, I'll share a practical framework to help you live with Barakah, no matter how steeped you may be in Hustle Culture.

EMBRACING BARAKAH CULTURE IN THE CORPORATE WORLD: BRIDGING THE GAP BETWEEN FAITH AND PROFESSIONALISM

Whenever I present the idea of Barakah Culture as an alternative to Hustle Culture in the corporate world, I often encounter the most resistance from Muslims working alongside non-Muslim colleagues. This push-back may stem from an inferiority complex or fear of being seen as uncommitted to the prevailing work ethic or a feeling that Barakah Culture is simply not compatible to the Hustle Culture environment at work.

I believe that Muslim professionals have an important role to become ambassadors for Barakah Culture, showcasing the compatibility of success and spiritual beliefs in the modern professional world and demonstrating that it does not lead to reduced productivity or drive. Instead, it fosters balance, mindfulness, and long-term success and fulfilment.

Moreover, organisations should create safe spaces for discussing such topics and challenges related to balancing faith and work. These spaces can help Muslims feel more confident and supported in their pursuit of a Barakah-focused lifestyle. I hope this book provides Muslim professionals with a framework to present Barakah Culture to their colleagues and feel more confident to showcase and defend Barakah Culture at work.

CHAPTER SUMMARY

- This chapter highlights 11 aspects where Barakah Culture surpasses Hustle Culture, encouraging us to genuinely consider embracing a life of Barakah rather than being confined to Hustle Culture.
- Implementing Barakah Culture in our lives requires in-depth self-reflection and open discussions with family members and colleagues (refer to the thought experiments mentioned earlier).
- As Muslim professionals, it is our additional responsibility to represent and promote Barakah Culture in our corporate and business settings.

CHAPTER FOUR

A Framework for Barakah

What would it take to shift our mindsets, values, and lifestyle choices to live a life of Barakah?

As Muslims, we often overlook how our faith in God, belief in life after death, and adherence to sacred scriptures (Quran and Sunnah), impact how we think (our mindsets), what we believe and cherish (our values), and what lifestyle choices we make (our rituals). These three pillars – mindsets, values, and rituals – that we inherently embody as Muslims, are the necessary building blocks for Barakah Culture to exist and flourish at a personal, organisational, and societal level. The 'how' for bringing Barakah back into our lives is right in front of us. We simply need to tap into the mindsets, values, and rituals that are already fundamental to our Muslim identity.

But where do these pillars come from? They are based on three key characteristics of our faith that define the Islamic worldview as explained by Dr. Ali Gümüsay, in his 2019 paper on 'Embracing religions in moral theories of leadership'[5]:

1. **Belief in the Oneness of God** orients us towards a worldview in which God is the centre of our lives. Thus, we develop certain mindsets and ways of thinking

that a person who doesn't believe in God (or doesn't believe in the Oneness of God) cannot subscribe to. For example, a person who truly believes in God will develop the God-consciousness to do the right thing even under extreme circumstances and when no one is watching. Someone who does not believe in God may have a moral compass that guides them, but if tested, this might falter.

2. When a person **believes in the Hereafter**, they are essentially believing in an extreme level of accountability - where everything they do or say in this world will either help them or hurt them in the Court of God. Such belief in a life after death instils important values in a person's life, such as honesty, justice, and trustworthiness.
3. Finally, **believing in sacred scriptures** (Quran and Sunnah) which detail a way of life that entails subscribing to certain rituals and lifestyle choices that reinforce specific mindsets and values. Rituals such as fasting, prayer, and remembrance of God anchor a person's life with keystone habits that help them remain connected to the Divine.

These beliefs create the pillars that then form the basis of Barakah Culture, as represented by the below illustration:

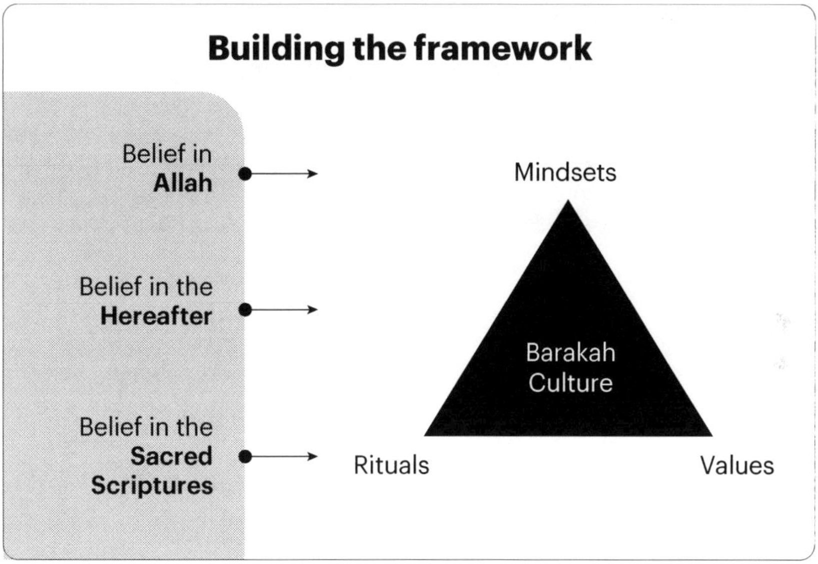

The embodiment of these mindsets, values, and rituals is Prophet Muhammad ﷺ. He was the living embodiment of Barakah and hence why everything that is attached to him, and his remembrance, is full of Barakah (we'll explore this theme more deeply in the chapter on the Barakah of sending blessings upon Prophet Muhammad ﷺ).

With this framework, the next step is to determine what specific mindsets, values, and rituals we need to practice and adopt to live a life of Barakah.

Mindsets, Values and Rituals of Barakah Culture

In our research trying to define and understand Barakah Culture, we've come up with 17 mindsets, 17 values, and 17 rituals that we believe every person who aspires to practice Barakah Culture needs to adopt in their lives.

	Mindsets	Values	Rituals
1	Forbearance & Forgiveness	Mercy & Compassion	Consult Allah & Others
2	God-Consciousness	Peace	Seek Beneficial Knowledge
3	Humbleness to Allah	Truthfulness	Making *Dua*
4	Contentment	Family	Keeping Ties of Kinship
5	Beautiful Patience & Perseverance	Modesty & Concealment	Eating with People
6	Reliance upon Allah	Beauty	Remembrance of Allah
7	Consistency	Justice	Reconciliation
8	Hereafter-focused	Generosity	Repentance & Constant Returning to Allah
9	Gratefulness	Excellence	Praiseworthy Planning

10	Steadfastness upon the Truth	Strength	Charity
11	Love for the Sake of Allah	Uprightness	Salah
12	Purpose & Impact-driven	Trustworthiness	Reciting Quran
13	Abundance	Easiness	Waking up Early
14	Introspection & Self-accountability	Moderation	Lowering the Gaze
15	Presence	Gentleness	Controlling the Tongue
16	Intentionality	Teamwork & Cooperation	Helping People
17	Taking Initiative	Responsibility	Sending Blessings upon Prophet Muhammad ﷺ

Go through the list above and pick one Barakah Culture mindset, value, and ritual that you'd like to work on[6]. Think practically about how you'll apply the Barakah Culture mindset, value, or ritual in your life in the following week.

FOR EXAMPLE, IN MY OFFICE, I HAVE THESE THREE CARDS PERMANENTLY DISPLAYED:

- **Value:** Peace
- **Mindset:** Reliance upon Allah
- **Ritual:** Sending Blessings upon Prophet Muhammad ﷺ

As I go about my working day, I challenge myself to have inner peace and be a source of peace (not fear or stress) for my teams or clients. Now, whenever I feel frustrated or anxious, I remind myself of this value and it helps calm me down and bring Barakah to my inner world as well as my relationships.

For reliance upon Allah, this mindset helps me make powerful business decisions and not fear the unknown. I'm reminded of the Prophetic tradition of seeking counsel and praying *istikhara*[7] prayer whenever I need to make a decision. Moreover, once a decision is made, I need to own it, act towards it, and ultimately rely upon Allah to bring the results we seek.

Finally, the ritual of sending blessings upon Prophet Muhammad ﷺ reminds me to dedicate time for *salawat* during my workday. In a later chapter, we'll discuss why this is an important part of attracting Barakah in one's life.

As simple as the above exercise may be, I've worked with many individuals and organisations that have found that consciously thinking about and experimenting with these Barakah Culture mindsets, values, and rituals was a necessary first step towards moving away from Hustle Culture.

As we practice this exercise and work towards adopting Barakah Culture, we must keep in mind this important value: sincerity. No amount of lip service to Barakah Culture will bring Barakah into our lives without the sincere intention of adopting these mindsets, values, and rituals for the sake of God.

Furthermore, we need to practice these mindsets, values, and rituals on a daily or weekly basis and not as a one-off exercise. To ensure they remain top of mind, consider journaling weekly or daily, outlining which Barakah Culture mindsets, values, or rituals you intend to practice that week.[8]

The Barakah Culture Manifesto

In the month of Rabi-Al-Awwal 1441H (November 2019), I had the privilege of visiting Medina - the city of Barakah, cherished by the Prophet Muhammad ﷺ. The Prophet had prayed for Barakah for his city, saying: "O Allah, bestow Barakah upon our city, our fruits, our *mudd*, and our *sa's*, granting us abundance upon abundance" (MUSLIM). He also said: "O Allah, endow Medina with double the Barakah You bestowed upon Mecca." (BUKHARI)

With a desire to share the core elements of Barakah Culture, I had planned to write a small book on this subject during my visit. However, upon my arrival, I discovered that I had left my writing pad behind, and there was no nearby stationery store to purchase writing paper. All I managed to find were a few pieces of hotel notepad.

At that moment, an idea occurred to me. Instead of a book, why not craft a manifesto that encapsulated the fundamental principles of Barakah Culture? This would be the ultimate exercise in achieving more with less!

So, during the sacred time after *asr* (afternoon) prayers, on the blessed day of *Jumuah* (Friday), near the revered resting place of Prophet Muhammad ﷺ, Allah guided me to compose the following 100 words, encapsulating the essence of Barakah Culture:

Bismillah.

Start every action with sincere intention,
and ask Allah for help.
Life is not about you,
it's about serving your Lord with excellence.
Thank Allah for what you have,
and seek his sustenance beautifully.
Be like a gardener: focused, hardworking, gentle,
and trust Allah with the results.
Cherish your parents,
and treat them with mercy and compassion.
Plant seeds whose harvest will benefit
generations to come.
Pray and persist for your goals,
until you achieve them or are guided to what's better.
Remember death often to stay focused on what matters.
Send abundant *salawat* upon Prophet Muhammad ﷺ
Alhamdulillah.

In the next part of the book, we'll expand on each of the principles above, why they are important for Barakah Culture, and how we can practically apply them in our lives.

CHAPTER SUMMARY

- Our faith in God, belief in the Hereafter, and adherence to the Quran and Sunnah help us develop the necessary mindsets, values, and rituals to live a life of Barakah.
- We can intentionally attract Barakah in our lives by focusing on specific mindsets, values, and/or rituals each week and finding ways to practically implement them in our daily or weekly routines.
- If you find engaging with the 51 mindsets, values, and rituals too daunting, the Barakah Culture manifesto offers a concise overview of the core principles for living a life of Barakah and can serve as a valuable guide for integrating Barakah into your journey.

PART

02

Living with Barakah

"'Bismillah, In the Name of God', is the start of all things good."

SAID NURSI

CHAPTER FIVE

Bismillah

Once upon a time, there lived a devout woman who always uttered "Bismillah" (In the name of Allah) before undertaking any action. She wholeheartedly believed that by doing so, Allah would protect her and guide her in all she does. One day, her neighbour entrusted her with a valuable ring before leaving on a trip. The woman recited "Bismillah" and placed the ring in her cupboard, confident that Allah would keep it safe.

Her husband, growing increasingly irritated by his wife's constant invocation of "Bismillah", sought to challenge her faith. He secretly removed the ring from the cupboard and tossed it into a river, intending to confront her about the ring later that day, fully expecting it to be lost.

However, Allah's plans were different. That very afternoon, the woman went to the market to buy fish. As she cleaned the fish at home, she discovered the missing ring in the fish's stomach. Surprised, she returned the ring to the cupboard, once again saying "Bismillah".

When her husband asked about the ring later that day, she immediately retrieved it from the cupboard. He was left in awe, admitting what he did, and understanding the true power and significance of reciting "*Bismillah*".

In Barakah Culture, every act is performed in the name of God; from signing a major deal, to the most intimate act between husband and wife. In fact, scholars caution that anything done without saying '*Bismillah*' lacks Barakah.

To foster this Barakah in our lives, we learned to say *Bismillah* at a very young age. Our parents and Islamic studies teacher reminded us to say *Bismillah* before we eat, drink, and study, until it becomes a habit. Yet, we still fail to appreciate the significance or impact of *Bismillah* in our daily lives.

When you invoke the phase "*Bismillah*", you're acknowledging that what you're about to do is all going to be possible by Allah's will and blessing. Moreover, you're asking Allah to place His Barakah in the act so that the outcome becomes far more beneficial than you expect.

In his book Risale-i Nur Collection, 19th century Muslim theologian Said Nursi wrote a parable to help us understand the importance of saying Bismillah:

> Someone who makes a journey through the deserts of Arabia must travel in the name of a tribal chief and enter under his protection, for in this way he may be saved from the assaults of bandits and secure his need. On his own, he will perish in the face of innumerable enemies and needs. And so, two men went on such a journey and entered the desert. One of them was modest and humble, the other proud and conceited. The humble man assumed the name of the tribal chief, while the proud man did not. The first travelled safely wherever he went...but the proud man suffered indescribable calamities through his journey.

When you say *Bismillah* consciously and sincerely, it's as if you enrolled in an army and therefore, you act in the name of the government you're representing.

You don't rely on yourself and your meagre means, but rather, you're doing everything in the name of the One. As the Prophet Muhammad ﷺ said: "When a man goes out of his house and says: "In the name of Allah, I trust in Allah; there is no might and no power but in Allah," the following will be said to him at that time: "You are guided, defended and protected." The devils will go far from him, and another devil will say: How can you deal with a man who has been guided, defended and protected?" (ABU DAWUD)

Why does a simple phrase hold such power? In *Words Can Change Your Brain*, authors Andrew Newberg and Mark Waldman argue that words can literally alter your brain. Focusing on positive words can impact how you perceive yourself and others. If we extend this idea, a conscious and sincere *Bismillah* can guide your intellect and spiritual heart towards the Divine, attracting Barakah in even the most mundane activities. Additionally, *Bismillah* can serve as a deterrent against inappropriate acts (after all, if you can't say *Bismillah* before performing an act because it's sinful or inappropriate, you probably shouldn't!).

Bismillah is your starting point to live a life of Barakah. So be mindful when you pronounce it and recognise the Divine name you're starting the act with.

PRACTICAL TIPS FOR INCORPORATING BISMILLAH INTO YOUR DAILY LIFE

The simplest way to add Barakah to your life is to say *Bismillah* consciously and regularly. Here are some practical tips to help you:

1. Say *Bismillah* consciously before every sip of water.
2. Set your phone or desktop background as a reminder to say *Bismillah* when unlocking your phone or opening your laptop.
3. Place *Bismillah* stickers on household appliances to remember to recite it before performing chores.
4. Never leave or enter the house without saying *Bismillah* and the appropriate *dua* - add a sign on your door as a reminder.
5. Encourage your family to remind one another to say *Bismillah* and hold a friendly competition to see who can remember most often.

CHAPTER SIX

Start Every Action with Sincere Intention and Ask Allah for Help

"You have good intentions."

These were the words of my grandfather whenever I shared an achievement with him.

My grandfather, Rubeya Abdullah Faris, grew up in the harsh valley of Hadhramout, south of Yemen, herding camel and living a simple life.

When he became a young adult, he ventured with his friend to East Africa and started his life from scratch, first as a vegetable seller, and eventually a successful wholesale trader with properties in Tanzania and Yemen.

My grandfather and his generation and many generations before him lived and breathed Barakah Culture. They understood that success was not due to sheer effort and grit, but rather something Divine that comes to those with good, sincere intentions.

Why Intentions Matter

Barakah Culture is an intentions-driven culture. Specifically, it's a culture that aims to make worshipping God its main intention in every action.

In a famous *hadith*, Prophet Muhammad ﷺ said: "Actions are judged by intentions..." (BUKHARI) A reminder that it's not what you do that matters, but your intentions behind it that matter more.

I learned good intentions from a sugar cane juice seller. My father and I would stop by *Ammo (uncle)* Omar's shop after Friday prayers to enjoy the cold sweet drink and cool ourselves from the summer heat. *Ammo* Omar - a pious-looking Sudanese man - would greet us with his calm, big smile, uttering words of praise and thanks of God whenever we asked how he was. After taking our orders, you'd see his sincerity in action: he'd pick the best sugar cane in his stock, go out of his way to ensure that the order is to our liking, and even pour extra juice for us with a smile. This was not a man who simply sold juice or provided excellent customer care. This was a man who worshipped God through selling juice, ultimately encapsulating the 'Barakah Effect.' We could feel Barakah in him and his shop - a feeling of peace and ease that I can still remember to this day.

If you want to attract Barakah in anything you do - no matter how small or big - start with a pure intention to worship God in all acts. Intentions are a hidden force that can propel you to success beyond your imagination. The more pure and sincere your intention is for God, the greater the Barakah

Effect in an action. You might produce incredible work, but if you don't have good intentions attached to it, you lose the Divine gift of Barakah. But if you have good intentions, you'll see the Barakah either in your lifetime, or future generations will benefit from it.

The word intention in Arabic is *niyyah*. It has the same root as the word 'seed' in Arabic, *nawat*. The image of intentions being like seeds, reminds us that we need to bury or hide our intentions deep in our hearts, and water them with our efforts and actions, expecting God to sprout this seed beyond our expectations and give this intention life. Allah says in the Quran:

> *It is God who splits open the seed and the fruit stone: He brings out the living from the dead and the dead from the living- that is God- so how can you turn away from the truth?* (QURAN 6:95)

Moreover, just like one seed may sprout a tree that would give countless fruits, a single powerful intention may produce outcomes that go far beyond the initial intention despite the circumstances, as seen in this story related by Prophet Muhammad ﷺ:

"A small deed may be magnified by an intention and a major work may be shrunk by intention."

IBN ATA'ILLAH

A man expressed his intention to give charity, so he came out with charity and placed it in the hand of an adulteress. In the morning, the people were talking and saying: charity was given to an adulteress last night. He (the giver of *sadaqa*) said: O Allah, all praise belongs to you, an adulteress! He then again expressed his intention to give charity; so he went out with the charity and placed it in the hand of a rich person. In the morning the people were talking and saying: charity was given to a rich person. He (the giver of charity) said: O Allah, all praise belongs to you to, a well-to-do person! He then expressed his intention to give charity, so he went out with charity and placed it in the hand of a thief. In the morning, the people were talking and saying: charity was given to a thief. So (one of the persons) said: O Allah, all praise belongs to you, (what a misfortune it is that charity has been given to) the adulteress, to a rich person, to a thief! There came (the angel to him) and he was told: your charity has been accepted. As for the adulteress (the charity might become the means) whereby she might restrain herself from fornication. The rich man might perhaps learn a lesson and spend from what Allah has given him, and the thief might thereby refrain from committing theft. (MUSLIM)

Allah says in the Quran:

> *But those who spend their wealth in order to gain God's approval, and as an affirmation of their own faith, are like a garden on a hill: heavy rain falls and it produces double its normal yield; even if no heavy*

rain falls, it will still be watered by the dew. God sees all that you do. (QURAN 2:265)

The Barakah Effect in the above verse is the rain that produces double the normal yield. Even in tough circumstances where there's no rain, the garden is still cared for by the dew. And the reason for this Barakah is the sincere intention that one spends in God's path.

Intention is a deep and subtle concept but a critical one if we want to align our lives with Barakah Culture and see the Barakah Effect in our lives. Salim Bin Abdullah wrote to the Caliph Umar Bin Abdul-Aziz and told him: *"Know that Allah helps a servant according to their intention. So, whoever's intention is complete, Allah's help will fulfil his intention. And if his intention decreases, Allah's help will decrease accordingly*". Now, let's dig deeper into what intentions exactly are.

What Are Intentions?

According to Imam Al-Haddad, there are two meanings for intentions

1. Heartfelt desire, purpose, motive for doing something, i.e. the why.
2. The decision and determination to do something, i.e. the drive.

Let's explore these further.

1. Intentions as Heartfelt Desires

Heartfelt desire does not mean how you feel about something or the emotions behind an action, but rather, your purpose behind it. The book *Ethics in Islam* shares the following illustrative example:

> *A man saw a woman and, thinking her to be a stranger, made advances to molest her, but found to his surprise that she was his own wife. Then, suppose another man came across a woman and, thinking her to be his wife, made advances and touched her, but found that she was not his wife. In the first case, the man would be considered guilty of committing an evil deed, whereas in the second, the man did not commit any sin.*

The above scenario highlights the importance of intentions in defining moral conduct. As the author concludes, "good conduct is founded entirely upon intention i.e. on heartfelt will".

To attract Barakah, we need to think about having good and sincere intentions even in mundane aspects of our life. Prophet Muhammad ﷺ said, "Whatever you spend seeking thereby the Pleasure of Allah, will have its reward, even the morsel which you put in the mouth of your wife". If you want Barakah in your marriage, or career, or children, then turn the daily activities into acts of worship by making the heartfelt desire that you're doing those actions for God. Imam Al-Haddad said: "Utter no word, do no action, and decide no matter without the intention of drawing nearer thereby to God..."

Moreover, you can attach as many good intentions as you want to any act, thus multiplying the Barakah it attracts. You may have come across the story of the scholar who, when someone knocks on their door, thinks of 70+ intentions before opening the door. For example, he'll intend to greet the person, to give them charity if they ask for charity, to honour them as a guest, to give them good advice, etc. Think of the level of mindfulness and presence that it takes a person to be conscious of the quantity and quality of intentions even in mundane activities that may not seem outwardly spiritual. Then think what sort of Barakah this person attracts in their lives each day when they are thinking about the intentions in every small or major act. It's a subtle, but extremely powerful way of living that we need to spend time cultivating.

Our heartfelt desires are hard to control; you can't force yourself to have a specific intention behind something. Imam Al-Ghazali describes intentions as sitting between knowledge and action. You might know what to do, and have the ability to do something, but it's the intention that sits in the middle that governs whether your heart will spring forth and do the action or not. That's why one of the supplications that we need to keep making is to ask Allah to grant us the heartfelt desires or intentions that please Him and to remove any that are not for His sake.

2. Intentions as Decisions and Determinations

The second meaning for intention is when you decide and are determined to act on something. There are three levels for this meaning of intention:

1. You decide to act and stay determined to act until you fulfil your intention.
2. You decide to act but fail to act while able to (due to lack of determination, laziness, or procrastination).
3. You decide to act but fail to act because you're not able to.

What's surprising about Barakah Culture is that it rewards all three types of intentions, even the unfulfilled ones.

The Messenger of Allah ﷺ said that Allah, the Glorious, said: "Verily, Allah has ordered that the good and the bad deeds be written down. Then He explained it clearly how (to write): He who intends to do a good deed, but he does not do it, then Allah records it for him as a full good deed, but if he carries out his intention, then Allah the Exalted, writes it down for him as from ten to seven hundred folds, and even more. But if he intends to do an evil act and has not done it, then Allah writes it down with Him as a full good deed, but if he intends it and has done it, Allah writes it down as one bad deed." (BUKHARI)

Why does Allah reward all three? First off, every intention in the above scenarios is a sincere intention, meaning the person firmly resolves to do something. These are not wishful-thinking intentions.

Secondly, if someone has the habit of resolving to do something and they fail at it - either because they lacked determination or they were not able to - the fact remains that this is a person who is still trying to do good. Usually, it's only a matter of time before this person acts on their good intentions. Similarly, if someone resolves to do bad deeds but then decides against it, or is unable to do it, Allah rewards him *depending* on what stops him. If it's fear of God, then that's a sign that his heart is purer than the inclinations of his self. And if circumstances simply didn't add up, the realisation that the sin would've caused serious harm will deter him from having such intentions in the future.

Thirdly, sometimes, you want to achieve something sincerely for God, but life circumstances get in the way. Instead of giving up hope and thinking that you're not worthy to achieve this high status with God, you're encouraged to make sincere intention anyway. This is not about wishful thinking. This is about people who are constantly thinking about how to please God, and sometimes all a person has is their sincere intentions, given their circumstances.

The Barakah of Sincere Intentions

Once upon a time, two close friends embarked on a trade journey through the vast desert. They carried their money securely in belts that they tied around their waists. As they made progress on their expedition, they decided to take a well-deserved rest. One friend hung his money belt on a nearby tree and lay down to sleep, while the other remained awake to prepare lunch.

Suddenly, a bird swooped down and snatched the money bag hanging from the tree, thinking it was red meat. The friend who was awake felt sad for his friend's loss, so he selflessly decided to place his own money belt on the tree so his friend wouldn't lose from this journey.

When the sleeping friend awoke, he didn't notice anything amiss and assumed the money belt hanging from the tree was his own. However, he was puzzled when his companion, who had stayed awake, informed him that he couldn't continue the journey and made various excuses to turn back. Despite his confusion, the man pressed on alone, determined to complete the trade mission.

After some time, he stumbled upon another money belt lying on the ground, identical to his own. Realisation dawned upon him: his friend had sacrificed his own fortune to protect him from loss. Overwhelmed with gratitude, he picked up both money belts and continued to the city to trade. His endeavours proved fruitful, and he returned to his hometown with a caravan laden with goods.

Upon returning to his hometown, he headed straight to his friend's house and declared that half the profits belonged to him. Astonished, the friend asked how he could have made such wealth without traveling and trading himself. The man replied with a smile: "your *niyyah* was your ride" (your good intention and selfless act travelled and traded on your behalf).

Setting sincere intentions for Allah can propel us to achieve things we never imagined possible. This clarity of intention can also empower us to overcome reluctance, lack of support from family and friends, and self-doubt about our abilities. A prime example is the experience of new Muslims during their first Ramadan. They've never fasted before and have no idea what it's like to abstain from food or drink for 12 hours or more. Many don't have the support of their family or community, particularly if they live in remote areas with few fellow Muslims. Moreover, they might lack confidence in their ability to complete a full month of fasting. And yet, their heartfelt sincerity and desire to worship God carries them through this challenging period.

When someone connects their deepest desire to the Divine and the unseen, celestial world, they access a level of drive and purpose that is unstoppable. Moreover, God in his Infinite Mercy and Knowledge, sees those intentions, and places His Barakah in them.

When Imam Malik wrote his famous book *Al-Muwatta*, other scholars in Medina at that time were also creating their own versions. People questioned Imam Malik, saying that others were doing the same as he had done. In response, Imam Malik said: "What is done for Allah will truly have a lasting impact". Sure enough, today, we don't know any other *Muwatta* than the *Muwatta* of Imam Malik.

Imam Malik's sincerity in writing the *Muwatta* was so deep that he put himself to the test. After completing his work, he threw it in the water, stating that if it got wet, that means he wasn't sincere, and he had no need for it. Miraculously, the book remained dry – a clear sign of Allah's acceptance of his sincere intention in his work.

Whenever I think about Imam Malik and other scholars who wrote timeless books that have benefitted millions of people for generations to come, I can only smile and remember my grandfather's words: "*their intentions were good*".

In the next section, we'll explore how intentions form, as well as the different levels of intentions.

How to Craft Good and Sincere Intentions

To attract Barakah in our lives, we need to get better at crafting good intentions that are sincerely for Allah. In fact, some of the early scholars would say: "Seek the intention for the deed, before you do the deed".

To achieve this, we must understand two key processes that occur in our hearts concerning intentions. Firstly, how we transition from a prompt to an intention, and secondly, how to elevate our intentions from being worldly and self-serving to those that are purely for God.

Let's explore both concepts below:

1. The Journey from Prompts to Intentions

Where do intentions come from? This is the question that Dr. Samir Mahmood, a lecturer at Usul Academy, explores on his blog.

He describes a process in which intention is the final step of a series of internal stages within the heart, beginning with a *khatir* (prompt) and culminating in intention. This process can be visualised as follows:

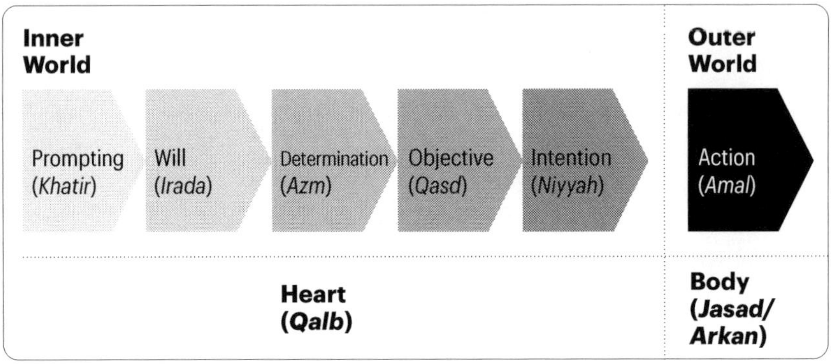

This process clarifies the *hadith* we examined earlier, explaining why Allah rewards someone who intends to do good but doesn't act on it. They have reached a point of certainty in their heart with the intention; hence they are deserving of the reward.

To better understand the process, consider the following examples:

EXAMPLE 1: BUYING A SHIRT

- Prompt: I think I need a new shirt
- Will: I want a new shirt
- Determination: I will buy a new shirt
- Objective: I will go to the store today and buy a new shirt
- Intention: This is the shirt I want to buy because it'll make me look so good in front of my peers and I'll feel good about it.
- Action: Bought the shirt

EXAMPLE 2: SPIRITUAL ACT

- Prompt: It's *asr* time
- Will: I need to pray soon
- Determination: Going to make *wudhu* to pray *asr*
- Objective: Going to the mosque to pray *asr*
- Intention: I'm praying *asr* in the mosque sincerely for God
- Action: I pray *asr*

So, how can we cultivate good intentions using this knowledge?

- **Capture Good Prompts:** According to Dr. Samir Mahmoud, good prompts originate from God, the Angels, and your Higher Self that seeks to connect with the Divine. When you have good thoughts, move them quickly through the stages to intention and action, thereby inviting Barakah into your life. Don't procrastinate on these good thoughts, or you may miss out on the reward for your intention. For instance, if a thought crosses your mind to give charity to a poor person on the street, act quickly to reap the Barakah of giving charity.

- **Beware of Bad Prompts:** Just as there are good prompts, we also have bad prompts from *shaytan* and our lower self that seeks to fulfil base desires. When you have bad thoughts, try to halt their progression before they become will, determination or objective. The more resistance you create against your bad thoughts, the less likely you are to act on them, thus attracting more Barakah by avoiding sins and harmful deeds. As Ibn Al-Qayyim advised:

"Repel the thought, for if you don't, it becomes an idea. So repel the idea; for if you don't it will become a desire. So fight against that (desire), for if you don't, it will become a determination and a passion. And if you don't repel that, it will become an action. And if you don't replace it with its opposite, it will become a constant habit. So at that point, it will be difficult for you to change it."

2. From Worldly Intentions to Spiritual Intentions

While it's essential to transform thoughts into intentions, it's equally important to delve deeper and evaluate the sincerity behind our intentions. Not all intentions are created equal and understanding the 'why' behind them is crucial.

The strength, sincerity, and drive behind an intention can differ from person to person and task to task. Some intentions are incredibly sincere and powerful, attracting God's Barakah to someone's life beyond expectations. In contrast, other intentions can be ego-centric and worldly, turning even an act of worship into a self-serving deed.

The late Nabeel Al-Azami, author of the book *Muhammad: 11 Leadership Qualities that Changed the World*, summarised the work of Sh. Sulaiman Nadwi on intentions shown in the diagram. In this hierarchy, intentions are ranked higher or lower based on their level of selfishness and service to Allah. The more elevated an intention, the more sincere it is in its service to Allah.

The Barakah Effect we receive from deeds is directly related to the purity and sincerity of our intentions:

- If our intention is solely for Allah, we will attain maximum Barakah.
- If the intention is only for ourselves or to show off to others, we will achieve the least Barakah (and Barakah may be removed from our life).
- However, if the intention is mixed - partly for Allah and partly for people - we will receive the reward and Barakah of that intention according to our sincerity.

Imam Al-Ghazali draws an analogy to a person on a diet for medical reasons. If you follow your diet strictly, you're more likely to heal and enjoy good health. If you have regular cheat days and waver with your diet, you'll benefit from it as much as you can adhere to it.

Sh. Sulaiman Nadwi's hierarchy of intentions classifies our intentions based on this concept of sincerity:

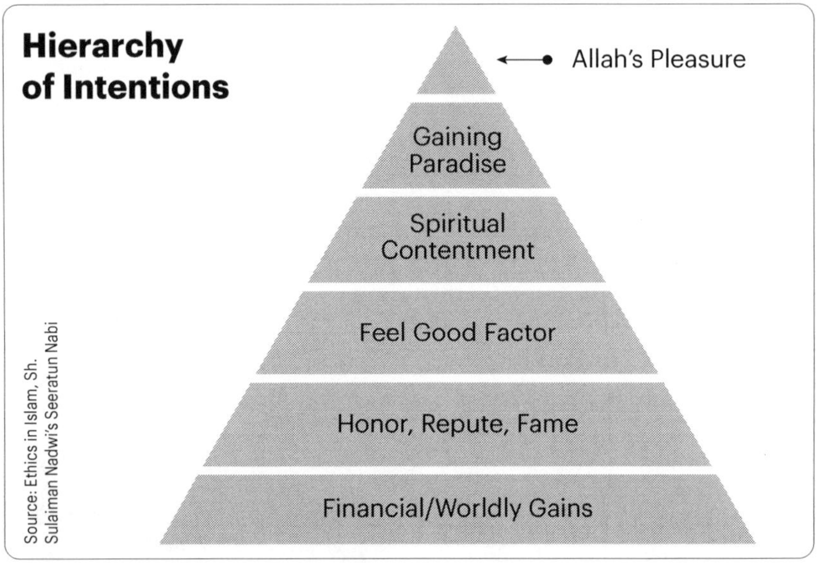

According to Sh. Sulaiman Nadwi, there are six levels of intentions.

HUSTLE CULTURE – THE FIRST THREE LEVELS

These first three levels of intentions – financial or worldly gain, honour/reputation/fame, and feel-good factor - are the three types of intentions most prevalent in Hustle Culture. They closely match the three levels of motivations found in most corporate culture, known as:

- **Achievement Motivation** - the focus is the 'need to achieve' (financial or worldly gain)
- **Affiliation Motivation** - the focus is the 'need to be liked' (honour/reputation/fame)
- **Power Motivation** - the focus is building a power base

or what makes them feel ‘strong’ about themselves (feel good factor)

Let’s dig into each level a little further.

Financial/Worldly Gain

The intentions that attract the least Barakah are those that are solely for financial/worldly gain, such as a promotion at work, more money or more material goods. People trapped in Hustle Culture set this type of intention every day as they strive towards their worldly goals. They’re motivated by the infamous question: what’s in it for me? While you may experience temporary euphoria and a dose of happiness if you achieve your worldly intention, you will likely feel empty afterwards. And if you’re like the majority of people and don’t achieve lofty financial/worldly intentions, you’ll feel frustrated, stressed, and trapped in the rat race of life.

Honour, Reputation and Fame

Some followers of Hustle Culture eventually upgrade their intentions to seeking honour, reputation and fame. They’ll do acts of service even if they won’t personally benefit from it to gain appreciation and respect. Their driving question is: what would people think of me? Although this level of intention is more purposeful than financial/worldly gain, ostentation or ‘showing off’, ultimately corrupts our sincerity.

Not only does the honour, reputation and fame intention corrupt the sincerity of our intentions - ultimately derailing our hope to receive Barakah - but it also severely impacts our mental health. If you do things for people's praise and you don't get the praise that you feel you deserve, you feel spiteful and insecure, perhaps even envious of others who achieved praise for similar acts. Fear of failure (and sometimes fear of success) become like ghosts that keep chasing you to self-sabotage your own work. Sometimes you might feel guilty and suffer from imposter syndrome when you feel that the honour, reputation and fame you got is not something you deserve - since who you are in public doesn't match who you really are in private. We see the drama of people trapped in this level of intentions among social media influencers, celebrities and politicians, where their desire for recognition drives more absurd and erratic behaviour.

OVERCOMING OSTENTATION FOR A LIFE FILLED WITH BARAKAH

Let's define ostentation and why it's particularly problematic for living a life of Barakah. Ostentation can be defined as the act of performing deeds with the motive of impressing others, in order that they regard one as a pious and saintly individual.

There are two types of ostentation. The first is one that is obvious and which people generally detest: the humble-braggers, attention-seekers, and self-promoters who like to boast about their achievements and seek admiration for the work they do. They boast about how much charity they gave or how many times they went to *hajj* or of their service to the community. And in the professional domain, they brag about how hard they worked and take credit for all the work done. This type of ostentation is the most prevalent in today's Hustle Culture.

Many Barakah seeking professionals struggle to see a way to succeed in Hustle Culture without falling victim to this form of ostentation. They reason: if I don't brag about my work and role, I won't get noticed and others will take credit for my work. But the answer to this is found in Surah Yusuf, where Prophet Yusuf when asked to be advisor to the king, he openly told him:

> *Joseph said, 'Put me in charge of the nation's storehouses: I shall manage them prudently and carefully.'*
>
> (QURAN 12:55)

Yusuf stepped up to the role when he was best fit for it - not to show off or take on work that he can't do, but because he knew he was the best fit for the work at hand.

The second type of ostentation is more subtle. “The sign of this type of ostentation is a man’s desire to be honoured when he meets others: that he be appointed to a position of prominence and leadership, with others serving him. When he is honoured, he becomes elated. When such honour is not forthcoming from people, he is stung with surprise. This attitude indicates that the person’s efforts and deeds are motivated by the desire for name and fame, and to gain service from people.” (COMMENTARY BY SH. ABDULLAH GANGOHI, BOOK OF WISDOMS).

In 2017, I was invited to give a keynote presentation at the World Domination Summit - a summit of entrepreneurs, authors, and speakers. It was my first major TED-like talk in front of a mainstream audience and I chose to speak about Barakah.

As I was preparing for my speech, I noticed something about my *nafs* - it was imagining the appreciation and standing ovation that I would get after the speech; it wanted to be recognised. I realised that if I don’t rid myself of this desire, the Barakah of the speech would be removed.

The morning of my keynote, I went for a long walk and talked to my *nafs*. I reminded my *nafs* that Allah had blessed me with this opportunity to speak in front of a large audience (mostly non-Muslims) and if I sincerely wanted the Barakah of my speech to enter the hearts of listeners, I would need to be more sincere and remove any desire for wanting recognition or fame from the speech.

Sitting at a breakfast table, I made a counter-intuitive *dua*: "O Allah, don't let me see a standing ovation for this speech, I just want you to accept it and put Barakah in it".

Leading up to the keynote, I kept reminding myself to stay sincere. As I walked on stage, I said Bismillah and delivered a 20-minute speech on Barakah. As soon as I was done, I walked straight off stage and was glad it was over. Moments later, my host reached out to me and was upset because apparently, I was getting a standing ovation but I wasn't there to witness it. Alhamdulillah.

You might think: well, what's wrong with being motivated by a standing ovation or some praise? Wouldn't that increase your performance and force you to do better?

Once again, this comes down to the difference between Hustle Culture and Barakah Culture. Hustle Culture is ego-centred, whereas Barakah Culture focuses purely on God. Seeking recognition and praise from those besides Allah, means that we have other people in our heart and not God.

Another common question people ask is: what if people praise me or I derive pleasure and joy when someone praises me? Does that mess up my intention or remove its Barakah?

It is normal and human to feel good when you do a good deed and people praise you for it, but these feelings alone should not be the primary incentive for doing a good deed or stopping a bad habit.

The Feel-Good Factor

There are people whose intentions are not about financial/worldly gain, nor about honour, reputation and fame. Their intention is to simply feel good about whatever they intend to do - even at a financial or reputational cost. These are the good citizens whom we honour in society; the heroes who stand up to truth and justice. They are driven by the question: how will this make me feel? Although this is a more sincere level of intention, since it doesn't want anything in return from society, it still falls short from the higher levels for intentions we'll explain below. Why? For one, it's not reliable. What makes one person feel good about something may not necessarily be good for others. For example, volunteer tourism or 'voluntourism' is an emerging travel trend linked to doing good when visiting poor countries for tourism. Unfortunately, there have been many concerns that people who engage in volunteer tourism may not actually be helping those who they are serving and may instead be perpetuating patronising ideas about the countries they visit. Another reason why the feel good factor is not reliable is that what makes someone feel good one day, may not make them feel good the next day. For example, I may feel good today to help my parents around the house. But what if I don't feel good about it tomorrow? Do I stop helping them? People who are stuck at this level of intention will do just that – they won't be helpful to others because it doesn't feel good anymore. We see a lot of this in volunteer organisations where volunteers join an organisation to support a cause and the moment it doesn't feel good anymore, they leave.

People whose motivation is 'what makes me feel good' are still operating from an ego-centric perspective with all its desires, weaknesses and whims. They are still stuck in the 'what's in it for me' mentality and their intention doesn't' take them beyond that.

BARAKAH CULTURE – THE TOP THREE LEVELS OF INTENTIONS

To experience a life filled with Barakah, we must elevate our intentions to one of the top three levels of intention shown in the pyramid: spiritual contentment, seeking paradise, and *ikhlas* (sincerity). Let's explore these crucial levels in more detail:

Spiritual Contentment

To break from Hustle Culture and set the intentions that will bring Barakah and Barakah Culture into your life, you need to embrace a God-centric, Hereafter-focused, spiritual lifestyle that guides your intentions. When you make this switch, you'll be able to access the next level of intention, which is about spiritual contentment. At that level, you're not focused on doing things that simply feel good, but rather, doing things that feel good spiritually. Your intentions will now focus on cultivating spiritual wellbeing, beyond the whims and desires of the self. In other words, you'll ask yourself: what intention would make me sleep peacefully at night or reach the end of my life and not feel guilt or shame? Every now and then, you might be pulled to lower levels of intention, but the sweetness of spiritual contentment in your heart will push you up again.

Yet even this spiritual level of intention is hostage to how spiritual the self feels at any point in time. People who arrive at this level of intention may find that when they're in a 'spiritual' mood, they'll tap into more of their spiritual side to make decisions and carry on actions, and if they are in a less spiritual mood, they might falter and slide back into low levels of intentions. We see this in the infamous post-Ramadan dip. People experience a spiritual high during the month of Ramadan, especially the last 10 nights, and then after Ramadan, their spirituality drops, and they are unable to maintain even half the level of spirituality they had during the blessed month. The challenge: when the spiritual feel-good factor of Ramadan is over, we lose that environment and find it hard to sustain that level of spirituality. The solution? We need to upgrade our intentions even further to the next level.

Gaining Paradise

The next level up in the intentions hierarchy is the intention to achieve success in the Hereafter, captured by entering the Eternal Garden of Paradise. All action one does in this world becomes a measure of whether it'll attract God's Mercy and enter them in Paradise, or protect them from God's Punishment, the Eternal Hellfire. Setting intentions not based on worldly goals but the Hereafter keeps one focused on the bigger picture of life - specifically, the question Allah poses to humanity in the Quran: "So where are you [people] going?" (QURAN: 81:26). Moreover, since we never know when death will come knocking on our doors, it sparks a sense of urgency in us to do the right thing on a moment-to-moment basis, so that we die in the state most pleasing to Him. The Prophet ﷺ said, "Everyone will be raised in the condition in which he dies" (MUSLIM). Seeking the Hereafter is a level that's commended in the Quran, Allah says:

> *If anyone desires a harvest in the life to come, We shall increase it for him; if anyone desires a harvest in this world, We shall give him a share of it, but in the Hereafter he will have no share.* (QURAN 42:20)

Focusing on the Hereafter is a powerful way to stay connected to the Divine and it's what Allah reminds us to focus on in many parts of the Quran. However, many people are unaware of an even higher level of intention that transcends the pursuit of rewards in the Hereafter. This pinnacle of intention is to act sincerely for God alone. Ibn Ata'illah offers a profound insight on this matter:

> *"Whoever worships Him for something he hopes for from Him, or in order to stave off the arrival of chastisement, has not concerned himself with the real nature of His Attributes."*

Commenting on this maxim by Ibn Ata'illah, Sh. Abdullah Gangohi says: "If the servant's purpose in rendering worship is the acquisition of Paradise and salvation from Hell, then Allah-willing - he will achieve these goals. However, [in this scenario] he has desired personal pleasure by way of worship. He thus remains trapped in the web of the ego; he has not discharged the right of Allah's lofty attributes. The servant's attribute of excellence is that his worship should be purely for Allah's greatness and glory, not because of the sole desire for Paradise or fear of Hell. The duty of the slave is to serve, whether the Master favours or rebuffs him."

Seeking Ikhlas

Hasan al Basri was asked: "Which would you choose first: to pray two *raka'at* (unit of prayer) ? Or to enter Paradise?" He answered: "I would pray two *raka'at* first." When asked "why?", he replied: "Because praying two *rak'at* pleases Allah, whereas entering Paradise pleases me. And a polite slave will choose what pleases Allah over what pleases himself or herself."

Embracing true *ikhlas* is the ultimate goal in our spiritual journey, as it entails acting purely for Allah's sake without any desire for personal gain in this world or the next. This unwavering devotion to God serves as the most potent catalyst for unlocking abundant Barakah in our lives.

Based on the above analysis of the six levels of intentions, I've expanded the model developed by Nabeel Al-Azami to capture the full spectrum of the hierarchy of intentions, especially in relation to Barakah Culture vs Hustle Culture.

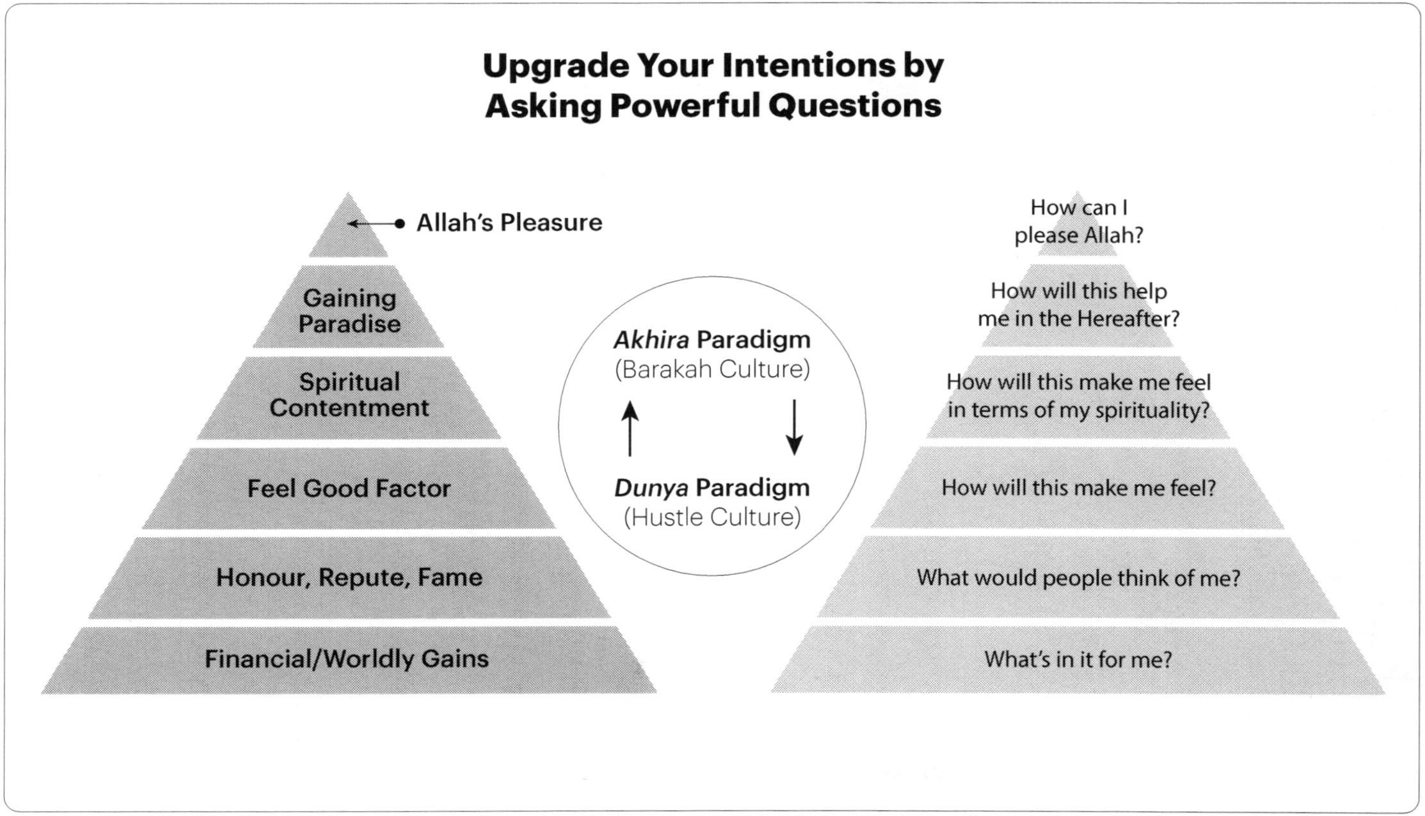
Upgrade Your Intentions by
Asking Powerful Questions
Allah's Pleasure
Gaining Paradise
Spiritual Contentment
Feel Good Factor
Honour, Repute, Fame
Financial/Worldly Gains
Akhira Paradigm
(Barakah Culture)
Dunya Paradigm
(Hustle Culture)
How can I please Allah?
How will this help me in the Hereafter?
How will this make me feel in terms of my spirituality?
How will this make me feel?
What would people think of me?
What's in it for me?

Grasping the hierarchy of intentions enables us to assess our current level of sincerity and strive towards purifying our intentions to attain the state of *ikhlas*. This purification process entails separating the true essence of worship from any impurities that may tarnish it. As a result, some scholars liken this refinement of intention to alchemy - converting the base metal of our ego-driven and selfish deeds into the precious gold of pure acts of worship that we humbly offer to Allah. Let's run through an example to see how the hierarchy of intentions can be used in practice to attract Barakah in your life.

Levelling Up Intentions in Practice

Suppose you want to exercise. Your initial intention may be for honour/reputation/fame. You want people to look at you and comment on your physique, how healthy you look, and how you fit nicely in a new set of clothes. You can upgrade your intention and seek a feel good factor. This is a welcome upgrade. You don't care much about what people say and simply want to feel good about your body after a good workout. After exercising for a few weeks, you realise that exercise is linked to your emotional state and its feel good factor can fluctuate based on so many factors in your life. Or perhaps you've become so obsessed with how good exercise makes you feel, that it's now a means of escaping other life challenges.

When you hit an intention plateau and you feel trapped in world-centred intentions and don't see the Barakah in your actions, it's time to break from the Hustle Culture levels of intention and level up to Barakah Culture intentions.

After much reflection, you realise that exercise helps you feel good spiritually. When you exercise, you feel grateful about your body and overall health, and your spiritual awareness increases. You start to contemplate God's intricate miracle in how your body works, adapts and grows. Moreover, on some days you choose not to exercise because your spirituality is calling you to fulfil other responsibilities with family or work. You become less selfish and it's less about you and your gym time and more about increasing movement and exercise in your body so you can be a better person overall.

At this point, you can stop or reflect deeper and try to make exercise a pathway to paradise. How? You realise that on days you exercise, you have more energy to perform acts of worship that you normally don't have on other days. You're less stressed and treat those around you with goodness and charity. You find that exercise helps you spend excess energy - energy that would have been wasted in pointless pursuits or sinful activities.

You're doing great - you've levelled up your intention from simply how you look, all the way to being a better person. Now, push yourself further. What if you upgraded your intention for exercise and made it purely for Allah's sake? You're not exercising to look good or feel good or boost your spirituality, or even seek paradise. You exercise because you realise that this body is a trust from Allah - a gift from your Creator - and maintaining this gift shows not only how grateful you are, but also your love and devotion to the Bestower of this Gift.

Can you see the power of intentions in upgrading simple daily activities into acts of worship? Now think of a person who upgrades such mundane activity to the highest level of intention. Don't you think Allah will put so much Barakah in their health for that sincere intention?

If this seems overwhelming, remember that the process of cultivating *ikhlas* doesn't happen overnight. **For now, see if you can upgrade your intentions in the following domains:**

1. Cooking a meal for your family.
2. Submitting a report to your boss.
3. Reciting Quran with a beautiful voice.

HOW SINCERE ARE YOUR INTENTIONS?

If you're unsure where your intentions fall in the hierarchy of intentions, conduct the following sincerity tests:

1. **The Benefit Test:** When contemplating different deeds or actions within your day, ask yourself: would you do these actions if you didn't get any praise, recognition or worldly benefit from it? If yes, you know that at a minimum, your intention is above the honour, reputation, fame intention in the pyramid.
2. **The 'What If It Fails?' Test:** What happens to your heart when your efforts don't bear fruit? By detaching from the results of an action, both success and failure won't impact your heart, and you'll concentrate on sincerity and seeking God's acceptance by giving your best effort. If your heart is easily swayed by failure (or success), this is a reminder to elevate your intentions and remain sincere for His sake.

3. **The Criticism Test:** How do you respond when someone criticises you or your work or when you receive constructive or negative feedback? When your intentions are sincere, though negative feedback may be hurtful, the opinions of others won't deter you from doing what's right. If you're easily discouraged by others' opinions, your intention may be closer to honour, reputation and fame than you realise.

Practical Tips to Cultivate Sincerity and Reap the Barakah

One of my favourite verses in the Quran is the following verse from Surah Al-Ankabut:

> *But We shall be sure to guide to Our ways those who strive hard for Our cause: God is with those who do good.*
>
> (QURAN 29:69)

Sincerity is something that we can cultivate. It needs practice, but we can keep reorienting our intentions until they ultimately settle in the service of God. While only Allah can truly gauge our sincerity, taking steps towards it can help us find, and stay on, the path to attracting Barakah in our lives.

Although I don't claim to be an expert in cultivating sincere intentions, I have collected some practical tips over the years that can help us develop sincerity.

1. Don't Force an Intention

One of the paradoxes of sincere intention is that you can't force yourself to be sincere. Think of love. Can you force yourself to love someone? All you can do is prepare your heart as best as you can for those moments of sincerity. The first step is self-awareness and to recognise the battle for sincerity that's taking place in your heart.

2. Don't 'See' Your Work

Part of preparing your heart for sincerity is try not to 'see' your work or notice it. A lot of us when we do good work, we'll spend days admiring it even if we don't tell others about it. We see and notice the hours we recited Quran or the amount of money we gave in charity or the mentorship we gave a young colleague. Sincerity is to do the good work and just move on. Don't dwell and admire it and think you're great.

Below are three strategies for resisting self-admiration:

1.Recognise how poor the work you're doing is compared to the Majesty of your Lord.

One way to help you stop seeing and noticing your work is to reduce the significance of your work and realise that it's nothing in the grand scheme of Allah's work. I once observed an ant as it crawled on my kitchen table. It was busy scurrying around searching for food. In an instant, I reflected on how the ant must feel very accomplished for carrying a piece of grain from one end of the kitchen table to the other. But in the grand scheme of creation, this achievement doesn't mean much. Like the ant in our lives, we're less significant in size and impact than an atom in the sight of Allah, and therefore we shouldn't feel too proud of our good deeds as if we're doing a favour for Allah.

2. Don't give into your ego and never be satisfied with it.

No matter what you sacrifice for God's sake, you'll never fulfil the overwhelming debt that we owe to Allah. Prophet Muhammad ﷺ related to us the story of a worshipper who spent years worshipping His Lord and so when he died, God said that he should enter Paradise with His mercy. The worshipper protested and said I spent my entire life in your service, shall you not enter me to Paradise according to all the good deeds I did? So, Allah asked that his good deeds should be weighed on one side of the Eternal Scale and the blessing of eyesight should be weighed on the other. The blessing of eyesight outweighed all his good deeds. The worshipper asked God for forgiveness and asked to enter Paradise with His mercy.

3. Understand how much shaytan (the devil) has influenced your work.

***Shaytan* can come to you in many ways to trick you away from sincerity, as Imam Al-Ghazali explains in the following scenarios:**

- Scenario 1: He'll come to you to tell you to improve your good deed, so that people see that you're pious. Most spiritually intelligent people won't fall for this, as it is obviously ostentation.
- Scenario 2: He'll come to you to tell you that you're a good person and people look up to you. Do good, he says, and they'll follow you and you'll get their reward. You might believe he's right, but in reality, he's just feeding your ego.
- Scenario 3: He'll come to you while you're doing something in secret and try to make you imagine how would others react if they saw you.

A righteous man was used to praying in the first row at his mosque for 30 years, and one day he was late, and he felt shy of people seeing him not at his usual first row spot. Then, he realised that perhaps his 30 years of diligence was simply ostentation, and it made him repent. This is the subtlety of the trick of *shaytan*.

The key to sincerity is that it shouldn't matter whether a person, an animal or any creature sees you or not. You wouldn't do anything differently. And this is the crux of being sincere. As Sh. Sulaiman Nadwi puts it:

> *Until we believe that there is a Being who is the Knower of all secrets, omniscient and aware of every movement and action of our hearts; and until we believe that we shall be accountable and answerable to that Being for our deeds, no sincerity of purpose or detachment from worldly desire can be produced in our hearts, and, as a result no noble and unselfish conduct can ensue.* (ETHICS IN ISLAM)

As I observed that ant crawling across the table, busy with its life, I imagined how it'd react if it knew that there was a human being watching it as it moved around. I then realised how forgetful I'd been of my own Lord watching over me and how, when I engage in a good deed, I forget the Ever-Watchful.

It's ok to admit our own mixed intentions. Intentions are complex; we are works in progress and Allah will reward us according to our intentions. This is not to relax but to recognise that we need to work harder even if we may not be able to reach perfection. Sh. Khalil advised that I repeat this phrase often: *ilahi anata maqsudi wa ridaka matluby* (O Allah, you're my purpose and your pleasure is what I seek).

We spent a lot of time diving deep into intentions because this is the crux of Barakah Culture: if you focus on nothing else but sincere intentions, you'll unlock a multitude of Barakah in your life.

In the mid-2000s, I visited renowned scholar Sh. Abdullah

Bin Bayyah in Jeddah and asked him for advice. After a moment of silence, he said, “have sincere intentions and work hard” – **that is the essence of Barakah Culture.**

CHAPTER SEVEN

Life is Not About You, it's About Serving Your Lord with Excellence

> *Say, "Surely my prayer, my worship, my life, and my death are all for Allah—Lord of all worlds.* (QURAN 6:162)

A couple of years ago, I was planning my trip to Mecca. Like many people, I looked for the best deals online and found a great five-star hotel with a beautiful room that overlooked the *Ka'ba*. It had everything I could ask for, including a coffee machine that brewed to perfection.

But when I opened the windows and looked out at the *Ka'ba*, I felt something was off. Here I was, in a luxurious hotel room, towering over the holiest shrine on earth. Was this really service to God? I felt embarrassed and awkward for trying to personalise my *umrah* experience and making it more about me than serving my Lord.

Don't get me wrong – there's nothing wrong with enjoying a comfortable *umrah* experience or the modern amenities around the Holy Mosque in Mecca. But my experience made me think about the ego-centred lifestyle that has seeped into our acts of worship. A few decades ago, no rooms existed with a view of the *Ka'ba*, and for centuries, the journey to *umrah* or *hajj* was extremely difficult.

It's almost as if *hajj* and *umrah* were meant to remind us that life is not about us – it's about serving our Lord with excellence.

For me, my experience felt like the opposite of what the builder of the *Ka'ba*, Prophet Ibrahim, stood for. He was willing to sacrifice his child, his family, and himself for the sake of God. It made me think about the importance of humility and putting our own desires aside in our acts of worship. If we can adopt this mindset, we can unlock Barakah in our lives.

We live in strange times.

Each one of us have become individuals worshipping our own selves and desires, thus removing the Barakah from our lives.

We try to personalise everything in our lives for our individual needs and become upset if an action or circumstance doesn't meet or serve our individual desires.

When you adopt this individualistic mindset, you reduce the Barakah in your life, since life will be about you and you won't be willing to make the necessary sacrifices for God or others in society. This is the antithesis to Barakah Culture. Allah says in the Quran:

> *Say, 'O Prophet,' "If your parents and children and siblings and spouses and extended family and the wealth*

> *you have acquired and the trade you fear will decline and the homes you cherish—'if all these' are more beloved to you than Allah and His Messenger and struggling in His Way, then wait until Allah brings about His Will. Allah does not guide the rebellious people."*
>
> (QURAN 9:24)

The COVID-19 pandemic has been a global wake-up call that reminds us that our actions have significant impact on others. When we refused to wear masks, stay indoors, and reduce social gatherings in the name of personal freedom, we put the lives of vulnerable people at risk. Sadly, our ego-centric mindset didn't seem to care.

When people started hoarding toilet paper and hand sanitisers, it became apparent that extreme individualism has a painful cost. The pandemic revealed the consequences of putting personal interests before the collective good. If we continue to live selfishly, we may not survive as a society the next time a pandemic or natural disaster hits us.

In contrast, the Prophet ﷺ described a tribe called Al-Ashareen and their selfless behaviour during difficult times. They would gather all the provisions they had and divide them equally among themselves. The Prophet ﷺ said, "They are of me, and I am of them," showing the beauty and Barakah of sacrificing for the common good.

As human beings, we have always understood that we are stronger when we work together. Throughout history, our ancestors lived in tribes and clans, recognising the importance of community. Moreover, Islam emphasised the importance of community and congregation in many verses of the Quran and sayings of Prophet Muhammad ﷺ:

> *Abu Al-Darda reported: I heard the Messenger of Allah ﷺ saying, "If three men in a village or in the desert, make no arrangement for salah in congregation, Satan must have certainly overcome them. So observe salah in congregation, for the wolf eats up a solitary sheep that stays far from the flock."* (ABU DAWUD)

If we leave people to 'live their life' as individuals without responsibility to society, we're essentially creating a recipe for societal disaster as described in the following *hadith*: "The likeness of the man who observes the limits prescribed by Allah and that of the man who transgresses them is like the people who get on board a ship after casting lots. Some of them are in its lower deck and some of them in its upper deck. Those who are in its lower deck, when they require water, go to the occupants of the upper deck, and say to them: 'If we make a hole in the bottom of the ship, we shall not harm you.' If they (the occupants of the upper deck) leave them to carry out their design, they all will be drowned. But if they do not let them go ahead (with their plan), all of them will remain safe." (BUKHARI)

The five pillars of Islam are all reminders that life is not about you, and giving up some of your desires for the sake of worship is beneficial:

- The first pillar - *the shahadah* - is about giving up worshipping anything but Allah (including yourself).
- The second pillar - *salah* - is about giving up some of your busy schedule to dedicate a portion of it for prayers.
- The third pillar - *zakat* - is about giving up some of your wealth for the poor and needy.
- The fourth pillar - fasting during the month of Ramadan - is about giving up on our basic desires of food, water, and sex for a set number of hours for 30 days.
- The fifth pillar - *hajj* - is about giving up time, energy, wealth, and the conveniences of life, so you can journey to God.

Instead of accepting the above five pillars as they are, we try to bend these acts of worship according to our individual needs:

- We try to squeeze *salah* in our busy schedule by rushing through it, combining all prayers together, or giving up on praying five times a day altogether.
- We look for fatwas that ease the obligation of *zakat* on some of our assets so we can spend more money on things we want.
- We biohack our fasting with pills and supplements so we can carry on with Ramadan without it impacting our per-

formance at work.
- And we want to customise our *hajj* experience so it's as painless as possible.

Hustle Culture has warped our understanding of sacrificing for God, and we need to reclaim it back if we want to see Barakah in our lives.

Why We Became Ego-Centred?

Before discussing strategies for living a God-oriented life rather than an ego-centred one, we must first examine how we developed such high degree of selfishness in our modern world. While Hustle Culture has played a significant role, there are other socio-cultural factors that have contributed to our self-interest. Until we acknowledge and confront the ways in which we have engineered this behaviour, we cannot eradicate it.

1. Survival Instincts that Don't Trust God

One cause of our ego-centricity is our human survival instinct. While this is helpful to a certain extent, such as protecting us from danger and ensuring that we take care of ourselves, when it crosses a certain threshold - particularly when it exceeds the limits set by God and those we are responsible for - this survival instinct becomes corruptive.

This survival instinct mainly comes from our lack of trust in God and His provision. We feel that in order to survive (or thrive), others need to fail or not be as successful as we are.

This leads to envy and toxic competition and thus removes Barakah from our lives.

2. Deteriorating Communities and Family Ties

Secondly, and perhaps most importantly, we've lost our ability to be patient with others and be part of something greater than ourselves. We want to bend everything (and everyone) around us to our desires and if they do not comply, we get annoyed, upset or break our relationship with them. Little do we realise that this individualistic mindset is the cause of so much strife and hardship in our lives and the loss of Barakah.

Consider the fact that for centuries it was common to see families living together in a multi-generational home or piece of land. From great-grandparents to extended cousins, you'd see them all living in the same vicinity with loving memories, family dramas, and tangled social experiences. Love it or hate it, this interconnectedness brought Barakah in the home as people shared memories, ate together, and took care of the elders and children as one big family. Living together - as challenging as it may seem - does not allow for an ego-centred lifestyle since resources are shared, boundaries are shared, and unless you want to be an outcast, you'll try to find a role for yourself in the wider context of the family.

Nowadays, we have lost this sense of interconnectedness and live independently. This has led to a loss of Barakah in many ways, such as wasting resources, neglecting the elders, losing our ties of kinship, and losing our social safety net.

1. **Wasting resources:** Instead of sharing resources with the extended family, every time we move to a new home, city or country, we need to start from scratch and buy new furniture, appliances, vehicles etc. This additional material burden, especially at the beginning of one's life, traps you in Hustle Culture and workism. You need to earn more and more money to support your independent life.
2. **Neglecting the elders:** 'What do we do about parents?' is a common question most adult children ask when their parents reach a certain age. We have designed and built our lives so independently that caring for our parents seems like an extra burden and rarely part of our life plan.
3. **Losing the ties of kinship:** In a multigenerational household, you'd know all your relatives well and spend quality time with them. Nowadays, you might not know half of your family or what's happening in their lives because you live halfway across the world. And our children? They probably couldn't recognise their own relatives if they bumped into them at an airport!
4. **Losing the social safety net:** We are constantly worried about what will happen to our kids after we die - especially if we're poor. As a collective, we've stopped taking care of orphans and there's no 'social guarantee' that our own children will be taken care of by those close to us. David Brooks in an Atlantic article explains:

"If you want to summarise the changes in family structure over the past century, the truest thing to say is this:

We've made life freer for individuals and more unstable for families. We've made life better for adults but worse for children. We've moved from big, interconnected, and extended families, which helped protect the most vulnerable people in society from the shocks of life, to smaller, detached nuclear families (a married couple and their children), which give the most privileged people in society room to maximise their talents and expand their options. The shift from bigger and interconnected extended families to smaller and detached nuclear families ultimately led to a familial system that liberates the rich and ravages the working-class and the poor." – The Nuclear Family Was a Mistake, The Atlantic.

The above account is only one example of how an individualistic mindset can truly destroy not just a family, but an entire generation.

When Allah described this *ummah* as the best community, he didn't describe us as a community of superhuman individuals, but as a successful community of believers that work together, support each other, and hold each other accountable:

[Believers], you are the best community singled out for people: you order what is right, forbid what is wrong, and believe in God. If the People of the Book had also believed, it would have been better for them. For although some of them do believe, most of them are lawbreakers- (QURAN 3:110)

The Prophet Muhammad ﷺ described believers as one body. If we are not able to be one body with our own families, how will we be one body as a community or *ummah* at large?

3. Personalised Consumerism

Additionally, modern consumerism drives the ego-centred life. Everything can be personalised to the nth degree to fit our exact desire and serve our egos in highly specialised ways. From the type of food we eat, to the brand of coffee we drink, everything can be customised to our egos. Even gadgets that should be standard tools can be customised with personalised engravings of our names on the device. This explosion of personalisation and customisation of products and services to our individual needs keeps feeding the ego-centred lifestyle.

We need to take off the expensive, pompous clothes of individualism and wear the clothes of servitude to Allah if we want Barakah in our lives.

HOW SHAYTAN EXPLOITS OUR INSTINCTS

From the very beginning of human existence, the choice between living an ego-centred life or a God-centred life has been present. When Allah created Adam, he was intended to live a life of worship and to be God's vicegerent on earth. However, *shaytan* exploited Adam's *nafs*, or inner desires, and led him to make the mistake of eating from the forbidden tree.

When Adam was in Jannah, *shaytan* promised him two things:

1. Immortality
2. Power and Kingdom that never ends.

> *But Satan whispered to Adam, saying, 'Adam, shall I show you the tree of immortality and power that never decays?'* (QURAN 20:120)

If you think about this, these are the two things every human being desires: to live as long as possible, and to own as many items or have power as much as possible. These two desires are what Hustle Culture exploits to convince us to worship ourselves (or work) instead of Allah.

Interestingly, even though Adam was already in Jannah, which should have fulfilled his desires for immortality and ownership, *shaytan* exploited his human weakness and made him turn away from the Barakah in Jannah. In our own lives, we may also have everything we need for a life of Barakah, yet still feel like something is missing. *Shaytan* takes advantage of this feeling to make us desire things that are not permissible and lead us astray from the path of Allah.

Of course, the story doesn't end there. Although *shaytan* did convince Adam to disobey Allah, Adam and *Hawa* (Eve), realising their mistake, sought God's forgiveness and they were forgiven - a reminder that just because you turn towards Hustle Culture and an ego-centred life, it never means the door to Barakah is shut in your face.

From Selfishness to Selflessness

In our pursuit of selfish desires, we've lost sight of our true purpose in life: to worship Allah and serve His creation. Our innate need to serve and sacrifice for a higher cause is natural, but we often direct it towards fleeting and temporary things that cannot fulfil us in the long run.

In 1908, Josiah Royce - a Harvard philosopher - asked himself: why is food and shelter not enough for us? Do we crave more in life than simply being safe and alive? He reached a conclusion that as humans, we have an intrinsic need to live for a cause beyond ourselves. He believed that when we have something worth sacrificing for in our lives, we give our lives meaning. He called this The Philosophy of Loyalty.

The question is: <u>**what is worth sacrificing to make life truly meaningful?**</u>

- You may sacrifice your life for **a loved one**, but they may abandon you, disappoint you, leave you or die.
- You may sacrifice your life for **your country,** but countries rise and fall, and your social values keep changing until you don't recognise your country anymore.
- You may sacrifice for **an ideology or principle,** but your ideology or principle may be proven wrong or you may change over time.
- You may sacrifice your life for **work**, and we've all seen where that leads...(hint: workism).

When you sacrifice your life for anything other than Allah, you're essentially sacrificing your life for a transient cause that will never truly fulfil you. Even though some of the above are worthy causes, Barakah Culture puts Allah first and everything else after.

One of the challenges of living a God-centred life vs an ego-centred life, is that you don't see the immediate benefit of living a God-centred life (at least not rationally).

Living an ego-centred life feels better and happier yet continually following our desires is exhausting. Imagine a day where you wake up and can eat and drink anything you want. You have a great breakfast, a wonderful lunch and an exquisite dinner. By the end of the day, even though you're satiated and should feel happy, you feel full, bloated, and a bit guilty from all the calories you consumed.

Compare that to waking up in the morning and deciding to fast instead. Yes, you'll feel hungry and tired and groggy throughout the day, and you'll probably question the decision of fasting multiple times. But by the end of the day, when you break your fast with a single date and a glass of water, not only do you find a deep sense of spiritual contentment and gratitude, but your day feels full of Barakah, which no amount of food can ever compensate for.

The challenge for us is to be spiritually intelligent enough to make the daily commitment to live a God-centred life, even when it's inconvenient or tiresome, knowing that Allah is the most gracious and no effort or pain will pass in vain.

Living an ego-centred life may feel comfortable in the short term but it's like chasing a mirage - we'll never truly quench our thirst for meaning and purpose. When we commit ourselves to living a God-centred life, we tap into the wellspring of Barakah that Allah has promised us, and we discover the joy and contentment that comes from fulfilling our true purpose in life.

Living a God-Centred Life

The human journey is a journey of submitting to Allah until we reach the highest state of *ubudiyya* - slavery to God[9]. The sooner we accept our role in life as His slaves, the sooner we will let go of our ego-centric tendencies and see the Barakah in our lives. If we don't opt-in to be a slave of God, by default we'll opt-in to the individualistic, Hustle Culture mindset and be slaves to our own desires.

Accepting that we're God's slaves is the first step to recognising that life is not about you, but about serving your Lord and His creatures with excellence. This mindset is essential to live a life of Barakah, and it has significant implications on our personal and professional lives.

When you live as a slave of God, you embody the notion that you have a Master and that you won't do anything in your life without your Master's permission.

In traditional Islamic books, you'll often read the parable of the king who sends one of his slaves to a special town to fulfil certain duties. However, when the slave reaches that town, he gets distracted with its beauty and glamour and gets busy trying to establish a business and build a life for himself in that town. One day, the king calls him back and asks the servant if he fulfilled his duties in the new town. How do you think the king should treat the servant when he finds out that the servant did not fulfil his duties as per the king's command?

When we acknowledge that we are slaves of Allah, rather than being the masters of our own destiny as some self-help books suggest, we understand that every experience we have in life is a test from our Creator. He wants to see how we respond and if we recognise His presence during both good and bad times.

WHEN YOU'RE GOD-CENTRED

- Your daily concern is **how can I please Allah in every moment of my life.**
- You're willing to sacrifice your personal desires, comforts and even some of your rights in order to seek a higher reward from Allah.
- Your cost benefit analysis is not worldly focused but Hereafter focused. You're always analysing what's the benefit of doing something for the Hereafter vs just for this world. This characteristic explains why the companions of the Prophet Muhammad ﷺ made such huge sacrifices with their property, wealth, and lifestyle. The cost and benefit analysis were so clear to them, and doing things for Allah always seemed more beneficial than the traditional worldly cost benefit analysis.
- You can commit to the mindsets, values and rituals that attract Barakah in your life, despite them being difficult at times.

- You live with a sense of responsibility rather than entitlement.
- You recognise that your wealth, health, family and everything you own or know is a trust from God that you'll be questioned about. Therefore, you work hard to protect, nurture and grow these blessings from God.
- You truly understand the meaning of "We belong to God, and to Him we shall return" when calamities hit you.

> *Those who say, when afflicted with a calamity, 'We belong to God and to Him we shall return.' These will be given blessings and mercy from their Lord, and it is they who are rightly guided.* (QURAN 2:156-157)

The benefits of living a God-centred life are undeniable and unmatched. You'll not only feel closer to Allah and aligned with His purpose, but you'll also better tackle the ups and downs of life.

HOW BARAKAH CULTURE HELPS YOU DEAL WITH LIFE

According to Islamic tradition, we constantly live between four states:

1. Bounty
2. Calamity or Difficulty
3. Obedience
4. Disobedience

These are the four states that our lives revolve around.

In Hustle Culture, how do we normally manage each of these four states?

1. When we are in a state of bounty: we are not grateful and if anything, we assume we deserve this bounty because we worked hard for it.

2. When we are in a state of calamity: we are upset, anxious and get stressed thinking about how this calamity will impact our personal lives and make our lives more difficult, without regard for how this will impact others in society.

3. When we are in a state of obedience: we do acts of worship with the mindset of 'what's in it for me?' *Salah* becomes meditation. Fasting becomes weight loss. *Hajj* becomes tourism. And *zakat* becomes a way to show off how much good we do in society.

4. When we are in a state of disobedience: we justify our sins and try to convince others that this is part of our personal freedom and God will forgive us because we're so special.

Compare this with how adherents to Barakah Culture approach the four states.

1. When we are in a state of bounty: we react by being thankful and recognise that all blessing and all success comes from Allah.

Solomon smiled broadly at her words and said, 'Lord, Inspire me to be thankful for the blessings You have granted me and my parents, and to do good deeds that please You; admit me by Your grace into the ranks of Your righteous servants.'

(QURAN 27:19)

2. When we are in a state of calamity or difficulty: we react by being patient and persevere through the calamity beautifully.

Their father said, 'No! Your souls have prompted you to do wrong! But it is best to be patient: may God bring all of them back to me- He alone is the All Knowing, the All Wise,' (QURAN 12:83)

3. When we are in a state of obedience: we do acts of worship sincerely for Allah, seeking nothing in return but His pleasure.

'We feed you for the sake of God alone: We seek neither recompense nor thanks from you.'

(QURAN 76:9)

4. And when we are in a state of disobedience or sin: we recognise that God has rights over us, and it leads to feelings of regret and remorse. We attempt to balance between hope and fear, as we try to rectify our relationship with God through repentance and good deeds.

Prophet Muhammad ﷺ said "When a servant acknowledges his sin and repents, God forgives him."
(BUKHARI)

When we live a Barakah-culture, God-centred life, regardless of the state we are in, we have no perpetual fear of the future and no perpetual sadness over the past. This is the promise of Allah, when He said:

We said, 'Get out, all of you!' But when guidance comes from Me, as it certainly will, there will be no fear for those who follow My guidance nor will they grieve (QURAN 2:38)

The Barakah of Being a Slave of God

Some may question whether living as a slave means living a lowly life. However, this is a fundamental misunderstanding of what it means to be an *abd* (slave) of Allah.

Let me illustrate with an example. If you were appointed as an ambassador for your country, would that be a lowly or high title? It's an honourable title, and even though you're considered a 'public servant', it's viewed as a prestigious position in society.

Similarly, Allah appointed us as His slaves and public servants for His creation. This is the highest station any human being can attain in life, and it's open to anyone who submits to it. This was the station that Allah prescribed for His Prophet Muhammad ﷺ in the Quran.

Living an individualistic life that centres solely around ourselves, our titles, and our own legacy may give us a temporary sense of honour, but in practice, it can lead to anxiety, grief and a loss of Barakah. Conversely, when we centre our lives on the One who created us and act as His slaves on this earth, we live a truly God-centred life that elevates us in this life and the next. **Specifically, choosing to be a slave to God brings about the following changes:**

1. **Your *nafs* attaches itself to its true Creator and Sustainer and doesn't revolve around itself.** It feels fulfilled and calm, knowing that its *Rabb* (Lord) will take care of its needs, and will look forward to its return to Him:

> *'[But] you, soul at peace: return to your Lord well pleased and well pleasing; go in among My servants; and into My Garden.'* (QURAN 89: 27-30)

2. **Shaytan recognises that you've established a connection with your Lord and is less likely to try to influence you.** *Shaytan* promised his Lord that he'll not be able to mislead those who were devoted to Allah:

> *Iblis then said to God, 'Because You have put me in the wrong, I will lure mankind on earth and put them in the wrong, all except Your devoted servants.'*
> (QURAN 15:39-40)

3. **You start making spiritually intelligent decisions that bring Barakah to all the different aspects of your life,**

even when the decisions might not make sense from a worldly perspective: We see an example of this in the Quran when Allah talks about a "few sincere people" overcoming a large army of disbelievers:

> *When Talut set out with his forces, he said to them, 'God will test you with a river. Anyone who drinks from it will not belong with me, but anyone who refrains from tasting it will belong with me; if he scoops up just one handful [he will be excused].' But they all drank [deep] from it, except for a few. When he crossed it with those who had kept faith, they said, 'We have no strength today against Goliath and his warriors.' But those who knew that they were going to meet their Lord said, 'How often a small force has defeated a large army with God's permission! God is with those who are steadfast.'* (QURAN 2:249)

Just imagine the liberation and Barakah you'll get from not having to always try to serve the needs of the self and being truly free from your desires. As the famous saying goes, "If you don't worship Allah, you'll worship something or someone else." What more Barakah can one have than not being a slave to themselves and being the slave of the Most High?!

How to Reorient Yourself to Become a Slave of God

Imagine bumping into a random person on the street that stops you and asks the question: who are you? How will you answer? Most likely, you'll respond with one of the usual labels of life: name, profession, ethnicity, nationality etc.

Now, imagine that you just woke up from a deep coma, you've lost your memory and someone asks you: who are you? What would your answer be if you had no idea what your name, profession, ethnicity or country of origin are? In other words, if we were to take away all the labels of life from ourselves, who are we at our most basic level?

The answer you'll probably say is **'human being'.** If we were to step back and think of who we are as human beings at a basic spiritual level, we'd recognise that there are two parts to us: a physical (earthly) side which is our body, and a spiritual (heavenly) side which is our *ruh* (spirit). Together, these two parts come to form the *nafs* - the self or ego or the 'I' as we know it.

If we hope to attract Barakah in our lives, we need to re-orient our *nafs* and recognise that life is not about us but about serving our Lord with excellence.

Since you're reading this book, I'm sure you're ready to truly submit your *nafs* to your Lord and attract Barakah in your life. **The question is: where do you start?**

Step 1. Recognise Where Your Self Came from and Compare Your Self to the Grandeur of Allah's Creation. This step requires some quiet reflection, thought and pondering over verses of the Quran that remind us of where we came from:

> *Did We not create you from a liquid disdained?*
>
> (QURAN 77:20)

Allah reminds us of the lowly beginnings of our journey into this world. We were made from a fluid that we quickly want to wash off. Part of that fluid settles in the womb of our mothers and the process of creation begins until we come to this world as a child.

In his TED talk, Image-maker Alexander Tsiaras shares a powerful video, showing human development from conception to birth and as Alexander himself admits: "Even though I am a mathematician, I look at this with marvel of how do these instruction sets not make mistakes as they build what is us? It's a mystery, it's magic, it's divinity."

Our beginnings compared to the vastness of Allah's creation humble us and make us recognise our position in this world. When the sun, moon, trees, sea and birds all obey God's command, who are we to think that we're independent and not submit to God?

> *Do you not realise [Prophet] that everything in the heavens and earth submits to God: the sun, the moon,*

> *the stars, the mountains, the trees, and the animals? So do many human beings, though for many others punishment is well deserved. Anyone disgraced by God will have no one to honour him: God does whatever He will.* (QURAN 22:18)

Recognising our humble beginnings and our space in this universe is the first step to understanding who we truly are - as slaves of the Most High - and accepting our position as God's *khalifah* on earth.

Step 2. Act Like a Slave of God

We all go through life feeling confused about our identity and where we belong, especially third-culture children: born in one place, studied in another, and currently living somewhere else. What if, instead of trying to find an identity label that fits you, you remove all labels and go back to your basic identity as a slave of God?

How will this identity shift impact the way you conduct yourself, the way you carry yourself, and the way you deal with day-to-day challenges?

Imagine from the moment you wake up until you sleep, the only question on your mind is: how can I be the best slave of God today? How will this drive your motivation to live a life of Barakah and serve God and His creation with excellence?

This identity will develop true humbleness and humility for

Allah in your heart, which will then affect how you speak, act and deal with others. Allah describes the believers in the Quran:

> *The 'true' servants of the Most Compassionate are those who walk on the earth humbly, and when the foolish address them 'improperly', they only respond with peace.* (QURAN 25:63)

To be clear, acting like a slave of God and being humble to Allah is not about acting lowly or humiliating yourself. As Umar bin Al-Khattab rebuked the young man who was walking hunched over out of display of humility: *"O Young man, raise your head. True humility is in the heart and not shown through the body and face. If anyone shows his humility through his body more than what is contained in his heart, then he is a hypocrite."*

Being a slave to God also doesn't mean you can't excel at work. On the contrary, being a slave to God blesses you in the following ways:

1. Spiritually: we know that when we humble ourselves sincerely to God, we'll be elevated in status among people. Prophet Muhammad ﷺ said: "... and none humbles himself for Allah but Allah raises him." (TIRMIDHI)

2. Psychologically: when we adopt the identity that we're slaves of God, we'll develop what confidence coach, Hafsah Adham, calls "spiritually-centred" confidence. This confidence is rooted in our trust in Allah instead of our flimsy egos. It was best shown by Prophet Yusuf who confidently asked the king to be made the treasurer of Egypt because he knew that he was best fit for the job and would do it well.

3. From a team dynamics perspective, when you're humble for a greater cause - and in our case, that's humbleness to God - you'll come across as more honest and sincere as a professional and will be respected by all your peers (and this means you'll be more influential in your team since people will listen to you and respect your opinion).

The best example we have of someone embodying what it means to live life as a true slave of God is the Prophet Muhammad ﷺ. We see him throughout his life not acting like a king even though he had every right to do so. He would sit on the floor, eat with his hands, help around the house and sit at the end of the gathering and not at its centre.

A man came to the Prophet ﷺ and his voice trembled out of awe as he spoke to him. The Prophet said to him: "Be calm, for I am not a king. Verily, I am only the son of a woman who ate dried meat". (IBN MAJAH)

When Prophet Muhammad ﷺ entered Mecca as a conqueror, he had every right to enter Mecca with his head high as any victor would. Instead, he entered Mecca lowering his head out of humility to God who gave him this victory.

Step 3. Serve with Excellence

Once you recognise who you are as a slave of God, the next step is to engage in the life-long process of improving yourself and serving your Lord with excellence.

The beauty about serving Allah with excellence is that it's an all-encompassing personal development journey.

From your desire to serve Allah with excellence in your acts of worship, you'll learn how to best follow the Prophetic lifestyle.

You'll want to serve Allah with excellence with your family, so you'll be the best family member you can be, for Allah's pleasure.

You'll want to serve Allah with excellence in your career, performing your craft with brilliance; not to please people, but to please Allah. It's as if you're submitting that work to Allah first before you submit it to your boss or client.

This continuous journey of serving Allah with excellence will attract Barakah in your family life, your career and your time. When Allah sees that He is your first priority from the moment you wake up until you sleep, He'll unlock doors of Barakah for you that you won't even expect.

The Barakah effect comes from the congruence of personal and professional life centred on *tawhid* (oneness of God).

PRACTICAL TIPS FOR LIVING A GOD-CENTRED LIFE AND BECOMING HIS SLAVE

1. Start your day by making remembrance of Allah instead of checking your phone.
2. Protect your first hour in the morning by filling it with prayer and remembrance.
3. Read the Quran after your *fajr* prayer to start your day with guidance from your Creator.
4. Break your ego by fasting and doing uncomfortable acts for the sake of Allah, such as giving charity, praying *tahajjud* (voluntary night prayers), sacrificing for Him, and apologising when you're wrong.
5. Make it a habit to regularly pray istikhara for any small or major decision you need to make.
6. Each day, make a specific dua for something you want or need.
7. Before going to sleep, hold yourself accountable for acting like a slave of Allah that day and think about what you can do differently the next day.
8. Always be on the lookout for opportunities to serve Allah on earth, even if it's just picking up trash from the road.
9. Be Allah's deputy publicly and privately and do good to His creation, even if you don't receive approval or appreciation from others.
10. Prioritise *salah* at work and assert your right to pray.

11. Always make ethical choices, even if it means putting your own professional interests at risk. Refuse bribery, never lie to win a business deal and maintain *adab* (ethical decorum) when dealing with colleagues, suppliers and clients.
12. Set a timer to remind you to consciously remember Allah every hour throughout your workday.

The Prophet Muhammad ﷺ said that Allah, the Exalted and Glorious, said: "When My servant draws close to Me by the span of a palm, I draw close to him by the cubit and when he draws close to Me by the cubit, I draw close to him by the space (covered) by two arm spans, and when he comes to me walking, I go in a hurry towards him." (MUSLIM)

Let's run towards Allah and seek His Barakah in our lives.

CHAPTER EIGHT

Thank Allah for What You Have, and Seek His Sustenance Beautifully

Remember that He promised, "If you are thankful, I will give you more, but if you are thankless, My punishment is terrible indeed." (QURAN 14:7)

In Rajab 1443H, I walked into the Al-Bughsaan mosque in Jeddah, Saudi Arabia for *isha* prayers.

I chose to visit this mosque because I had beautiful memories coming here with my dad during Ramadan for *tarawih* prayers. Sh. Ali Jaber - may Allah have mercy on him - used to lead prayers in this mosque after he retired from leading prayers in Mecca.

The *adhan* (call to prayer) was not called yet, and I had some quiet reflection time before *isha* prayers started.

During those moments of reflection, something special happened: for what felt like the first time in my life, I experienced real *shukr*.

I felt this deep sense of overwhelming gratitude towards Allah for all the blessings He has bestowed upon me my entire life.

It hit me how all my experiences - the good and the bad - all my life events, the coincidences and all the people I had met, were all part of my *Rabb*'s plan for me. I was deeply moved because I felt unable to thank Allah enough.

A few days later, a gift came from Allah that I did not expect: I landed two major contracts for my business, neither of which I made any particular effort for. I couldn't help but make the connection between how experiencing *shukr* even for a few moments a couple of days earlier had opened the doors of Barakah for me. "If you are thankful, I will give you more..." (QURAN 14:7)

You've probably heard and read a lot about gratitude and the importance of being grateful in all aspects of life. In fact, there's a whole cottage industry that has formed around the topic of gratefulness from gratitude journals to gratitude retreats.

The science and research behind gratefulness is well-documented and we can all appreciate the need for us to be more grateful in our lives. What I will explore in this chapter is the link between gratefulness and Barakah Culture, and how Hustle Culture makes us ungrateful creatures instead.

There's a *hadith* of Prophet Muhammad ﷺ that says that if you wake up in the morning and you're safe at home, have food for one day, and in good health, then it's as if you have the whole world at your feet.

> *"Whosoever begins the day feeling family security and good health; and possessing provision for his day is as though he possessed the whole world."* (TIRMIDHI)

The *hadith* sets the standard for what 'enough' means using three parameters:

- Are you safe in your home and family?
- Are you healthy?
- Do you have provision and food for today?

If you answered yes to all three, then you should be overwhelmed with gratefulness, for the world is at your feet. If you're missing one or all of the above, it also means you should be grateful for the times you had all three but were ungrateful instead.

For those of us who have been blessed with privileged upbringings but still complain about our blessings or feel anxious about our financial status, the *hadith* mentioned above should be a humbling reminder. It begs the question: why do we struggle to maintain a state of gratitude, even when we have so much?

The following *hadith* from Prophet Muhammad ﷺ might give us a hint:

> *"Whoever is focused only on this world, Allah will confound his affairs and make him fear poverty constantly, and he will not get anything of this world except that which has been decreed for him. Whoever is focused on the Hereafter, Allah will settle his affairs for him and make him feel content with his lot, and his provision and worldly gains will undoubtedly come to him."*
>
> (IBN MAJAH)

Our obsession with this world drives our lack of gratitude. We're caught in a vicious cycle, in which our dissatisfaction with our present situation makes us more addicted to Hustle Culture – trying to eventually find happiness in the next big thing, which makes us even more ungrateful. We've succumbed to *shaytan's* promise when he said:

> *I will come at them- from their front and their back, from their right and their left- and You will find that most of them are ungrateful.* (QURAN 7:17)

Our materialistic and consumerist culture make us constantly aware that others have more than us and we need to keep up. This induces constant financial anxiety in our minds and spiritual hearts.

From a very young age, society tells us that to be successful, you have a certain amount of wealth and certain lifestyle factors. We make all our decisions about which school to attend and where we live to achieve a 'successful' life. We try so hard to attain this 'successful life' that we're willing to borrow on *riba* (interest) and end up burdening ourselves and our children with debts due to the unrealistic social expectations.

Unfortunately, for many people, this promised life is never achieved, and we become like the children of Israel who were lost in the desert for 40 years before poor health, debt and old age throws us to the side of the road, having not achieved anything meaningful in life, and lost the Barakah along the way.

For those of us who 'make it' and live the social standards of success, we have a sense of entitlement over what we have. We feel that we worked hard for this success, and it came purely from our efforts, forgetting the One who bestowed those favours upon us. It reminds me of the story of the three men of the Children of Israel and how two of the men failed the gratefulness test:

"There were three men among the Children of Israel, one leper, one bald and one blind. Allah wanted to test them.

He therefore, sent to them an angel who came to the leper and asked him what he would like best. He replied: "A good colour, a good skin and to be rid of what makes me loathsome to people". He (the angel) rubbed him and his loathsomeness vanished and he was given a good colour and a good skin. He then asked him what type of property he would like best. The leper replied that he would like camels...He was given a pregnant she-camel. The angel invoked for Allah's blessing on it.

The angel then went to the bald man and asked him what he would like best, and he replied: "Good hair and to be rid of what makes me loathsome to people". The angel ran his hand over him, and he was given good hair. He then asked the man what property he would like best. He replied that he would like cattle, so he was given a pregnant cow. The angel invoked Allah's blessing on it.

The angel then went to the blind man and asked him what he would like best, and he replied: "I wish that Allah restore my sight to me so that I may see people." Thereupon the angel ran his hand over him, and Allah restored his sight. The angel then asked what property he would like best. He replied that he would like sheep, so he was given a pregnant ewe.

Flocks and herds were produced for the three men, the first having a valley full of camels, the second one, a valley full of cows and the third one full of sheep. Then the angel came in the form of a leper, to the one who had been a leper, and said: "I am a poor man and my resources have been exhausted in my journey, and my only means of reaching my destination are dependent on Allah and then on you, so I ask you by Him Who gave you the good colour, the good skin and the property, for a camel by which I may get to my destination". He replied: "I have many dues to pay." The angel then said: "I think I recognize you. Were you not a leper whom people found loathsome and a poor man to whom Allah gave property?" He replied: "I inherited this property through generations". The angel said: "If you are telling a lie, may Allah return you to your former condition".

The angel went in the form of a bald man to the one who had been bald and said the same as he had said to the former and received a similar reply. So he said: "If you are telling a lie, may Allah return you to your former condition". The angel then went to the one who had been blind and said: "I am a poor traveller and my resources have been exhausted in my journey. My only means of reaching my destination are dependent on Allah and then on you,

> so I ask you by Him Who restored your eyesight for a sheep by which I may get to the end of my journey". He replied: "Yes, I was blind. Allah restored my eyesight, so take what you wish and leave what you wish. I swear by Allah that I shall not argue with you today to return anything you take, as I give it for Allah's sake". The angel said: "Keep your property. You have all simply been put to a test, and Allah is pleased with you and displeased with both of your companions." (BUKHARI)

It's easy to think that if you were in the two men's shoes and you were given so much blessing, you'd be generous and grateful like the blind man. However, when asked to give to others, many of us default to miserliness and ungratefulness. We adopt the Hustle Culture scarcity mindset and refuse to part with even a small fraction of our wealth and other blessings and privileges. We think we worked so hard to earn them and we don't want to just give them away. We become like mini-Qaruns, saying, "I was only given it because of knowledge I have." (QURAN 28: 78)

If we don't practice gratefulness on a daily basis, when we are tested, it might become hard for us to pass the test. We should remember that all our blessings are simply loans from Allah and soon we need to return them back to Allah, either willingly (through charity and giving, which leads to Barakah) or unwillingly (through death, accident, or loss of Barakah).

Gratefulness and Contentment vs Ambition

When we talk about gratefulness, several Hustle Culture enthusiasts might turn around and argue that being grateful and content is the antithesis of living an ambitious and successful life. After all, if you're always grateful for what you have, how will you aspire for higher goals in life?

This question reveals a deep misunderstanding of the difference between contentment and ambition. More importantly, this dilemma has created two camps in the *ummah*. Those who say: "*Alhamdulillah*, I'm content with what I have. Why should I be ambitious and strive for more?" And those who take the other extreme position and say: "We will *not* be content or grateful until we achieve societal levels of success" (i.e. wealth, fame and economic prosperity).

In fact, one of the most common questions I get whenever I train people on Barakah Culture is: "Isn't Barakah Culture the reason why the *ummah* is so backward? We're so laid back as an *ummah* and we don't have ambition anymore". The assumption is that because we neglected this *dunya* (world), other nations and civilisations rose to power and made advancement in technology, science and economy. And, presumably, it's hard for the Muslim world with its gratitude or contentment mindset to catch up.

In my previous book, *The Productive Muslim: Where Faith Meets Productivity*, I argued that the notion that *dunya* is bad and should be avoided at all costs, without making the distinction between '*dunya'* (this world) and '*hayat al-dunya*' (worldly distractions), has led the Muslim world to lose its edge among nations[10]. However, the implied solution that Muslims should be more ambitious in the *dunya* and adopt a Hustle Culture mindset isn't the key to economic progress.

What we need instead is a generation of Muslims with ambition and high-aspiration intentions, not for the sake of competing with the West and modern civilisation, but for sake of lifting God's name on earth. We need a generation of Muslims that are eager to bring Barakah back on earth.

As I discussed in the last two chapters, when you set your ambition along the Barakah paradigm of doing something in this world for the sake of Allah and serving His creation, you'll think far beyond the myopic worldly paradigm that only thinks of profit and the economy.

Imagine Muslims exploring the latest technologies such as biotech, space exploration and artificial intelligence from the perspective of God's deputy on earth, and using these sciences and technology to please Allah. Think of the Barakah this will unlock for the world!

I once chatted with the Chief Technology Officer of an IT company who was struggling with this idea of serving God through his work. He said that all he does as a software engineer is write code. How can he unlock Barakah Culture by writing code? I asked him which of the 99 names of Allah he loves the most. He said that he loved the name *Al-Jamil* (The Most Beautiful). I asked him whether there was such a thing as beautiful code? Can he serve Allah by writing beautiful code? His eyes lit up and I could see that this level of thinking opened a whole new perspective on what it means to be truly ambitious.

This approach to ambition is what unlocked the years of scientific advancement in the Golden Era of the Islamic Civilisation. Those advancements were not made because people were ambitious in their careers or hustling for the sake of hustling. They were made because some of the greatest scholars, scientists and mathematicians of that time had sincere intentions to do what's good for society and be God's *khalifah* on earth.

Fatimah Al-Fihri, the incredible woman who built the first university in the world, was ambitious and God-centred. She built the university seeking God's pleasure to spread beneficial knowledge on earth and fasted during the entire period that the university was being built to attract Barakah to her project.

So to the Hustle Culture enthusiasts, my answer is that being grateful and content does not negate ambition or achieving high-*himma* (aspiration) intentions in life or for our *ummah*. If anything, it might unlock success and Barakah for the greater good.

Humans are ambitious by nature. The desire to achieve something and be something is innate in our psyche and is part of mental wellbeing. However, what we choose to be ambitious about is the key between approaching ambition with Barakah or with a hustle mindset.

The companions of Prophet Muhammad ﷺ understood the difference well. If not for their ambition, Islam would not have spread so quickly after the Prophet's death. Yet, at the same time, they were content with what Allah gave them regardless of the circumstances.

Abu Hurairah once narrated: “People say that I have narrated many a*hadith* (Prophet’s narrations). Had it not been for two verses in the Quran, I would not have narrated a single *hadith*, and the verses are: “Verily those who conceal the clear sign and the guidance which We have sent down.. (up to) Most Merciful.” (QURAN 2:159-160). And no doubt our Muhajir (emigrant) brothers used to be busy in the market with their business (bargains) and our Ansari brothers used to be busy with their property (agriculture). But I (Abu Huraira) used to stick to Allah’s apostle, content with what will fill my stomach and I used to attend that which they used not to attend and I used to memorise that which they used not to memorise” (BUKHARI). Abu Hurairah ambitiously memorised numerous *ahadith* of the Prophet ﷺ, yet he was also content with his restricted provision in this world.

As Muslims, we’re encouraged to have high-*himma* ambitions when it comes to matters of the Hereafter and serving God, and have contentment when it comes to matters of this world.

Our Prophet ﷺ said: “The distance between every two levels of Paradise is like the distance between the sky and the Earth, so if you ask Allah for anything, ask Him for the Firdaus, for it is the last part of Paradise and the highest part of Paradise, and at its top there is the Throne of Beneficence, and from it gush forth the rivers of Paradise.” (BUKHARI)

And in numerous places throughout the Quran, we are told to hasten and compete for *Jannah*, not letting our comforts weigh us down.

> *O you who have believed, what is [the matter] with you that, when you are told to go forth in the cause of Allāh, you adhere heavily to the earth? Are you satisfied with the life of this world rather than the Hereafter? But what is the enjoyment of worldly life compared to the Hereafter except a [very] little.* (QURAN 9:38)

Regarding contentment, Allah says in the Quran:

> *"Nor strain thine eyes in longing for the things We have given for enjoyment to parties of them, the splendour of the life of this world, through which We test them: but the provision of thy Lord is better and more enduring."* (QURAN 20: 131)

Finally, as the Prophet ﷺ beautifully put it: "Riches does not mean having a great amount of property, but riches is self-contentment." (BUKHARI)

Being grateful and praising Allah for what you have means that you're always content and pleased with God's decree at any given moment of time across all areas of your life. You don't face the doubts, agony or anxiety of someone who feels that their life is not where it is supposed to be - either financially, physically or socially. This contentment does not negate having ambition or what I call 'high-*himma* intention'. Rather, you seek God's bounty that's written for you in this life and the next, and serve His *ummah* in the best possible way.

Gratitude in Hardship

> *How desperate and ungrateful man becomes when We let him taste Our mercy and then withhold it! And if We let him taste mercy after some harm has touched him, he is sure to say, 'Misfortune has gone away from me.' He becomes exultant and boastful. Not so those who are steadfast and do good deeds: they will have forgiveness and a great reward.*
>
> (QURAN 11: 9-11)

People struggle with being grateful when things don't go their way or worse, when things go worse than they expected.

Allah teaches us how to think about those situations through a story that is recited weekly on fridays: Surah Al-Kahf (The Cave). In this chapter of the Quran, Allah presents the story of Prophet Musa and Khidr - a righteous person - who was tasked with teaching Prophet Musa some of the knowledge that had been imparted to him, particularly his understanding of *qadr* (destiny). The story presents three case studies:

CASE STUDY 1

A group of poor people who owned a boat offered a ride to Musa and Khidr. When Khidr jumped on the boat, he started making a hole in the boat, effectively making it defective. Khidr later explained that these poor people were about to pass by a tyrant king who confiscates any working boat. The hole saved the boat from seizure by the king.

Think of this case study from the perspective of the poor people. They probably were upset when they found that their boat had a hole that made it defective. Yet later, as they passed the tyrant king's territory and saw how other boats were confiscated while theirs was left alone, they would have been extremely grateful for the hole they had in their boat and thanked Allah for the defect.

This is the example of when something bad happens to you and then you realise days or years later that it was actually good for you. The challenge for us is to be grateful when we discover that hole in our life - when we see that sickness, rejection letter or challenging family situation - as a hole that perhaps we won't know the benefit of it until years later.

CASE STUDY 2

Khidr sees a young boy playing with other kids. He approaches the child and kills him without any apparent reason. Again, Khidr later explains that this young boy would have grown to become a disbelieving tyrant, who would have made life horrendous for his parents.

I think of this story from the perspective of the parents whose boy was killed. They never knew the reason why their son was murdered and perhaps would spend the next 30-50 years mourning the loss of their child and wondering why this happened to them.

This is the case of when bad things happen to us and we have no idea why, nor will we ever. Yet again, we're reminded to be grateful because we don't know the goodness in something even if it seems evil and beyond our comprehension.

This is perhaps the hardest situation to be grateful for but our certainty in Allah's wisdom should enable us to be thankful, despite the horrifying situation we are dealing with.

CASE STUDY 3

Khidr and Musa pass by a town and ask the townspeople for some provision for their journey but no one offers their support. They then pass by a wall that is about to collapse, which Khidr proceeds to fix without asking for any compensation. Khidr explained that the wall belongs to two orphans, whose father was a righteous man and left them a treasure underneath the wall. If the wall collapsed, the people of the town may have confiscated the wealth from the boys. So, Khidr rebuilt it so it would stay upright for a few more years, until the orphans were old enough to discover and protect their wealth.

This case study shows how sometimes good things happen to us that we are not aware of. For instance, a person may leave for work five minutes early and completely miss a horrible accident they would have experienced if they'd left on time. They would get into work and not realise the immense blessing Allah just gifted them.

Scholars say that the majority of *qadr* is in the third category. Allah takes care of us and we're not aware of it. Just think of the immeasurable number of processes that go through your body at this very moment - Allah is making it all function - and yet we are still ungrateful.

> *If you tried to count God's blessings, you could never take them all in: He is truly most forgiving and most merciful.* (QURAN 16:18)

These three case studies make it clear that regardless of the destiny that we're dealt with, we should remember the *khair* (goodness) that Allah bestows upon us and be thankful. Take the following story, for example:

> Once upon a time, there was a king who had a loyal servant that would always say "*fiha khair*" (there's good in this) no matter the situation. One day, the king and his servant went out hunting, but an unfortunate accident led to the king losing a finger. Despite the king's anger, the servant still said "*fiha khair*". The king was so upset that he ordered for the servant to be thrown in jail. But even in jail, the servant continued to say "*fiha khair*". The following week, the king went hunting without his servant and ended up lost in the jungle.

A group of cannibals captured him and decided to sacrifice him for their gods. However, when they discovered that the king was missing a finger, they deemed him unworthy and let him go. The king finally understood that there was khair in losing his finger for it saved his life.

When the king returned home, he called for the servant and asked why he had said "fiha khair" when he was thrown in jail. The servant replied calmly, "Your Majesty, if I had been with you on your hunting trip this week, the cannibals would have sacrificed me instead!"

Always remember *fiha khair*, even if you can't explain where the *khair* is in the moment. Allah does not intend evil for you - even if the circumstances seem evil.

> *Aisha reported: When the Messenger of Allah ﷺ saw something he liked he would say "All praise is due to Allah by whose favour good deeds are accomplished"* (IBN MAJAH). *And when the Prophet ﷺ saw something he disliked, he would say "All praise is due to Allah in every circumstance."* (IBN MAJAH)

Lastly, reflect on the story of Prophet Yusuf. As a young boy, he was thrown into a well by his own siblings, sold into slavery and sent to prison for a crime he did not commit. Despite all these negative circumstances, Prophet Yusuf never showed signs of ungratefulness. Commenting on this story, Dr. Meraj Mohiuddin, author of the sirah book *Reve-*

lation, mentioned to me in an interview that Prophet Yusuf focused on how to be the best version of himself through these trials.

- When he was thrown into the well, he displayed **patience**.
- When he was sold into slavery, he made the most of the situation and **learned about the operations of the treasury.**
- When he was accused wrongfully and sent to prison, he **invited his companions in prison to Islam**.

If Prophet Yusuf had agonised over his circumstances, he would not have been mentally or spiritually equipped to handle the situations he faced. He would've fallen into a victim mindset and failed to see the opportunities for personal and spiritual development in front of him. Instead, Prophet Yusuf exhibited gratitude and towards the end of his story, recognised that these trials were all part of Allah's plan.

> *And he raised his parents upon the throne, and they bowed to him in prostration. And he said, "O my father, this is the explanation of my vision of before. My Lord has made it reality. And He was certainly good to me when He took me out of prison and brought you [here] from bedouin life after Satan had induced [estrangement] between me and my brothers. Indeed, my Lord is Subtle in what He*

wills. Indeed, it is He who is the Knowing, the Wise.

(QURAN 12:100)

He was not vengeful but rather thankful, generous and humble.

Praising Allah and thanking Allah for what you have and what you're going through, no matter the circumstances, attracts Barakah to one's life even if that Barakah appears years later like in the story of Prophet Yusuf.

Seek *Rizq* (sustenance) Beautifully to be More Grateful

> *[The nature of] man is that, when his Lord tries him through honour and blessings, he says, 'My Lord has honoured me,' but when He tries him through the restriction of his provision, he says, 'My Lord has humiliated me.'* (QURAN 89:15-16)

The biggest driver for lack of gratefulness is a complete misunderstanding about our relationship with *rizq*.

As a father, husband and son, every now and then, I worry about whether I'll be able to provide for my family or care for my elderly parents. I recognise that these worries make me less grateful than I should be and stem from the Hustle Culture mindset I grew up with. Usually, these worries resolve themselves when I'm able to shift to a Barakah mindset.

Someone once told me: "We believe in Allah, but we don't

believe Allah". When Allah tells us in the Quran that our sustenance is guaranteed, many of us who grew up in Hustle Culture, don't seem to sincerely believe it. We feel in control of our *rizq* and our desperation for finding more *rizq* make us addicted to the religion of work.

A bedouin Arab heard these verses: "In the sky is your sustenance and all that you are promised. By the Lord of the heavens and earth! All this is as real as your speaking" (QURAN 51: 21-22). He was shocked that Allah would have to take an oath upon Himself to convince us that our sustenance is guaranteed.

Moreover, as mentioned earlier, 21st century Muslims seem to have adopted a version of the prosperity gospel advocated amongst conservative Christians in America: we equate our levels of sustenance with closeness to God. We think that if we are blessed that means Allah loves us, and if we are not blessed, this means that we're not doing something right.

To shift our perspective on sustenance from the Hustle Culture mindset of scarcity and prosperity gospel, to the Barakah Culture mindset of abundance, contentment and gratitude, we need to understand that:

1. <u>Rizq is not just material wealth.</u> *Rizq* is anything that supports your wellbeing, including your physical, mental and spiritual health, as well as your family, friends, the network you have and the services you enjoy. When you think of *rizq* holistically, you'll recognise the immense blessings that deserve your gratefulness, no matter your financial circumstances.

2. **We should seek *rizq* beautifully.** Prophet Muhammad ﷺ said: "O people, fear Allah and be moderate in seeking a living, for no soul will die until it has received all its provision, even if it is slow in coming. So fear Allah and be moderate in seeking provision; take that which is permissible and leave that which is forbidden" (IBN MAJAH). The word for 'moderate in seeking a living' in Arabic is *"ajmilu"* which means to seek something beautifully. It's as if Prophet Muhammad ﷺ is trying to remind us that when we seek our sustenance, we should be like slaves knocking on the doors of our Master, and asking him beautifully for our sustenance, and grateful for whatever He provides even if we think in our limited understanding that it's not enough.

4 Steps for Seeking *Rizq* Beautifully

How should we seek rizq beautifully?
There are four steps to do so.

1. Recognise that sustenance is only from Allah

When I left my full-time job to run my business, the transition was tough. Shifting from the certainty of a pay check to the unpredictability of business dealings was frightening. However, this transition helped me to truly understand who my Sustainer was and to have *tawakkul* in Allah that He'll provide.

Barakah Culture calls upon us to have confidence that all *rizq* is ONLY from Allah – *Ar-Razzaq* (the Sustainer) and not from people.

This understanding is inspiring because you don't end up humiliating yourself trying to get sustenance from your boss or your customers, and you have a high sense of dignity in your business and work dealings.

Moreover, don't hand over your means of sustenance to others. This is why I personally encourage Muslims to have a side business even if they are full-time employees. You want to be semi-independent from people, so your livelihood is not based on the whim of a corporate leader.

2. Have the right manners when asking for *rizq* from Allah

If you're trying to get Barakah in your sustenance, then you need the right *adab* when asking from Allah. This includes:

i. Remembering the **importance of being God's slave** and acting as God's slave – so asking only Him for your sustenance and *rizq*.

ii. Being **on top of your prayers and acts of worship** and prioritising them over seeking *rizq* (e.g. have a clash between a meeting and prayer time? Choose prayer!)

iii. Have **complete trust and reliance in Allah** whilst seeking your *rizq*, and not attaching your heart to your means of sustenance. As Prophet Muhammad ﷺ said: "If you were to rely upon Allah with the required reliance, then He would provide for you just as a bird is provided for, it goes out in the morning empty, and returns full." (TIRMIDHI)

iv. Be in a constant state of **remembrance during your work.** Prophet Muhammad ﷺ said, "If anyone constantly seeks pardon (from Allah), Allah will appoint for him a way out of every distress and a relief from every anxiety and will provide sustenance for him from where he expects not." (ABU DAWUD)

v. Not being upset **when *rizq* doesn't show up** on time or there's delay in your *rizq*. As the Prophet said: "The supplication of every one of you will be granted if he does not get impatient and say (for example): 'I supplicated my Lord but my prayer has not been granted'." (BUKHARI).

3. Seek God's sustenance in *halal* and ethical ways

From the 2008/2009 financial crisis, to the plethora of corporate scandals in the news every day, Hustle Culture is rife with people seeking sustenance in unethical ways.

Seeking beautifully entails seeking God's sustenance in ethical, halal ways, even if this comes at a personal cost and sacrifice. Perhaps the scholar who was most known for his ethical business practices is Imam Abu Hanifa, and the following showcase an example of the Barakah Culture mindset that's hard to imagine in a Hustle Culture driven world:

Imam Abu Hanifa used to own a garment shop with a partner. One of the cloths had a defect in it, and he told his partner to inform any potential buyer of the cloth's defect. Later that day, Imam Abu Hanifa came back and asked if the defective cloth was sold. The partner said yes. He asked him if he told the buyer of the defect. The partner said no. Imam Abu Hanifa was so upset that he first tried to look for the buyer in the market, and when he couldn't find the buyer, he donated the money of the cloth to charity.

On another occasion, a woman came to Imam Abu Hanifa wanting to sell a piece of cloth that was very expensive. But she didn't know the true value of the cloth. Instead of cheating her and buying the cloth at a very low cost, he told her the true value of the cloth and gave her a fair price for it.

We read these examples and more in our history books and biographies of great Muslim scholars and merchants, yet we fail to adopt such mindsets in our business or work dealings. We forget that this approach to seeking sustenance in ethical and honest ways is what made Muslim traders the best ambassadors for Islam. They are the reason why millions of people converted to Islam, especially in Southeast Asia - now that's Barakah!

4. Be content with your sustenance to bring Barakah

Being grateful and content for your sustenance relieves you of the burden of doubts, agony or anxiety that comes from the constant need for more. The Prophet Muhammad ﷺ said, "Successful is the one who enters the fold of Islam and is provided with sustenance which is sufficient for his day's needs, and Allah makes him content with what He has bestowed upon him." (MUSLIM)

Moreover, there's a beautiful relationship between contentment in your sustenance and seeing Barakah in your life, illustrated by the story mentioned by Sh. Omar Abdul-Kafi in one of his videos on Barakah[11]

> A man used to earn five dirhams for his work, and he went to Imam Abu Hanifa and complained that five dirhams was not enough to live by. The sheikh told him to ask his employer to pay him four dirhams instead. The man was surprised: how can he live on four dirhams when five dirhams was not enough? However, he did what he was told and came back a few weeks later complaining that four dirhams was not enough to live by, so Imam Abu Hanifa told him to ask his employer to pay him three dirhams instead.

> Again, the man was surprised but he did what he was told and asked his employer to pay him three dirhams. After a few weeks, the man came back and thanked Imam Abu Hanifa, telling him that the three dirhams were sufficient for him and he's no longer complaining of money not being enough. Those around Imam Abu Hanifa were surprised and asked why the reduction in pay worked. The Imam said that this person's work was not worth more than three dirhams, so when he used to earn more than what he deserved, there was no Barakah in his pay and that money didn't last. But when he earned exactly his due, there was Barakah in his rizq and it was sufficient for him.

This story might sound counter-intuitive to how we are told to seek sustenance and why we should always ask for more even when we know that our work doesn't really deserve that much more. Being content with a small amount of *halal rizq* is better than having loads of undeserved wealth devoid of Barakah.

Being thankful and grateful for what's little might seem like a meek and lowly way, but nothing is more empowering and stress-free than recognising the Barakah of more with less.

This is not a call to live austere lives and abandon the pleasures of this world, but rather, a reminder that our hearts and sense of gratefulness should not be attached to what we have or don't have. We should seek sustenance beautifully and be sincerely grateful so that Barakah will come into our lives.

Practical Tips for Gratitude

If we want to see Barakah in our lives, we need to practice gratitude until we reach the status of *Abd Shakour* (a grateful slave).

The first step to becoming *Abd Shakour* is to live a God-centred life and not an ego-centred life (see previous chapter). When life revolves around your desires and goals, frustration and FOMO (fear of missing out) replace feelings of gratitude. Moreover, comparing where you are with where others are - either in real life or on social media - adds fuel to the fire of ungratefulness and dissatisfaction with God's decree. Living a God-centred life gives you the mental clarity to recognise the innumerable blessings upon you.

When you recognise that you're a slave of God, you're thankful for anything that comes from your Master, no matter how small. You understand that you're extremely indebted to Him, and that the only way to thank Him is to sell your body, soul, and your life to Him, expecting nothing in return (even though out of His generosity, He promises you Paradise):

> *Indeed, Allah has purchased from the believers their lives and their properties [in exchange] for that they will have Paradise.* (QURAN 9:111)

Here are other practical tips to be grateful to Allah.

1. Get uncomfortable to be grateful

Most of us who live in urban areas grow up with comforts of life that were not available a century ago. From fast transportation to health facilities and supermarkets, we take these basic life comforts for granted and rarely pause to reflect on the immense blessings we have.

One way to develop gratefulness is to try to deprive yourself from your urban living comforts every now and then so you can develop appreciation and gratefulness for all the blessings you enjoy.

Start with taking a simple camping trip or going to a country where the infrastructure and facilities are very basic.

When you take away the comforts you're used to in life, two things start to happen:

1. You'll be <u>more grateful</u> for what you have.
2. You'll start wondering whether some of those comforts that you swore you can't live without are <u>really necessary</u> (do you really need that salted caramel mocha latte with two pumps of vanilla substitute and a scoop of vanilla bean powder?!)

Being uncomfortable will help you appreciate the small things in life and help you break away from the frivolous urban luxuries that get people addicted to the grind.

2. Be reflective on the story of your life

Like my experience in that mosque in Jeddah, spending a few minutes being grateful about different aspects of your life, including your heath, your relationships, the opportunities you had in your life, books you read (including this one, hopefully!) can really help you feel that sense of overwhelming gratitude.

This is not about following some new-age spirituality hack that uses the positive psychological effect of gratitude to numb your senses and get back to the grind. This is about deeply connecting your blessings to your *Rabb* and recognising that everything you can think of (and cannot think of) is from Allah and that we should feel complete and utter indebtedness towards Him.

3. Look at problems or challenging situations in your life from the perspective of gratefulness

Think of a problem or challenge you're going through and force yourself to think of three to five reasons you should be thankful for your situation, no matter how difficult. Al-Sha'bi reported: Shuraih, may Allah be pleased with him, said:

> *Verily, if I am afflicted with a calamity, then I praise Allah four times. I praise Him that it was not worse than it was. I praise Him when He provides me patience to bear it. I praise Him when He guides me to supplicate appropriately and hoping for reward, and I praise Him for not making it a calamity in my religion*
>
> (SIYAR A'LAM AN-NUBALA)

So, whether you've stepped over that Lego piece, had a fight with your spouse, lost your job or a loved one, ask yourself how you can be thankful for that situation and even if you can't, practice saying *"Nahmadullah wa nashkuruh"* (we thank Allah and are grateful to Him). Sometimes the practice of the tongue enters the heart, and your spiritual heart becomes grateful as a result of your words.

4. Be grateful to others - no matter how small

When people remember you, do they remember you as a grateful person?

Being a person of gratitude means expressions of gratitude are constantly on your tongue.

You're grateful to your spouse, parents, children, family, team, co-workers and everyone that supports your personal and professional development. And you make your gratitude known.

Express your gratitude in words, in writing and in giving gifts, and be thankful without waiting for a "you're welcome" in return or an appreciation of your thankfulness.

A member of our team constantly says: "I appreciate you". Her consistent appreciation to the entire team makes her someone everyone respects and enjoys working with.

Finally, I want to take this opportunity to be grateful to you for reading this book thus far and I pray that you derive benefit from it, and that you continue benefitting from the chapters to come. Ameen!

CHAPTER NINE

Be Like a Gardener — Focused, Hardworking, Gentle and Trust Allah with the Results

A man was once in the desert when he heard a voice from the Heavens instructing a cloud to go to a garden and pour rain over it. The man watched the cloud float above a garden in the middle of the desert, pour rain, then move on.

Intrigued, the man approached the garden and saw a gardener directing the fresh rainwater to his plants. He told the gardener about the voice and the cloud, and asked the man what could have caused such a miracle?

"I don't do anything special," the man replied. "But every year, I give one-third of my crops to the needy, I keep one-third for my family, and I re-invest a third back in the land."

Every one of us are gardeners working hard to make the gardens of our life bear fruit. Whether we're starting companies, nurturing a family or attempting to solve a human problem, we all recognise the metaphor of the garden and gardener.

Gardeners recognise there are things within their control, such as how much time they invest in their gardens, and things outside their control, like the weather and the number of plants that grow. Similarly, some things in our lives are within our control, such as how much time and money we spend on a project, who we build relationships with etc. and other things are outside our control, like that next big idea, market conditions or an economic downturn.

We are often taught by Hustle Culture to manage what's within our control and ignore everything else. Yet the gardener in the parable managed to attract good fortune – or Barakah - to his garden, despite its unlikely location in the desert, through the practice of giving one-third of his harvest to those in need. This concept is not a one-off story, but rather an argument for a way of being. To live a life of Barakah, you must adopt the gardener mindset. The following story I received from one of my students illustrates the importance of this gardener mindset:

> There once lived a man known for his generosity, kindness, wisdom and reason. His home served as a sanctuary for the underprivileged, the impoverished and the disheartened. As was his custom, he shared a tenth of his harvest, regardless of the crop or quantity, four times each year. When he turned wheat into flour and baked bread, he distributed a tenth of it as well.

One day, he imparted this wisdom to his children: "When I am no longer with you, continue this tradition so that Barakah fills your harvests. The yield from your fields comes from the Divine, for it is Allah who provides. If you give back from His abundance, you shall see doors of prosperity open...

The devil constantly taunts you with the fear of poverty. Do not become his victim. Instead, let us pursue and defeat him. A sultan's hawk should never be hunted by a mere partridge."

The Gardener Mindset vs The Carpenter Mindset

The Quran warns of adopting the opposite of the gardener mindset, referred to as the carpenter mindset.[12] With this mindset, which is common in Hustle Culture, you seek control over every aspect of life and ignore the spiritual elements at work. The Quran tells the story of a group of men who inherited a beautiful garden from their father. Their father used to offer some of the harvest to any poor person who visits his garden. However, when the sons took over, they vowed that no poor person would enter their garden. The next day, they went to their garden and found that it was destroyed by a powerful storm. Allah says in the Quran:

> *We have tried them as We tried the owners of a certain garden, who swore that they would harvest its fruits in the morning and made no allowance [for the Will of God]: a disaster from your Lord struck the gar-*

den as they slept, and by morning it was stripped bare, a desolate land.

Still they called each other at daybreak, 'Go early to your field if you wish to gather all its fruits,' and went off, whispering, 'Make sure no poor person enters the garden today!'––they left early, bent on their purpose, but when they saw the garden, they said, 'We must have lost our way! No- we are ruined!' The wisest of them said, 'Did I not say to you, "Will you not glorify God?"'- they said, 'Glory be to God, Our Lord! Truly, we were doing wrong!'- and then they turned to each other in mutual reproach. They said, 'Alas for us! We have done terrible wrong, but maybe our Lord will give us something better in its place: we truly turn to Him in hope.' Such is the punishment [in this life], but greater still is the punishment in the Hereafter, if only they knew. (QURAN 68:17-33)

How many of us act as gardeners, and how many as carpenters? What does it mean to be a gardener versus a carpenter? We'll explore this next.

The Carpenter Mindset

The carpenter mindset is a popular approach to planning in our fast-paced world. We set specific goals and work hard to achieve them using all our skills, efforts and tools. But what happens when things don't go according to plan? We get frustrated, annoyed and often blame ourselves or the tools we used.

Planning life as a carpenter is stressful because we're constantly attached to the results and feel no satisfaction in life until the results meet our expectations. Unfortunately, this only works when we have ultimate control over all outcomes in life, but let's face it: we don't.

Think about how this carpenter mindset negatively affects many aspects of our lives:

- We have specific ideas of how our relationships should be, and when people disappoint us, we become upset and resentful of them.
- We have specific plans and hopes for our children, and if they don't achieve them, we feel disappointed in them.
- We set milestones marking where we should be at certain stages in life, and if our lives don't follow that timeline or plan, we become depressed and feel like a failure.
- We are less likely to engage in spiritual practices that attract Barakah because we feel that it doesn't make sense and it's outside our control.

Allah challenges this carpenter mindset in the Quran with a powerful set of questions in Surah Al-Waqia. He says:

Consider [the semen] you eject-

do you create it yourselves or are We the Creator?

(QURAN 56: 58-59)

Consider the seeds you sow in the ground-
is it you who make them grow or We?

(QURAN 56:63-64)

Consider the water you drink-
was it you who brought it down from the rain-cloud or We?

(QURAN 56:68-69)

Consider the fire you kindle-
is it you who make the wood for it grow or We?

(QURAN 56:71-72)

In each of these rhetorical questions, Allah exposes the fallacy of control over our lives. The immediate answer to all the above questions is: no, we're not in control.

For people steeped in Hustle Culture, this is a hard pill to swallow. "What do you mean detach from results? I've put *so* much effort into this, I better get results!" We are taught from a very young age that we are in control of our destiny and the self-help section of any bookstore is full of titles of that promote a version of a carpenter mindset.

This is where spirituality and true *tawakkul* differentiates those of Barakah Culture versus Hustle Culture; we work hard as if everything is under our control yet at the same time, we completely trust that the results and the fruits of our labour are firmly in Allah's hands.

Allah is inviting us to adopt an alternative mindset - a gardener mindset - in which we take the means and sow the seeds we want to see in our life. The notion is to work hard, yet deeply recognise that ultimately the fruit of our labour (the result) is not in our hands but in Allah's hands.

The Gardener Mindset

Living life as a gardener means that we shift our mindset from one of control and outcomes, to one of nurturing and growth. Instead of trying to force results, we focus on cultivating the right mindsets, values and rituals in our lives for growth and Barakah.

Just like a gardener tends to their plants, we tend to our intentions and actions. We become focused on being process-oriented versus achievement-oriented and this usually leads to long-term success, learning and growth. We become less frustrated and anxious when we don't achieve the fruits of our labour fast enough.

This approach allows us to be more present in the moment and to appreciate the small victories along the way. We learn to embrace setbacks and challenges as opportunities for growth and refinement.

Living as a gardener also allows us to be more grateful for the blessings we have, recognising that they are a gift from Allah. We still act and make plans, but we trust in Allah's plan for us and accept that sometimes things may not go as we had hoped.

A good example of where a gardener mindset can be particularly helpful is with parenting. Children of Parents who adopt a gardener mindset do their best and do not stress about how their children might turn out. They tend to be more successful than parents who adopt a carpenter mindset and try to turn their children into the fixed image they have in their mind. These parents will feel like failures if their children don't meet their expectations, regardless of how hard they worked to raise them well.

I always think of Prophet Nuh and how he worked so hard to call his people to Allah, and then even his own son didn't believe in Him. Think of how he felt as a parent to see his son disbelieve in his message and then drown in front of his eyes? If Prophet Nuh didn't have a gardener mindset, he would have spent the rest of his life blaming himself for his bad parenting but that was not the case; he understood that he tried his best and the outcome was not up to him.

By adopting a gardener mindset, we can attract more Barakah into our lives and live in a state of contentment and gratitude, knowing that we are doing our part and leaving the rest to Allah. We become the embodiment of the *hadith*: "Tie your camel, and trust in Allah." (TIRMIDHI)

THE GARDENER EQUATION

Someone might argue that living as gardeners is being fatalistic; leaving things to the whims of destiny, but this is far from the truth. A gardener has a different understanding of destiny. They follow the gardener equation:

Free Will + Natural Laws + Allah's Will = Outcome

Let's break down the equation:

Free Will: As Muslims, we believe that Allah has given mankind the free will to make choices in their lives. We can choose to do good or choose to do evil, and that's why there's Judgement Day – to judge our choices and intentions (not the outcomes in our lives).

Natural Laws: This part of the equation recognises that we live in a cause-and-effect world, and we need to align ourselves to the natural laws of the universe. If we're trying to grow an apple tree, we need to use apple seeds. We can't expect an apple tree if we planted orange seeds, no matter how sincere our intention is. We need to align our actions and processes to the natural laws of how Allah created this world.

Allah's Will: Part of our creed as Muslims is that we believe that nothing happens without Allah's knowledge and will. No matter how strong our determination, and how aligned we are with the natural laws, if Allah does not will something to happen, it will not happen. Take these two stories from the Quran, for example:

- **<u>The people of Prophet Ibrahim had the will to burn him alive.</u>** They took the means and built the largest fire pit to throw him in, but Allah's permission did not come for the fire to burn, and Prophet Ibrahim had his best days in the fire pit! "But We said, 'Fire, be cool and safe for Ibrahim.'" (QURAN 21:69)
- **<u>Prophet Ibrahim saw in a dream that God commanded him to slaughter his son Ismail.</u>** He told the son the dream and the son agreed to be slaughtered since it was God's

command. They both submitted their will to the Will of God and Prophet Ibrahim took the sharpest knife and ran the knife on his beloved son's neck. But the knife did not cut. Allah's will for that knife to cut did not come and Ismail was saved, and they were both rewarded for their willingness to sacrifice for God.

You may have experienced something similar in your life. Sometimes Allah wills something to happen to you even though your intentions may not be there, and you didn't follow His natural laws. For example:

Imagine you slept late one day watching a TV show. You didn't have a strong intention to wake up for *fajr* prayers that morning. Your body is tired and under slept. Thus, you likely expected to skip *fajr* prayer that day. But, at the time of *fajr*, due to Allah's decree, you do wake up despite your late-night TV binge and you get up to pray.

When you understand the above equation, it changes your understanding of destiny and how you interact with destiny as a gardener. You recognise that you have a responsibility towards every element of this equation.

For Free Will: your responsibility is to set good intentions, make decisions, craft a plan to make your intentions a reality (instead of just wishful thinking), and determine the resources you need to execute your plan.

For Natural Laws: your responsibility is to learn what natural laws you need to tap into in order to make your intention a reality and seek knowledge and help if you don't know. For example, if you want to plant tomato trees, you need to know the type of seeds that grow healthy tomatoes in your area, the type of soil you'll need, how to manage the watering of your plant, how to protect the plant from pests etc. You might need to find an experienced gardener to teach you the ropes of how to plant the best tomatoes in your neighbourhood.

For Allah's Will: to say that we have nothing to do when it comes to Allah's will is a common misconception. In fact, as Muslims, we have three important responsibilities that we should fulfil:

1. Our first responsibility is to have greater hope and aspiration. We should never limit ourselves to what we think can be done, but rather think of the possibilities that Allah can bring forth. After all, Allah says in a *hadith qudsi*: "I am as my slave thinks of me." (TIRMIDHI)
2. Our second responsibility is to make *dua* and ask Allah for what we want based on the above belief. The Prophet Muhammad ﷺ taught us that nothing repels destiny or decree that has befallen someone except *dua*. (TIRMIDHI)
3. Finally, our third responsibility is to live a God-centred, Barakah Culture lifestyle. We must adopt the mindsets, values and rituals that attract Allah's Barakah in whatever endeavours we embark upon.

Prophet Muhammad ﷺ showed us an example of how to live this equation when he was preparing for the Battle of Badr – the first battle between the believers and disbelievers in the *sirah*:

- Free Will: He first sought council from his companions and saw that his companions made the intentional decision to go and fight.
- Natural Laws: He then prepared the army as best as he could and listened to advice on how best the army could position itself on the terrain to have a strategic advantage over the enemy camp.
- Allah's Will: He then stood in a long prayer beseeching God for victory as if he was not prepared for the battle at all.

Even though he was the Prophet of God, he still took the necessary steps to prepare for the battle and trusted in Allah's plan. He approached the battle like a gardener, tending to the process and leaving the outcome to Allah.

You might wonder then how to prepare for the second half of the equation: the outcome. This is the crux of the gardener mindset as we explained earlier: gardeners are not attached to the outcome or result because they know it's not from them. They can't control the outcome, so they are not obsessed with it. If the outcome is good, they are thankful, and if the outcome is bad, they are patient and repeat the gardening process and try to improve it for the better. We must remember that we aren't judged by the outcome itself, but by the reaction we have to it.

We test you with evil and with good as trial, and to Us you will be returned (QURAN 21:35)

It's also important to note that the gardener equation is circular, not linear. Meaning: when you set intentions, align with natural laws, ask for God's will, and receive an outcome, the process doesn't stop. The outcome creates a feedback loop for your spiritual heart to decipher and see what Allah wants you to do next, and you repeat the process until you reach your intentions or you're guided to what's better. The image below captures this process:

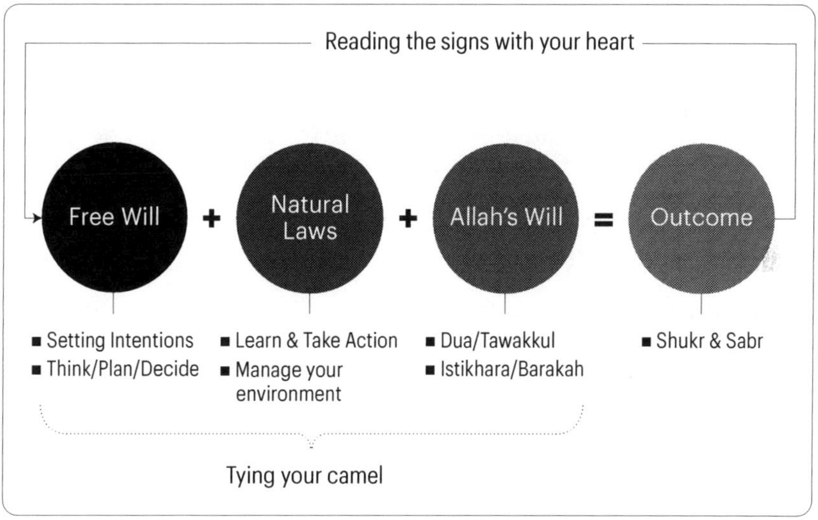

The Barakah Tree: Putting the Gardener Mindset into Practice

> *Do you not see how Allah compares a good word to a good tree? Its root is firm and its branches reach the sky.*
>
> (QURAN 14:24)

The metaphor of a tree is another great way to explain the gardener mindset and the Barakah effect that comes from being a good gardener.

If you want to see Barakah in your life, you first need to make sure that the intention (the seed) is pure of defects and placed in the right environment (soil). You then put energy, focus and time into nourishing this seed so that it ultimately has firm roots in the Barakah Culture paradigm of a God-centred, Hereafter focused life. If you consistently add Barakah Culture nutrients to the soil through the mindsets, values and rituals that attract Barakah, then you'll see the outcome of fruits exceed all expectations.

Below is a depiction of this metaphor:

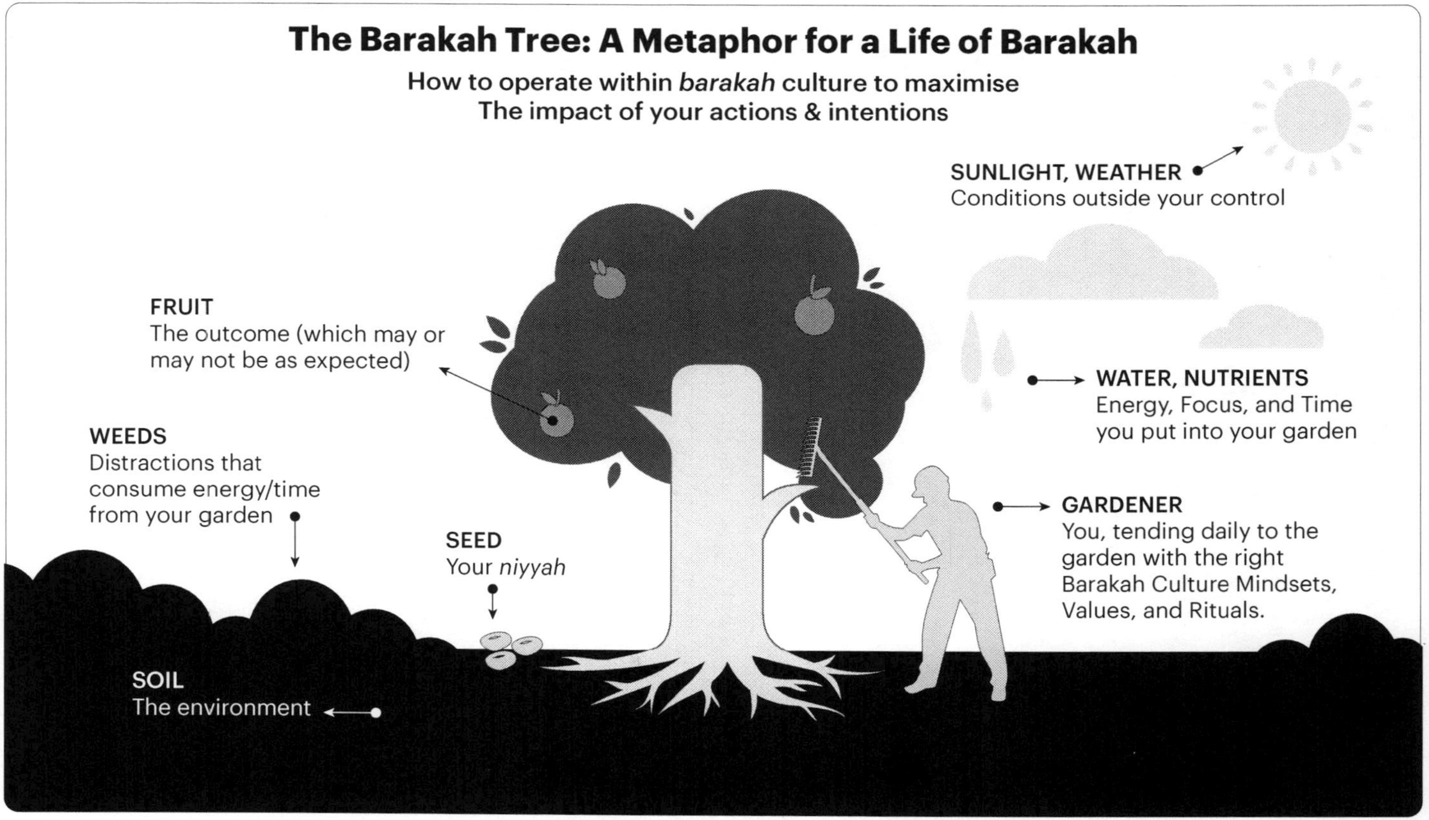
The Barakah Tree: A Metaphor for a Life of Barakah
How to operate within *barakah* culture to maximise
The impact of your actions & intentions
SUNLIGHT, WEATHER
Conditions outside your control
FRUIT
The outcome (which may or may not be as expected)
WATER, NUTRIENTS
Energy, Focus, and Time you put into your garden
WEEDS
Distractions that consume energy/time from your garden
GARDENER
You, tending daily to the garden with the right Barakah Culture Mindsets, Values, and Rituals.
SEED
Your *niyyah*
SOIL
The environment

The metaphor of a Barakah tree, as I call it, is helpful when you approach any project in life and want to see Barakah in it. Before beginning any endeavour, ensure that each step on the Barakah tree checklist is complete:

1. First, **check the intentions of your project:** is it God-centred and Hereafter focused? Allah told the Prophet ﷺ not to pray in a specific mosque because the intention behind building that mosque was for the hypocrites to create division in the community.

> *Then there are those who built a mosque––in an attempt to cause harm, disbelief, and disunity among the believers––as an outpost for those who fought God and His Messenger before: they swear, 'Our intentions were nothing but good,' but God bears witness that they are liars. [Prophet], never pray in that mosque. You should rather pray in a mosque founded from its first day on consciousness of God: in this mosque there are men who desire to grow in purity- God loves those who seek to purify themselves.*
>
> (QURAN 9:107-108)

Whether it's a project in your career, marriage or business, what's the intention? Is your project about serving your ego? Or is it centred on pleasing God?

2. **Check the soil:** How's the environment around the project? Is it conducive for the project to grow? Will the environment help the project bear fruit? Or will it be a stifling environment that will harm the project?

When it comes to our environment, there are elements we can change, e.g. whom we meet or hang out with or what we listen to etc. And there are elements we can't change, e.g. our family members and where we live. For the elements that we can't change, think about how you can best manage or minimise any negative impact. For example, if you live in a toxic family environment that's very negative, try to find a group of friends who are more supportive and positive to mitigate some of the negativity from your family.

Be like the gardener who – if needed – brings their plants to a special greenhouse, to protect them from the harsh environmental elements.

3. **Check the nutrients:** What will you feed this project with? Will you feed it with Hustle Culture pesticides of ego, pride and a scarcity mindset? Or will you feed it with Barakah Culture mindsets, values and rituals, such as abundance, *ihsan* (spiritual excellence), and *salawat*? The more you feed your project with good spiritual nutrients, the more you'll help your project establish firm, healthy roots deep in the soil.
4. **Check your processes:** How are you spending your energy, focus and time on this project? Are you dedicating

enough energy, focus and time for this project or not putting in enough effort?

Let's look at a real-life example of how you can apply the above steps:

Let's say you are struggling in your career and want to see more Barakah in your work. Here's how you can adopt the gardener mindset and grow a Barakah tree at work:

Step 1 – Check the foundation of your tree: If you've been career driven all your life, constantly chasing the next promotion, contemplate how you can rethink your career in a more God-centred, Hereafter focused way. Perhaps you can use your position and influence in the company to move the direction of the company towards something more meaningful and purpose and impact driven, than simply profit driven. Or you can be a champion for spirituality in the workplace, trying to encourage people to adopt Barakah Culture at work.

Step 2 – Check the soil and environment of your career: What is detracting Barakah from your career and what's attracting Barakah to your career? Some things may be hard to change, but can you take small steps to improve the workplace environment so it's more Barakah-friendly? I wrote an article on ProductiveMuslim.com on the impact of *shaytan* in organisations, and how if we don't check for *shaytan's* influence in our workplaces, it can remove Barakah from our places of work[13].

Step 3 – Check the nutrients: What are you feeding your career? With Barakah Culture mindsets, values and rituals or with the usual mindsets and routines of Hustle Culture? Perhaps you start praying *istikhara* before every major decision or make wudhu before entering a meeting or forgive those who wronged you at work, even if you were right.

Step 4- Review your process: How are you spending your energy, focus and time at work? Are you fulfilling the rights and responsibilities upon you at work or are you wasting time at work, endlessly scrolling through YouTube and chatting with your colleagues?

The Barakah tree approach demonstrates the importance of taking proactive steps to ensure our constant orientation towards Barakah Culture. It is important to remember that this is not a one-time process, but rather a lifelong process. Just like a gardener who tends to their garden every day, we must be constantly engaged in the process of nurturing our projects and ourselves to ensure that we are living a life of Barakah.

"Praiseworthy planning is planning that seeks to enhance one's relationship with God. Blameworthy planning is planning that revolves around the self and its appetites, heedless of one's debt to God, as well as God's remunerative generosity and spontaneous grace."

IBN ATA'ILLAH

Planning Your Life as a Gardener

As human beings, we enjoy setting goals and we're highly motivated to achieve them. Unlike animals, we are not content to simply sit, eat, reproduce and sleep; we have an innate 'meaning seeking' side to us that's part of our *fitrah* (natural disposition). Ultimately, we seek to fulfil our ultimate purpose, and that is to be a true slave of Allah.

The question is: if we're naturally inclined towards setting goals, how do we go about setting goals as gardeners versus carpenters? And more importantly, how do we achieve those goals as gardeners?

FAILURES OF HUSTLE CULTURE GOAL-SETTING TECHNIQUES

Most self-help books teach a goal-setting framework that originates from a carpenter mindset. The framework typically has the following basic steps:

- **Step 1:** Decide where you want to be X year(s) from now or at the end of your life. Complete exercises such as imagining your eulogy or creating a vision board.
- **Step 2:** Set long-term goals that will help you fulfil the above vision.
- **Step 3:** Set short-term goals or milestones that help you make progress towards your long-term goals.
- **Step 4:** Use a daily or weekly planner to stay focused on achieving your short and long-term goals.

Makes sense? Absolutely. Does it work? Not always.

In fact, after coaching several people on achieving their goals, I've realised that the above techniques usually work best with short-term 'SMART' (Specific, Measurable, Actionable, Realistic & Timebound) goals, and not so much with long-term, important goals that take several months or years to achieve. Here's why:

THE ABOVE FRAMEWORK MAKES TWO FLAWED ASSUMPTIONS:

1. It assumes you have the perfect vision for the future based on your current circumstances and life ambitions.
2. It assumes you have perfect control of every conceivable factor towards achieving your goals (hence making you ultimately responsible for any failures in achieving them).

A BARAKAH APPROACH TO GOAL SETTING

Below, I propose an entirely different framework for goal setting – one that is more rooted in Barakah Culture and in line with the gardener mindset discussed above. This approach to goal setting doesn't make impossible predictions nor sets you up for failure; rather, it helps you stay focused on your intentions, putting in the hard work and trusting Allah with the results.

The infographic provides a visual representation of the Barakah goal setting process, along with more detail about applying each step in the subsequent sections.

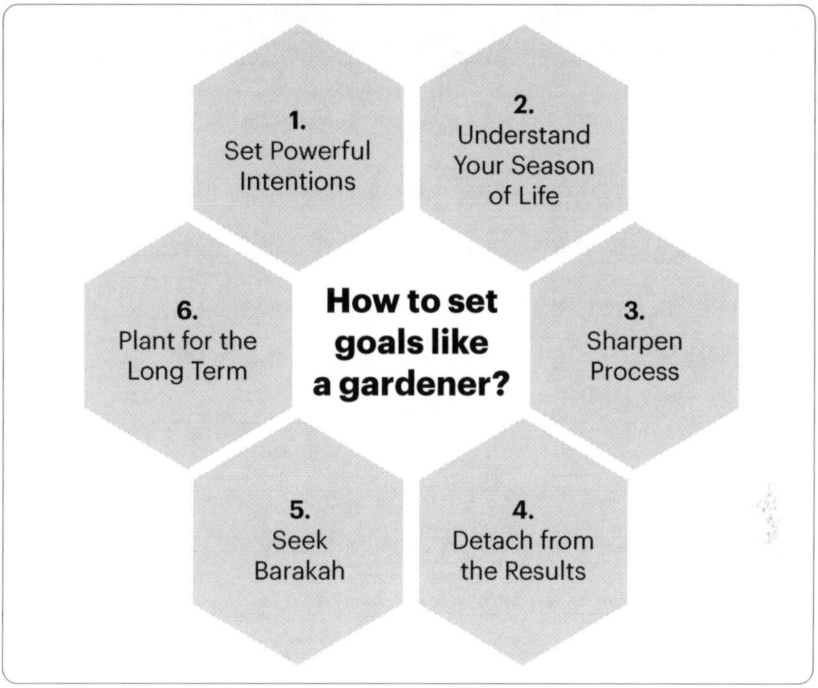

Step 1: Set powerful intentions – not visions

As we've discussed, when a gardener plans their garden, they start with an intention (seed) of what they want to grow.

Likewise, when you plan your goals, instead of focusing on the end result or crafting a vision board of how things 'should' be, focus on the intentions of your goals (i.e. the why).

Why Are Intentions Important for Planning?

- **Life circumstances should not dissuade you from your intention:** Our vision for the future changes with life's changing circumstances, but our intentions – if sincere – remain robust through the seasons of life. For example, you might have a vision of being a bestselling author (which may or may not happen), but your intention to spread beneficial knowledge wouldn't change regardless of whether you become a successful author or not.

- **Allah rewards intentions, not outcomes:** It's not what you do that matters, but the intention behind it that matters the most. The more sincere the intention, the greater the reward for the action – even if you don't achieve your goal. As Prophet Muhammad ﷺ said: "He who supplicates to Allah sincerely for martyrdom, Allah will elevate him to the station of the martyrs, even if he dies on his bed." (MUSLIM)

- **You have many sources of inspiration:** You can have multiple intentions associated with a single goal; so even if one or two of your intentions shift or are not conceivable, you can have other intentions that will drive your actions. Unlike having a single vision, if your vision doesn't work out, you aren't back at the drawing board trying to come up with a new one.

Step 2: Understand your season of life

One of the major flaws of traditional goal setting techniques and the carpenter mindset is the lack of appreciation for the changing macro and micro seasons in a person's life. You're considered a 'loser' if you can't achieve your goals even if things are outside your control and stacked up against you on a personal, business and socio-economic level.

Think of a gardener: they don't plant a seed just anytime in the year. They are in tune with the ebb and flow of the world around them and the changing seasons and climate, and they only plant the right seeds at the right time. Failure to do so would guarantee the failure of their crops. Becoming conscious of the changing seasons in your life helps you focus on when you should go for your goals and when you should wait until a better opportunity arises.

There are three types of seasons to be aware of in your life as you set your goals:

1. The Macroeconomic Season: We're affected by the economic cycles of life: the 2008 global recession, and the fallout from the pandemic are just a couple of the economic droughts in recent memory.

Part of being a smart gardener is to understand the implication of these seasons on the intentions you're trying to set.

The Quran tells us how Prophet Yusuf understood that the seven years of prosperity that Egypt was going through will be followed by seven years of drought. Hence, he set up systems for managing Egypt's resources to survive the drought years.

Be aware of the cyclical nature of the economy so you don't set your intentions up for failure.

2. The Business or Professional Season: Is your business or career going through a period of rapid expansion and growth or stagnation and decline? Understanding your business or professional season of life helps you decide which goals you should focus on for the upcoming year.

Should you focus on hiring, building systems and processes *or* cutting costs and developing products? Similarly, as a professional, should you focus on leading those important projects at work or fixing up your CV and upskilling yourself for your next career move?

Pay attention to the season of your business or career to determine what type of goals to set for yourself.

3. Your Human Life Seasons: Allah says in the Quran:

> *It is Allah Who created you in a state of weakness, then developed 'your' weakness into strength, then developed 'your' strength into weakness and old age. He creates whatever He wills. For He is the All-Knowing, Most Capable.* (QURAN 30:54)

When I was in my 20s, I read a powerful book that made me appreciate the different stages coming up in my life. It was called *The Seasons of a Man's Life* by Daniel J. Levinson. Levinson describes the different stages of an adult's life and the main characteristics of each stage:

Table 1 – Data from Daniel J. Levinson

"The Seasons of a Man's Life" 1978

Age	Season	Characteristics
18-20	Early adult transition	Seeks independence by separating from family
21-27	Entrance into the adult world	Experiments with different careers and lifestyles
28-32	Transition	Makes lifestyle adjustments
33-39	Settling down	Experiences greater stability
40-44	Transition	Makes adjustments to life based on experiences so far (sometimes referred to as mid-life crisis)
45-65+	Pay-off years	Is self-directed and engages in self-evaluation and thinks about what legacy they want to leave behind

Similarly, Imam Al-Haddad in his book, *The Lives of Man*, explains the stages of our worldly existence into the following categories:

- Birth and childhood
- Youth and maturity
- Seniority and death

Simply understanding what stage of life you're in can help you set appropriate intentions for yourself. For example, when you're in early adulthood (pre-30 years old), you might want to focus on seeking knowledge, going to college, and making career choices and marriage choices. Once you hit your 30s, you may want to focus on commitments related to family, where to live, and community service. During each stage of life, you might experience specific circumstances that re-prioritise your goals, focus and intentions e.g. you're going through a divorce, moving countries or receiving cancer treatment.

By acknowledging your human life cycle, you start thinking about how best to approach your life intentions in line with your natural strength and season of life. For example, if you're young, single and energetic, and one of your life intentions is to seek beneficial knowledge, then traveling and learning is a great use of your time. If, however, you're mid-career and you have family and responsibilities and are unable to travel to study, then you'll adjust seeking beneficial knowledge through online learning or learning from local scholars in your area.

Step 3: Sharpen the process

A gardener must follow a specific process to make their garden a reality. Not following the process or skipping some steps could mean the end of their gardening aspirations. The more the gardener focuses on the process, the more likely they are to achieve their gardening intentions.

Similarly, when setting up goals, I advise my coaching clients to set up process goals versus achievement goals, and focus on optimising the process rather than worrying about achievements. Here's the difference:

Goal	Process
I want to memorise the Quran in five years	I want to memorise half a page a day for three days a week
I want to lose 20lbs in 12 months	I want to run for 30 mins for three days a week
I want to be a published author in one year	I want to write 500 words a day

Why is this important?

Achievement goals turn the goals into a matter of success or failure – either you achieve it or you don't. Process goals, on the other hand, turn the goal into a habit or routine that will eventually help you achieve your desired outcome.

Moreover, process goals tap into the power of making progress and feeling the success momentum of taking concrete steps towards your goals. In contrast, achievement goals often feel like a mirage that you may never achieve.

Lastly, if for some reason you're not seeing progress, you'll question the process instead of questioning the goal itself. This happens a lot with people who want to memorise the Quran or learn Arabic. If they are not able to memorise the Quran or learn Arabic, they feel bad about it and usually give up. If instead, they focused on process goals, they'll question the approach they are taking to memorising Quran or learning Arabic and try a different process to see if it works better for them.

Process goals help people go farther, and not get discouraged along the way.

Step 4: Detach from the results

> *Anas bin Malik narrated that a man said: "O Messenger of Allah! Shall I tie my camel and rely upon Allah, or leave it loose and rely upon Allah?" He said: "Tie your camel and rely upon Allah."* (TIRMIDHI)

You've set powerful intentions, you've planted your intentions according to your season of life, and you've sharpened your process – congratulations, you've now fully "tied your camel" as the Prophetic saying goes. Now comes the next part of the *hadith*: "trust in God".

The beauty of detaching ourselves from the results is that our heart stays calm and sincere throughout all the ups and downs of trying to achieve our goals. If we achieve our goals, we give thanks. If things don't go our way, we are patient seeking the reward from Allah for the beautiful intentions we've set for the goals. Moreover, we need to recognise that Allah knows better than we do what is best for us (we just may not see it yet).

This approach connects us with Allah on a deeper level, as we start making daily supplications for the goals we're trying to achieve. Our goals become spiritual quests.

Just think of a gardener, who sets the intention of planting an oak tree, chooses the right seeds and season, focuses on the process of tending for the tree, then supplicates sincerely to Allah to make their tree a reality. What spiritual state would this person experience over the course of many years?

Whether the tree grows or not, what reward would Allah bestow for showing total dependence on Him?

Your whole experience with goal setting changes: instead of being a stressful or Hustle Culture endeavour, goal setting allows you to experience a spiritual endeavour that attracts Barakah and success in this life and the next – beyond your imagination.

Step 5: Seek Barakah

We always think of achieving our goals, but how often do we think about how we go about achieving our goals?

Imagine there are two people: each one set an intention to run a successful business. One person adopts an ego-centric, Hustle Culture mindset that harms his employees, his environment and even his own health. The other adopts a Barakah Culture mindset, that approaches the business with intentionality, mercy and balance. They both may end up with successful businesses but the one who sought Barakah whilst building their business will have far more positive impact than the one who didn't.

As you go set and chase your goals, make sure that you're following the process from a Barakah Culture perspective as explained in this book.

You need to be intentional about adding Barakah in your life through specific values, mindsets and rituals, just as you are intentionally taking multivitamins and exercising to add health to your life.

Step 6: Plant for the long term

> *"And whatever thing you [people] have been given – it is [only for] the enjoyment of worldly life and its adornment. And what is with Allah is better and more lasting; so will you not use reason?"* (QURAN 28: 60)

Yes, it's great to achieve all your goals and win awards but weighing this appropriately helps you stay focused on goals that service the Hereafter, rather than worldly goals that won't mean much after we die.

This doesn't mean we should neglect worldly goals, but we should try to focus our worldly goals on accomplishments that have an impact beyond our lifetime. Goal setting is about connecting your life's journey to your true destination in every moment of your life.

> *Anas ibn Malik reported that the Prophet ﷺ said, "If the Final Hour comes while you have a palm-cutting in your hands and it is possible to plant it before the Hour comes, you should plant it."* (AL ADAB AL MUFRAD)

Step 7: Track your intentions and duas

In the back of my Barakah journal,[14] I have written down intentions for the next five years of my life.

Every now and then, I take a look at those intentions and ask myself the same three questions:

1. Do these intentions still matter to me?
2. Am I actively working towards them with the right systems and processes?
3. Am I seeking Barakah in my approach to these intentions?

Seeing my intentions come to fruition over time is deeply moving.

You recognise that those tiny seeds you planted in your heart have come to bear fruit in this worldly life. And if you are sincere, you may see their real fruit in the Hereafter when they are measured on your scale of good deeds.

Track your intentions and actively make *dua* for them to see the fruits of your planning in your life. Because if you set intentions and forget about them or stop making active *dua* for them, don't be surprised when you feel that things are not going your way or other people are directing your life without your conscious approval.

PRACTICAL TIPS FOR BECOMING A GARDENER IN EVERY ASPECT OF YOUR LIFE:

- **Wake up early:** The Prophet taught us that there's Barakah in the early hours. As a gardener who wants to see Barakah in the fruits of their labour, we should wake up early and seek the Barakah in our projects and work in the early hours.
- **Plan your day or week with a gardening mindset:** Use our Barakah journal (BarakahJournal.com) to plan your life with Barakah. Unlike traditional productivity journals, the Barakah journal was designed based on the principles of planning your life as a gardener. You'll set daily or weekly intentions and respond to several prompts about putting Barakah first in your tasks and projects. It's a practical tool to help you experience Barakah on a daily or weekly basis.
- **Reset with breathing and *dua*:** When you find yourself trapped in the frustrations of a carpenter mindset, and upset that things are not going according to your plan, take a step back, breathe and remember "*fiha khair*" and ask Allah for ease and Barakah.
- **Apply the Barakah tree or the gardening equation to your next project:** When you approach a project as a Barakah project and you adopt the gardening equation or the Barakah tree metaphor, you'll think differently about how to position the project and how best to make the project succeed with Barakah.
- **Set annual intentions in Ramadan:** I highly recommend

that you spend some time in Ramadan to plan your annual intentions. It's a blessed time where you can set purer intentions for the sake of God on each aspect of your life. To learn more about planning your life in Ramadan, visit our annual intentions masterclass page at productvemuslim.com/AIM.

"Whoever desires
an expansion in his
sustenance and age,
should keep good
relations with his
kith and kin."

PROPHET MUHAMMAD ﷺ

CHAPTER TEN

Cherish Your Parents, and Treat Them with Mercy and Compassion

Once upon a time, there was a young man who lived with his father in a modest home. They didn't have much and life was tough for both of them. One day, a disgruntled man came to their home, demanding that the father repay a debt he owed. The heated exchange of words made the young man feel upset as he watched his father's spirit crumble beneath the weight of humiliation.

The young man interjected the exchange and gave the man all his savings, a modest sum that barely covered a third of the outstanding debt. He also promised to take personal responsibility for the remaining debt and pay it back over time. When the man left, the father felt deeply touched by his son's kindness. He knew his son had been saving to get married. Overcome with emotion, the father prayed fervently, beseeching Allah to bestow Barakah and success upon his son for his sacrifice.

The very next day, the young man's friend told him about a job opportunity with a wealthy merchant who was looking for someone honest and responsible to manage one of his businesses. The young man decided to go meet the merchant with his friend.

The moment the merchant laid eyes on the earnest young man, he knew he had found the right candidate. He extended an offer that was beyond the young man's wildest dreams: triple his current salary, a brand-new car, housing allowance and a staggering 10% of the company's sales.

The young man couldn't help but think of his father's prayer and became emotional. The merchant noticed and asked what was wrong. At first, the young man didn't want to share the story, but when the merchant insisted, he told him about what had happened with the debtor the day before and about his father's prayer for him.

Moved by the young man's story, the merchant decided to pay off the father's entire debt.

When I bring up the topic of attracting Barakah by cherishing and honouring our parents, I usually get a visceral reaction from people who have a difficult relationship with their parents. However, in this chapter, I'll try to strike a balance between what it means to seek Barakah from serving and honouring our parents, whilst not being a victim to psychological and emotional abuse that some parents afflict on their children due to their own personal challenges and upbringing.

Let's start by stating the obvious: parents are human beings, with their faults, challenges and personality issues. Moreover, the complex psychology that binds child to parent can sometimes make it harder for both parents and adult children to have a productive relationship. Having said that, we need to recognise that one of the saddest effects of Hustle Culture is the loss of respect and care for the elderly.

When a generation is brought up to worship materialism and centre their lives around their whims and desires, caring for parents seems like an afterthought at best, and a nuisance for many.

An article from the BBC came out in 2021 about the rising phenomenon of child-parent breakups. Basically, adult children who cut ties with their parents, usually due to differences of opinion on hot issues related to politics, religion or race.

Despite a lack of hard data, there is a growing perception among therapists, psychologists and sociologists that this kind of intentional parent-child 'break-up' is on the rise in western countries. Formally known as 'estrangement', experts' definitions of the concept differ slightly, but the term is broadly used for situations in which someone cuts off all communication with one or more relatives, a situation that continues for the long-term, even if those they've sought to split from try to re-establish a connection[15].

There are many factors that lead a child to break up from their parents including polarising society, rise of individualism and the ability for children to work and live anywhere in the world. Unfortunately, we don't recognise how these breakups lead to a loss of Barakah in our lives.

Honouring Parents with *Ihsan*

Allah commands us in the Quran to be good to our parents, even if they have a different belief system, and to only disobey them if they strive to make us worship other than Him:

> *We have commanded people to be good to their parents: their mothers carried them, with strain upon strain, and it takes two years to wean them. Give thanks to Me and to your parents- all will return to Me. If they strive to make you associate with Me anything about which you have no knowledge, then do not obey them. Yet keep their company in this life according to what is right, and follow the path of those who turn to Me. You will all return to Me in the end, and I will tell you everything that you have done.* (QURAN 31: 14-15)

The Arabic word used for "commanded" in the above verse is "*wassaynah*", which comes from the word "*wassiyyah*" or will – the last message or testimony that someone gives before they die. This message is a very important testament that is not to be taken lightly and should be carried out to the best of one's ability. Allah is giving us a *wassiyyah* to be good to our parents as a lasting testimony that we need to carry on in our lives for as long as we're alive.

Moreover, He doesn't just command us to be good with parents, but the word used to describe "good" is *husna*, a superlative form of "*ahsan*" or better. In other words: treat your parents to the best of your ability. In another part of the

Quran, the word "*husna*" is used to describe Jannah (paradise). It's as if Allah is telling us to treasure our parents as our paradise on earth (or the means to enter Paradise). Prophet Muhammad ﷺ was more explicit in making this link between a mother and child when he told a young man to stay with his mother "...for Paradise is beneath her feet." (AL NASA'I)

Another way to understand the choice of the word *husna* is that God was not prescriptive on how we should be good to our parents, nor did He put a criteria or limit for what *husna* is. Out of His Mercy, Allah will not judge us by a societal standard of what treating your parents with *husna* is but judge us by our intentions and our effort to care and be good to our parents, given our unique personal circumstances.

Towards the end of the above verse, Allah sends a strong reminder that we shall all return to Him and He will inform us of all that we'll do. All the issues we had with our parents will be presented to Him, and all the issues our parents had with us will be presented to Him, and He will judge us according to His Wisdom, Justice and Mercy.

It is a sad reality that we've become so spiritually weak in modern societies, unable to love our parents for who they are and willing to break relationships with our father and/or mother just because they don't align with our worldview. We need to have *husna* with our parents, even if they don't understand us or they don't communicate with us the way we like them to, even if we don't understand where they are coming from.

We need to lower our wing in humility towards our parents – and yes, that may mean we stop or slow down our flight in life sometimes – but it'll be worth it for the Barakah *inshaAllah*.

> *And lower your wing in humility towards them in kindness and say, 'Lord, have mercy on them, just as they cared for me when I was little.'* (QURAN: 17:24)

So how do we navigate seeking the Barakah of parents?

In this chapter, I argue that...

a. We need to recognise the **Barakah that parents bring** to our lives

b. Seeking the Barakah of parents **does not mean being slaves** to parents

c. As parents ourselves, we need to be **a source of Barakah** for our children.

The Underestimated Barakah of Parents

One of the richest Arabs in the Middle East, who runs a real-estate business, has a daily habit of spending at least an hour each morning with his mother before heading off to his work. Another well-known philanthropist in Malaysia is known to travel regularly to visit his mother in the village and is constantly in touch with her. You might assume that people in those positions will be too busy to care for their parents, perhaps hiring help instead. However, both men understood that the Barakah they were experiencing in their lives comes from their service to their parents.

People in their prime years often find themselves sandwiched between the demands of raising a young family and the expected and necessary care for aging parents. In this phase of life, if we don't see the Barakah in serving our parents, we might end up developing resentment towards them because we see our parents as a heavy burden and a roadblock to our success, or worse, become completely estranged from them.

I got a taste of this situation when my father who has stage four cancer fell and broke his hip. I had to drop everything and be next to my father whilst my family and I readjusted to his new reality. During this period, the hardest part of the challenge was trying to balance between caring for dad and managing all my other responsibilities as a father, husband and company director.

Despite the situation and personal challenge I went through, I honestly could still see the Barakah of being next to dad, even though outwardly, it looked like everything may be falling apart due to this situation.

If I didn't have this narrative in my mind that there's Barakah in serving parents, especially when they are most vulnerable, I might have found it hard to keep up with what was required of me at that moment.

During my stay, a family friend visited us and remarked: "what you're doing is *Jannah* – don't let go of it. Stay close to your dad". Just the sort of Barakah Culture message I needed to hear.

Understanding that serving our parents is a means of attracting Barakah in our lives helps us deal with the challenges of caring for them in old age. It makes it easy for us to forgive their shortcomings and changing moods, overlook their flaws and treat them with mercy and compassion.

The Barakah of Serving Parents

> *"Allah's pleasure results from the parent's pleasure, and Allah's displeasure results from the parent's displeasure."* (TIRMIDHI)

> *"A parent is the best of the gates of Jannah; so if you wish, keep to the gate, or lose it."* (TIRMIDHI)

A story narrated by Prophet Muhammad ﷺ, found in al-Bukhari:

> Three men walked along a road when suddenly, it started to rain. They decided to take refuge in a cave to wait out the storm. Soon, a rock fell on the mouth of the cave and blocked their only exit. The men said that nothing can lift them from their situation except praying to God with the sincerest action. One of them said, "O Allah! I had old parents and small children and I used to graze the sheep for them. On my return to them in the evening, I used to milk (the sheep) and offer the milk to my parents first before my children. One day I came late at night and found my parents sleeping. I milked (the sheep) as usual and stood by their heads.

I hated to wake them up and disliked giving milk to my children before them, although my children were weeping (because of hunger) at my feet till the day dawned. O Allah! If I did this for Your sake only, kindly remove the rock so that we could see the sky through it". So, Allah removed the rock a little and they saw the sky.

What I love about this story is twofold:

1. **The man's act of service to his parents was completely voluntary;** this was not something that was required for him to do, and I'm sure his parents wouldn't mind that he feeds his children first before feeding them. However, he simply wanted to treat his parents with husna above all else.
2. **His willingness to suffer pain for the sake of serving his parents,** even if he doesn't sleep and his children don't drink. Just imagine that scenario for a moment. Your kids are at your feet - yelling, screaming and crying, trying to grab that glass of milk - and you refuse to give them the milk as a matter of principle; wanting instead to serve your parents first. Many of us, even if we had every good intention to serve our parents, would just give the drink to our kids.

What level of *husna* does it take from us to be this sensitive and determined to serve our parents, even at personal inconvenience, and why have we lost the patience, the *adab* and the willingness to serve our parents even in small ways?

The issue is not whether I drink the milk first or my parents drink the milk first and which is right or wrong. The issue is adopting a Barakah Culture mindset and recognising that God wants me to serve my parents in the best possible way and therefore, I'll find those acts of service that I will prioritise for my parents and ask God to bless me through those acts.

Despite my opening remarks in this chapter, it's reassuring that the culture of honouring and serving parents is still prevalent in Muslim societies. However, part of me fears that unless we hold on to these concepts and culture, we risk losing them with the advent of modernisation that's sweeping the globe.

Service, Not Spiritual Blackmail

It's important to note that when I say serving or honouring your parents, I'm talking about serving parents with *ihsan*, *not* forfeiting your freedom to make your own choices in life.

I meet countless young men and women who struggle with this issue of honouring their parents. Some are even traumatised by it. They say that their parents are leveraging the 'be dutiful to your parents' spiritual stick to force them into life-altering decisions related to their marriage, careers, where to live or how to raise their children.

This often puts the child in a tough spiritual blackmail situation: on the one hand they don't want to lose their parents' pleasure, which they fear might anger God and make them lose Barakah in their lives but on the other hand, they don't want to live a miserable life where they feel that important life choices were made for them.

We tend to see two reactions in our community when it

comes to serving our parents. Those who are completely enslaved to their parents - not physically, but emotionally and psychologically - and will not do anything without their parents' permission. And those who rebelled against their parents and made it a point to be neglectful of their parents - perhaps not physically neglectful, but emotionally and mentally neglectful, silently wishing that their parents pass away so they can 'live life' and do what they want without the pressure of having them around.

Understanding how to navigate our relationship with our parents, and our obligation to them - without losing ourselves in the process - is the key to unlocking Barakah in our lives without compromising on the choices we make in life.

Below, I offer a framework of three principles that can help adult children navigate the fine line between serving parents and succumbing to spiritual blackmail.

The Barakah Framework for Serving Parents: Three Principles

Principle 1: Lay a foundation of mercy

The basis for the relationship between parent and child should always be mercy. This is what the Quran advocates when it says, "lower your wings of humility out of mercy". When you treat your parents from the perspective of mercy, you can respect their difference of opinion rather than go tit-for-tat against them. If you're a parent, you probably understand this concept when it comes to your children. Your children might do something that annoys you or even outright disobey you, but it's your mercy on them that helps you to forgive, forget and love and hug your children, even on a bad day. Try to have the same lens with your parents. They may be having a bad day or dealing with side effects from medication that make their mood swings go wild. Have mercy on your parent, and don't judge any command they give as them trying to control you.

I had a coaching client who had a difficult relationship with her grandfather. He was very strict and used the religious stick to compel her to make choices in life she wasn't comfortable with. She became resentful of her grandfather and felt bad about it. I asked her to view the relationship with her grandfather from the perspective of mercy, realising that as her grandfather is getting older, he probably feels like he's losing his grip on life and on his children, and rather unfortunately, his control of her was his way of holding on for dear life. This is not to justify the grandfather's actions but to simply understand where he's coming from. A few days later, she shared how this shift to mercy and reframing of the situation helped her develop greater love for him, rather than resentment.

Sometimes, adult children don't recognise that what their parents really want is a little attention and care from their children. Parents may act up or appear controlling because they try to demand this attention and respect, which unfortunately, children interpret as manipulation.

I tell adult children struggling with their relationship with their parents to look at situations from their parents' perspective: that controlling mother who doesn't like your wife? She may be feeling psychologically and emotionally insecure about losing her son's love after marriage. That demanding father who's hard to please? He may be struggling to come to terms with life after retirement and the advent of old age.

Understanding the motivations behind your parents' actions helps you meet their needs and better serve them (and oftentimes without comprising your own beliefs or needs).

Sometimes all that parents want is a kind smile, a daily call, a kiss on the hand and forehead, and a listening ear. Yes, you may not agree with everything they say or do, and they may drive you nuts, but if you follow God's command and lower the wings of mercy and humility to them, could you see a better way forward for your relationship with your parents?

Principle 2: Recognise that *husna* means something different to every generation

The fact that Allah asked us to treat our parents *husna* without defining what *husna* meant, requires us to manage the expectations of our parents. This is where generational values can clash on what it means to honour one's parent.

A parent who saw their parents or grandparents treated with the utmost respect, including standing up when they walk into a room, kissing the parents' hands and forehead when greeting them, and dedicating time and financial resources might expect similar treatment from their son or daughter, who perhaps didn't grow up seeing such examples. In the son or daughter's mind, *husna* could mean calling parents once a week, and making sure parents make it to their doctor appointment on time.

The point I'm making is that understanding, communicating and managing expectations of what it means to treat parents with *ihsan* is important for both the parents and children. Moreover, it's important to role model the behaviours we want to see in how our children treat us, by treating our parents accordingly.

Principle 3: Disagreements happen but disagree respectfully

Disagreements will happen between adult children and parents. To serve your parents doesn't mean you don't disagree, but that you navigate those difficult conversations with mercy and goodness so that you still have their blessings.

I learned about this first-hand when I wanted to leave my comfortable job working for a large Islamic bank to focus on running The Productive Muslim company full time. It was a difficult decision to make, and I wanted my parents' blessings before proceeding.

At first my parents were nervous about it. From their perspective, not only was I putting my future in jeopardy, but I also put their future at stake. They had expectations that with my comfortable salary at the Islamic bank, I'll be able to support them as they grow old and after they retire. Taking a plunge into running a risky business full time put those expectations at risk.

It took several conversations and listening deeply to their concerns before I got their blessings to proceed. And *Alhamdulillah*, despite the challenges in my early years of running the Productive Muslim company full time, I can see the Barakah of my parents' blessings as I became more established with my work.

A GUIDE TO DIFFICULT CONVERSATIONS: THE MODEL OF PROPHET IBRAHIM

Learning how to have difficult but productive conversations with parents is an important skill if we're trying to seek Barakah from Allah and serve our parents with *ihsan*. Successful conversations help bridge gaps between expectations of servitude, as outlined in the framework above, and help you recognise why someone is deserving of mercy or needs mercy – hopefully leading to shared understanding (and maybe even agreement).

Our role model is Prophet Ibrahim. The story below from the Quran shares how Prophet Ibrahim tactfully and politely navigated a tough conversation with his father, despite their entirely different belief systems:

> And mention in the Book [the story of] Abraham. Indeed, he was a man of truth and a prophet. [Mention] when he said to his father, "O my father, why do you worship that which does not hear and does not see and will not benefit you at all?

O my father, indeed there has come to me of knowledge that which has not come to you, so follow me; I will guide you to an even path. O my father, do not worship [i.e., obey] Satan. Indeed Satan has ever been, to the Most Merciful, disobedient. O my father, indeed I fear that there will touch you a punishment from the Most Merciful so you would be to Satan a companion [in Hellfire]."

[His father] said, "Have you no desire for my gods, O Abraham? If you do not desist, I will surely stone you, so avoid me a prolonged time." [Abraham] said, "Peace [i.e., safety] will be upon you. I will ask forgiveness for you of my Lord. Indeed, He is ever gracious to me." (QURAN 19:41-47)

We learn four conservation principles from Prophet Ibrahim's difficult conversation with his father:

<u>1. Honour the Relationship:</u> Prophet Ibrahim kept saying "O my father" to honour the father-son relationship. He didn't say "you infidel!" or make him feel that his position as a father was challenged because now Prophet Ibrahim has a different faith.

<u>2. Ask Questions:</u> Prophet Ibrahim did not jump into the conversation with advice and accusations. He started with a question. In another part of the Quran, Prophet Ibrahim asks a 'what' question, "When he said to his father and his people, "What are these statues to which you are devoted?"" (QURAN 21:52).

In the coaching world, we recommend asking questions – particularly what or how questions - to encourage the other person to think through their point of view, and potentially change their perspective.

3. Show Evidence: Explain your position using examples that make sense to your parents. In Prophet Ibrahim's story, the question, "Why do you worship that which does not hear and does not see and will not benefit you at all?" offered proof of his point. Your parents come from a different generation and sometimes they might not 'get you'. To bridge this gap, provide examples that make sense to them.

4. State Your Points with Kindness and *Adab*: Prophet Ibrahim calmly and firmly told his father about his belief system. He controlled his emotions and stated why it's important for his father to follow him and didn't lose his temper when his father said that he'll stone him or throw him out.

Treating our parents with *ihsan*, especially during difficult conversations, is a learned skill that you can develop and practice.

The Barakah of Being a Righteous Parent

In discussions of being good to one's parent – we often focus on the child and their duties and responsibilities towards their parent. However, we should remember, that this is a two-way relationship and just like we ask the child to be dutiful to their parent, the parent needs to be a righteous parent that attracts the Barakah to their progeny.

Let's revisit the story of Prophet Musa and Khidr (QURAN 18: 60-82) that I shared in chapter nine. The two men passed by a town whose people were inhospitable. Despite that, Khidr saw a leaning wall in this town and decided to reconstruct it with his own hands for free, even though the people of that town didn't deserve this generosity. Perplexed, Prophet Musa questioned this act of kindness to an undeserving town. Khidr explained:

> *"And as for the wall, it belonged to two orphan boys in the city, and there was beneath it a treasure for them, and their father had been righteous. So, your Lord intended that they reach maturity and extract their treasure, as a mercy from your Lord. And I did it not of my own accord. That is the interpretation of that about which you could not have patience."* (QURAN 18: 79- 82)

In an article on ProductiveMuslim.com on how to protect your children's future by Sh. Joe Bradford, Bradford comments on this story and says: "So, God brought al-Khidr and Prophet Moses to a place they weren't expecting to be, to do an act they weren't expecting to do, to preserve a legacy left for two minors they did not know, simply due to the honourable position their father had with Allah on account of the father's righteousness." Some narrations mention that it wasn't even the father, but the seventh great grandfather who was truly righteous, so this Barakah lasted seven generations!

Reciting this verse is tremendously moving for me. As a father, I recognise the role that my spiritual health and well-being has on the wellbeing of my children. It also makes me appreciate my parents, grandparents, and ancestors – some of whom were scholars and righteous men and women – and makes me wonder if I'm living off their Barakah. A scholar once said that whenever he sees his children, he increases his acts of worship, hoping that the Barakah of his acts of worship extends to his children.

Prophet Ibrahim was conscious of extending the Barakah of his prophethood to his children; in Surah Al-Baqarah, when Allah informed him that he'd be leader of a nation, he immediately asked for favour for his children.

> *And [mention, O Muhammad], when Abraham was tried by his Lord with words [i.e., commands] and he fulfilled them. [Allah] said, "Indeed, I will make you a leader for the people." [Abraham] said, "And of my descendants?" [Allah] said, "My covenant does not include the wrongdoers."* (QURAN 2:124)

Moreover, Prophet Ibrahim kept making *dua* for his progeny and seeking Barakah for them until Allah declared that every Prophet that came after him was from his progeny. He'd repeat prayers such as:

> *My Lord, make me an establisher of prayer, and [many] from my descendants. Our Lord, and accept my supplication.* (QURAN 14:40)

> *Our Lord, make us devoted to You; make our descendants into a community devoted to You. Show us how to worship and accept our repentance, for You are the Ever Relenting, the Most Merciful.* (QURAN 2:128)

In fact, it was the following prayer of Prophet Ibrahim that led to the Barakah of us having Prophet Muhammad ﷺ in our lives. As Prophet Muhammad ﷺ would say, "I am the supplication of my forefather Ibrahim" (TABARI). The Prophet ﷺ was referring to the following *dua* that Prophet Ibrahim made mentioned in the Quran:

> *Our Lord, and send among them a messenger from themselves who will recite to them Your verses and teach them the Book and wisdom and purify them. Indeed, You are the Exalted in Might, the Wise."*
>
> (QURAN 2:129)

In some historical accounts, when someone's mother passes away, angels descend and tell the person: "The one whom we used to honour you for has passed away, now do righteousness so we continue honouring you."

Cultivating Barakah of Parents at Every Stage of Life

I mentioned the book *The Seasons of a Man's Life* in the previous chapter, I repeat Levinson four seasons below to describe the dynamics between child and parents at each stage. The four stages are:

- Childhood and Adolescence
- Early Adulthood
- Middle Adulthood
- Late Adulthood

In each of these four seasons, the relationship between child and parent is different, and each stage presents a different way to cultivate Barakah.

Childhood and Adolescence

During early childhood, there's complete dependence of the child on the parent. Not just physically, but emotionally and psychologically, and even spiritually. The Prophet Muhammad ﷺ said: "The mother of every person gives him birth according to his true nature. It is subsequently his parents who make him a Jew or a Christian or a Magian. Had his parents been

Muslim, he would have also remained a Muslim" (MUSLIM). The *hadith* shows the total dependence that children have for their parents, including matters of faith.

At this stage, the seeds of the relationship between parent and child are established. If the foundation is strong: based on love, mercy, and guidance on the spiritual path, usually - not always - the relationship remains strong and respectful until old age. If the foundation is weak, either due to absence of one or both parents (thanks to Hustle Culture) or where love is only expressed materially (through gifts) and there's no deep bonding between parent and child, this is where the relationship can get complicated later in life.

In early childhood, we seek the Barakah of parents by obeying them, listening to them, and being the joy in their lives.

Early Adulthood

As the child hits puberty and reaches adolescence and early adulthood, the child wants to establish their independence and break away from the embrace of their parent. This happens even to the most dutiful children and the wise parent should not see this as a threat or disobedience from their child, but as the child wanting to explore life on their own terms. Parents at this stage should act as a sincere friend, and give advice to the children, rather than act as an authority figure who the child might then hate or resent. Having open conversations with the child as they grow is critical at this stage since you want the young person to foster an open dialogue around their thoughts, hopes, and dreams.

Ali Ibn Abi Taleb said, “Play with them for the first seven years (of their life); then teach them for the next seven years; then advise them for the next seven years (and after that)”.

In adolescence, we can foster Barakah by establishing communication channels early on. These channels ensure there’s a constant dialogue around our parents’ expectations and hopes, and our own expectations. For example, I used to have Fridays morning breakfast with my dad, which gave us an opportunity to communicate more deeply and discuss tough topics whenever we had a disagreement. It created a safe space for regular communication and exchange of ideas.

Middle/Late Adulthood

Once the young man crosses into middle adulthood (30s and 40s), the roles start shifting. The parent becomes more dependent on the adult child and roles reverse. This shift happens gradually, first with small requests to help - carrying something heavy, or getting an errand done – and then, as the parent gets older, the requests and responsibilities become more significant.

To foster Barakah at this stage, we must display humbleness and humility in conversations with our parents. We get stronger as they’ll get weaker, and the transition is difficult for both sides. At this point, we must also recognise that we may only have a few days left with our parents. Rather than letting *shaytan* get between you and your parents, cherish these moments before you lose them in this life.

PRACTICAL TIPS FOR SEEKING PARENTS' BLESSINGS

If you parents are alive, below are a few tips for developing a closer, Barakah-rich relationship every day:

1. **Spend time with them.** If you live with them or nearby them, make it a habit to visit them daily and spend quality time with them. If they live far or you can't visit, then call them daily.

   This daily routine of calling or visiting your parents is your daily dose of Barakah, which you do not want to miss.

2. **Get to know them on a personal level.** Sometimes because of the parent-child dynamic, we rarely understand who our parents are other than authority figures in our lives. What if we get to know them on a personal level, as we'd get to know a friend? What are their hopes, aspirations, concerns, and fears, and how you can help them?

3. **Develop a platform or channel for regular conversations.** Creating an easy means or opportunity for regular communication ensures that when you need to have difficult conversations, it's not as awkward. For me, it was the Fridays morning breakfast with dad and going shopping with my mom. It's in these mundane and regular meetups that we build an emotional buffer in

our relationship. If you live far, then the daily call and a message may serve the same purpose.

4. **Understand how they want to be shown respect and love.** I remember reading *The Five Love Languages* by Gary Chapman before getting married to my wife, and I found the advice useful not only for my marriage but for strengthening the relationship with my parents. I recognised that one of my parents felt love through quality time and another felt love through acts of service, and it made a world of a difference when I communicated with my parents using their preferred language of love.

5. **Get to know their friends, projects, and life plans.** This will be helpful when they pass away, and you need to pick up the pieces after they are gone. Get to know their friends through calls and visits. Accompany your parents when they go on trips to check on projects they worked on or are building. Make sure you understand what their wishes are after they pass away – be sure to write these down.

6. **Honour them after they die.** When your parents pass away, and they are no longer with you, honour them the way Prophet Muhammad ﷺ taught us to honour them by praying for them, giving charity on their behalf, keeping up with their relatives and friends, and being a good example for your children.

I pray that this chapter helped both parents and children better understand how to treat each other with love, compassion, and mercy and I pray that we find the Barakah of honouring our parents in every aspect of our lives.

CHAPTER ELEVEN:

Plant A Seed Whose Harvest will Benefit Generations to Come

> *"Every day two angels come down from Heaven and one of them says, 'O Allah! Compensate every person who spends in Your Cause,' and the other (angel) says, 'O Allah! Destroy every miser.'"* – Prophet Muhammad ﷺ

Born in West Africa in 1736, Yarrow Mamout's life took an unexpected turn when he was kidnapped by slave traders at the tender age of 16. Braving the harrowing journey to North America, he endured 44 long years of enslavement before finally buying back his freedom in 1796.

At 60 years old, Yarrow Mamout was determined to create a new life for himself and his family. After freeing his wife and son, he purchased a modest log house in Washington D.C. Here, he designated a small corner of his backyard as a prayer space, facing Mecca, and planted the foundation for a humble mosque. Little did he know, this small act would leave an indelible mark on history.

Yarrow Mamout may have passed away believing that his story and his mosque would be lost in the sands of time. Yet, centuries later, historians and archaeologists pieced together his incredible tale from his writings and objects discovered in his home.

As a testament to his enduring legacy, Georgetown University honoured Yarrow Mamout's memory by naming a new mosque after him in March 2023. The Yarrow Mamout Mosque now stands as a poignant reminder of the power of planting seeds for future generations.

Remember the gardener mindset concept from chapter nine about setting intentions, working hard, and detaching ourselves from the result? In this chapter, I want to take this concept one step further, and challenge you to think about sowing the seeds of a better tomorrow – not just for yourself but for generations to come.

When employing the gardener mindset, we often confine ourselves to reaping the rewards of our efforts in this world, focusing on our immediate gains within our lifetime. However, it's crucial to recognise the far-reaching implications of our actions on the generations that follow and our spiritual standing in the Hereafter.

As we nurture our families, establish businesses or engage in life pursuits, how many of us genuinely reflect on the lasting impact of our present-day actions? Adopting a gardener mindset in our Barakah Culture paradigm calls for planting seeds with the intent of seeking benefit not only in this life but also in the Hereafter.

Prophet Muhammad ﷺ emphasised this mindset in the

following *hadith*: "If the Final Hour comes while you have a shoot of a plant in your hands and it is possible to plant it before the Hour comes, you should plant it." (BUKHARI)

At first glance, this *hadith* may seem puzzling—why bother planting a tree if the Day of Judgement is imminent, and the world is coming to an end? This teaching invites us to maintain a focus on the Hereafter while leaving a lasting impact in this life, even in our final moments. Planting a tree with the intention of benefiting people, animals, and birds can result in rewards in the Hereafter, regardless of whether the tree bears fruit.

The Prophet ﷺ said: "No Muslim plants a plant or sows a crop, then a person, or a bird, or an animal eats from it, except that it will be charity for him." (TIRMIDHI)

Another important point is that the process of planting, of doing our part, even in the Final Hours of this world, shows our sincere commitment to the process of being slaves of God, trusting Him with the results.

Hustle Culture, on the other hand, tends to be myopic and self-centred in this world. The idea of a Hereafter, even if someone believes in it, seems distant and alien.

I was once in a meeting at an Islamic bank with several Muslim professionals, and one person made a comment about a project that we were discussing and whether it made sense from an *Akhira* (Hereafter) paradigm. People laughed at him. At that moment, it dawned upon me: even as Muslim professionals working for an 'Islamic' institution, we've fallen victim to Hustle Culture and forgotten the value of building projects and institutions for the Hereafter.

Occasionally, you might see someone from the Hustle Culture world seeking to build something that outlasts them, whether it's a charitable project or an endowment fund. Yet they will still approach the project in terms of leaving their personal legacy. They're guided by the 'what's in it for me?' intention, rather than building the project purely for God's sake and for the reward in the Hereafter.

Sowing seeds with a long-term perspective requires us to embrace a far-reaching view of life. Rather than perceiving ourselves as fleeting beings with a lifespan of 60-80 years, we must recognise our existence as part of a continuum that extends from Adam, until we stand before Allah on the Day of Judgement. Our engagement in various aspects of life—education, marriage, parenting, work, and the development of both commercial and charitable enterprises—contributes to the arc of human history. The impact we leave, either positive or negative, depends on our intentions and the values we uphold.

A Traveller Mindset

Once there was a wealthy merchant who desired for his son to follow in his footsteps and become a successful trader. To teach him the ropes, the father provided his son with a ship filled with valuable goods and sent him on a voyage across the seas.

For nine days, the ship sailed smoothly. But on the ninth day, a fierce storm struck, sinking the ship, and claiming everything on board. Miraculously, the merchant's son survived, washing up on the shores of an island with nothing but the clothes on his back.

Disoriented and frightened, the young man wept, unsure of what to do next. Suddenly, he heard the beating of drums and the sound of approaching villagers. The islanders gathered around him, dressed him in fine garments, and carried him to their village, where they crowned him their king.

The young man, bewildered by his sudden change in fortune, noticed an elderly man sitting quietly in a corner as the celebrations began to wind down. He asked the old man if he could stay and talk once the villagers had dispersed.

When everyone had left, the young man questioned the old man: "O *sheikh*, what is happening here? Who are these people and why have they made me their king? I was shipwrecked and washed ashore with nothing, and now they have made me their ruler. I don't understand".

The old man explained that the villagers had a tradition of selecting a new king every three years from the first person they encountered on the island's shore on a specific date. However, at the end of the three years, the villagers would strip the king of his royal garments, dress him in rags, and take him to a desolate island to perish.

Terrified by his impending fate, the young king sought the old man's advice. The wise elder counselled him to use his time as king wisely, enlisting the villagers to help prepare the deserted island with food, water and shelter so he could survive when the time came. The young king agreed, and the preparations commenced.

Three years later, as foretold, the villagers dethroned the

young man, clothed him in tattered rags, and brought him to the island. To his relief, the island was no longer barren but now contained essential resources for survival. After a few days on the island, a passing ship spotted the young man and took him home.

This allegorical tale from Islamic tradition symbolises the journey each of us takes from the womb to the grave and beyond, emphasising the importance of adopting a traveller mindset when going through this world.

Can you decipher which elements of the story represent different stages of life?

- **The three years** denote the three stages of one's life (childhood, adulthood, old age), while the white rags symbolise the shroud that cloaks you upon death.
- **The boat** that transports you to the deserted island embodies the angel of death, while the soldiers represent your deeds (good and bad) that accompany you to your grave.
- **The once-desolate island,** now a garden, signifies the grave, which can be a place of solace if prepared for or a desolate, unwelcoming space if neglected.

- Lastly, **the ship that rescues the young man** from the island represents the vessel that will carry us into the Hereafter to meet our Lord.
- **The ship** carrying the young man for nine days, with all its resources, signifies the mother's womb that nurtures a baby for nine months. The storm embodies the mother's labour pains, leading to the child's birth. Upon arrival in this world, the child is naked and crying.
- **The villagers** who clothed and crowned the young man represent the distractions, attractions, and illusions of power and control within this worldly life.
- **The wise old sheikh** symbolises the Quran, offering sound advice when consulted and guiding you toward the right actions if placed in charge of your affairs.

This parable and many similar parables to it have been taught by generations of scholars to help people understand the transitory nature of this world and the permanence of the abode of the Hereafter. These parables do not intend to instil in people a neglect of this world, but gently remind them that what they sow in this world will be harvested in the Hereafter and they should use the short time they have here to make long-lasting impact for generations to come.

Gardening from an *Akhira* Paradigm

For centuries, successful people understood that sacrificing present day comforts for long-term gains is a path to success.

- Exercising today helps your body adapt to old age better.
- Saving money today helps you prepare for retirement in the future.
- Investing in relationships today helps you in the future.

We intuitively understand this concept and appreciate the importance of making choices today that would affect us down the road.

Similarly, making choices today and sowing seeds today to harvest in the Hereafter is an important concept that is often repeated in the Quran:

> *Whoever should desire the immediate - We hasten for him from it what We will to whom We intend. Then We have made for him Hell, which he will [enter to] burn, censured and banished. But whoever desires the Hereafter and exerts the effort due to it while he is a believer - it is those whose effort is ever appreciated [by Allah].* (QURAN 17:18-19)

However, just like we struggle to make the right choices today in terms of our health, finances, and relationships, we also struggle to make sacrifices in this world that would help us succeed in the Hereafter. As humans, we tend not to be kind to our future selves since we can't seem to imagine ourselves

30, 40, or 60 years from now (never mind imaging ourselves in the Hereafter).

If we want the Barakah effect to enter our lives, and plant seeds for generations to come, we need to think and operate from an *Akhira* paradigm. We need to constantly be conscious and aware of the Hereafter and make choices in this world with full understanding of their impact in the Hereafter.

Consider the difference between someone who operates from a worldly paradigm versus someone who operates from an Akhira paradigm. When a worldly person wakes up in the morning, his first concern is this world. He wakes up and starts his day by checking his phone, reading his emails, news, social media feeds, and making sure he didn't miss anything. He gets out of bed and if he's motivated, he might exercise and pray. Prayer is usually done as a chore. He then showers, goes to work, engages in more chit-chat, social media, comes back from work, plays with his family, watches tv, and scrolls through more social media feeds before falling asleep with his phone in his hand. Does that sound familiar?

Now, think of a person who operates with an *Akhira* paradigm. She wakes up and her main concern is the Hereafter. She remembers God, wakes up before *fajr* to pray *tahajjud* or at least *fajr*. She spends some time with the Quran. She performs her duties - whether at work or home - whilst conscious that her words and actions are recorded by her assigned angels. She refrains from wasteful activities that don't benefit her and engages in beneficial activities like seeking knowledge, remembrance of Allah, and having an impact on those around her. At the end of the day, she holds herself to account and seeks forgiveness for any shortcomings. She thanks Allah for any good she sees and goes to sleep in a state of purity and remembrance.

Can you see the difference between a life lived in an *Akhira* paradigm versus a *dunya* paradigm? Can you see the difference in their sources of motivation?

When you're Hereafter centred, you're like a firm tree (the Barakah tree) that is firmly rooted and while the winds may shake you, they can't uproot you. This is because your source of motivation is pleasing Allah, having firm belief in the undeniable truth that you'll meet Him in the Hereafter.

When you're a worldly centred person, you're like an autumn leaf of a tree that's blown around by the winds of life. This is because you attach yourself to this temporal world instead of the permanence of the Hereafter.

COMMON MISCONCEPTIONS ABOUT ADOPTING AN AKHIRA PARADIGM ON LIFE

You might think that adopting an *Akhira* paradigm is simply a spiritual and intellectual exercise that has no benefit or use in our daily lives.

- **If you are a CEO of a company,** you probably don't want your employees to adopt an *Akhira* paradigm because you think that will make them lazy and not focus on their worldly tasks and projects.
- **If you are a parent,** you might be concerned about your child adopting an *Akhira* paradigm because you think they won't care about their studies and preparing themselves for the worldly future.
- **If you're an activist,** you don't want society to adopt an *Akhira* paradigm, because you worry people will lose interest in fighting for the social justice causes that you care about.

The above scenarios display **a misunderstanding of what it means to adopt an *Akhira* paradigm.** Embracing the *Akhira* paradigm doesn't entail neglecting this world or living in extreme poverty, apathy, with no hope of accomplishing anything meaningful in this life. You won't become a monk, hiding away in your monastery until your last breath. Rather, adopting the *Akhira* paradigm means:

- You're conscious and aware of the Hereafter and that the next world is your **final abode**.
- You're conscious and aware that **this world is a bridge** to the next world and is temporary.
- You're conscious and aware that what you do in this world will **impact what happens** to you in the Hereafter.
- You're conscious and aware that your actions and deeds will **impact those who'll come after you.**

Embracing the *Akhira* paradigm does not mean neglecting this world and having zero impact on society, rather it's the exact opposite. Therefore:

- If you're the CEO of a company, you want to encourage your employees to adopt an *Akhira* paradigm because they'll take a long view of the company's success, rather than a quarterly or five-year view. They'll come up with fresh ideas to maximise impact in the here and now, as well as in the distant future. They'll ensure that their ideas are sustainable and do not harm the environment, society, or future generations.
- If you're a parent, you want your children to adopt an *Akhira* paradigm because their values and life decisions about their careers and family won't be driven simply by economic opportunities and cost/benefit analysis, but what would be most pleasing to Allah in the Hereafter (including serving you with *husna* as discussed in the previous chapter).
- If you're an activist, you want society to adopt an *Akhira* paradigm because people will stop thinking about their short-term selfish needs and realise they need to do something about the bigger problems in society like climate change, racism, social inequity etc.

The Impact of Adopting a Hereafter Perspective

When you adopt the Hereafter perspective in your life, something interesting starts to happen. It's as if you start wearing a new set of glasses and you can see things more clearly. None of the glitters of this world excite you to leave your values, mindsets, and rituals, and that deep knowledge of the Hereafter helps you stay aligned with Barakah Culture always. This mindset informs a lot of your life choices:

- You're conscious of **what you eat and drink** not because of physical health alone, but because what you eat impacts your energy and wellbeing, which ultimately impacts your journey to God.
- You're conscious of **how you dress,** not because you want to show off, but because you know that God loves modesty, and you want to be on earth the way Allah loves to see His servants. Moreover, dressing modestly is a demonstration of your reverence of your position as God's slave on earth.
- You're conscious of **who you spend time with** as people can either remind you of the Hereafter and help you do good, or the opposite.
- You're selective of what **careers or businesses you get into** because this will impact your Hereafter.
- You're selective of **who your spouse** is because life partners can positively or negatively influence your faith.
- You're clear on the **values you want to impart to your children** even if those values are not popular in mainstream society.

- You're conscious of **your finances and future investments,** not to become wealthy for wealth's sake, but to start making investments for the Hereafter by helping orphans, the poor, and the needy.

The above changes are transformative, not only to you, but to those around you and that's how Barakah Culture starts to spread and become a reality in society. When people start putting their 'Hereafter goggles' on and see the world through the paradigm of the Hereafter, it changes how they live, play, learn and work. And that's when they experience Barakah.

The Three Most Important Investments in Your Life

> *The Messenger of Allah ﷺ said: "When a person dies, his deeds are cut off except for three: continuing charity, knowledge that others benefited from, and a righteous child who supplicates for him."* (TIRMIDHI)

The above *hadith* gives the blueprint for the type of long-term Hereafter centred investments a person should make in this life so they not only benefit him in the Hereafter, but also benefit generations to come.

We tend to oversimplify the above *hadith* and think that if we build a well somewhere, or distribute a book, or send our kids to a madrasah, that we're fulfilling the above *hadith*. But think of it deeply, and you realise that this *hadith* is not that simple to fulfil.

The Prophet Muhammad ﷺ is telling us that if we want to continue receiving good deeds in our graves, we need to invest in three types of good deeds – continuing charity, knowledge that others benefited from, and a righteous child who supplicates for us – and ensure that they continue and last for us beyond our life.

Beneficial Knowledge

We think that if we share a useful article we came across or write a book or upload a video, that we have acted upon this *hadith*. But if I were to ask you how you can ensure that this knowledge you're sharing or teaching can last for 1000 years, what would you say?

To answer this question, you'll need to use the gardener equation we introduced in chapter nine. You'll need to use your free will to do the thinking and planning of how best to preserve this knowledge. You'll then need to take practical means to preserve your knowledge. Then you need to ask Allah for acceptance and Barakah to preserve your knowledge.

Imam Al-Shafi once said that there's a scholar by the name Imam Al-Laith Ibn Sa'd, who was far more knowledgeable than the famous Imam Malik, but he had no students who wrote his knowledge down and spread it. This is not to reduce the position or the dignity of Imam Al-Laith, but it's a reminder that if we want beneficial knowledge to pass down generations, we need to actively think about how we can preserve it.

Having said that, sometimes Allah will accept and bless beneficial knowledge that will last for generations even though the means of distribution may not be there.

Think of the books that have been passed down to us for generations from the canon of Islamic intellectual thought; books that were written at a time when there was no internet, no computer, no word processor. Just pen and paper and volumes of books. See the Barakah that Allah placed in some of this knowledge. Centuries later, people still benefit from the works of Imam Bukhari, Imam Muslim, Ibn Al-Qayyim, Al-Ghazali etc.

When researching for this book, I came across a book about Barakah written by the Yemeni scholar, Muhammad Al-Hubaishi over 700 years ago! I marvelled at how Allah protected this book for centuries and guided this book to my hands as I was planning to write a book on Barakah.

This is the type of ongoing charity that benefits a person in their grave for generations to come.

So, if you want to spread and share beneficial knowledge, a Hereafter-centred person will start thinking long-term about preserving and sharing this knowledge whilst asking Allah for His acceptance and Barakah.

Ongoing Charity

Hustle Culture tells us that if we build a well in a remote part of the world, we've built an ongoing charity. Or if we built a mosque somewhere, this mosque is going to help us in the long-term. However, how many wells have we seen run dry in less than five years of operation? And how many dilapidated mosques have we seen on highways that have no one to maintain them after their benefactor died?

If you want to build an ongoing charity that lasts generations, you need to start thinking from a Barakah perspective and build a *waqf* (charitable trust) institution that continues to manage and operationalise your charity after you die. A *waqf* is a charitable trust under which an asset is donated to God and cannot be bought, sold, gifted or inherited, and the proceeds of which go towards charitable purposes. For example, you own a property and you donate that property to God. All the rent from that property goes towards building wells or maintaining a mosque - this is called *waqf*.

Thinking about building long-lasting *waqf* institutions is a hallmark of Barakah Culture - one that we have lost and need to revive.

In a paper published by Yaqeen Institute titled 'Financing Kindness as a Society: The Rise & Fall of Islamic Philanthropic Institutions (*Waqfs*)', Dr. Khalil Abdurrashid shares the power and impact that Waqf institutions had in the Muslim world:

> "By the early 1800s, according to one conservative estimate, more than half of the real estate in the Ottoman

> Empire was classified as endowed (waqf). According to another reliable source, charitable endowments (awqaf) comprised an estimated 75 percent of arable land in the area of today's Turkey, one-fifth in Egypt, one-seventh in Iran, one-half in Algeria, one-third in Tunisia, and one-third in Greece. At the end of the eighteenth century, an estimated 20,000 waqfs in the Ottoman Empire had a total annual income equal to one-third of annual government revenues, and perhaps including as much as one-half to two-thirds of arable land."[16]

Can you imagine half a country's real estate being donated to God, with proceeds going to charitable purposes? Or a third of a government's social programmes backed by charitable foundations that started generations ago? As Dr. Khalil remarks in his paper, "Muslims did not wait for governments to solve their problems but resorted to establishing waqfs to meet public needs".

The beauty of thinking about building long-lasting institutions is that you can be very creative about how you build your organisation and for what purposes you want to dedicate your ongoing charity.

The famous Muslim traveller, Ibn Battuta, describes of the glorious breadth of waqf institutions during his travel to Damascus:

> "There are endowments in aid of persons who cannot undertake the pilgrimage... There are endowments for supplying wedding outfits to girls, namely to families that are unable to provide them with the customary paraphernalia. There are endowments for freeing prisoners and endowments for travellers out of which they are given food, clothing, and the expenses of conveyance to their countries. There are endowments for the improvement and paving of the streets, because the lanes in Damascus all have a pavement on either side on which the foot passengers walk, while riders use the roadway in between...."

This is Barakah Culture at a society level - something we need to bring back to our modern societies.

One of the main reasons we're so trapped in Hustle Culture today is that we lost the social safety net that *awqaf* institutions used to provide in a society. One historian described the *waqf* institutions in Istanbul:

> "For many of the inhabitants of the city, it was a cradle-to-grave institution, for a man could be born into a waqf house, sleep in a waqf cradle, eat and drink from waqf provisions, read in waqf libraries, teach in a waqf school, take his wage from the waqf administration, and when he died, be put in a waqf coffin and be buried in a waqf graveyard. It was the waqf institution that fed, educated, housed, washed, and gave medical treatment to the population. It provided people

> with a livelihood and rescued them in times of natural disaster. They went shopping in the waqf shops, they prayed in the waqf mosques; and the physical features of their city were to a great extent shaped by the waqf. In short, life in Istanbul without the waqf institution was unthinkable."

You might wonder why we don't see *waqf* institutions in Damascus or Istanbul or across the Muslim world as described by historic accounts. Unfortunately, when colonial powers overtook Muslim lands, *waqfs* were the first institution to be attacked. Later, when nation states were born, *awqaf* institutions became bureaucratic government agencies instead of a true public philanthropic institution that serves society.

If we want to see the return of Barakah to our societies, we'll need to revive the free spirited *waqf* institution driven by individuals who are Hereafter-centred and think long-term about their charities.

Raising a Child Who Prays for You after You Die

This last deed is perhaps the most rewarding of the three Hereafter-centred investments you can make, and the hardest.

This deed isn't about sending your kids to an Islamic school or Sunday school and hoping for the best. It's about actively raising a child who a) is righteous enough to remember you and pray for you after you die, and b) loves you so much that they'd want to pray for you despite your shortcomings as a parent.

As parents, we can all the recognise the challenges of raising righteous children, especially in a Hustle Culture-driven world. However, our children can be glue that can bind all three of our Hereafter-centred investments together. For example, you might set up your educational project as a *waqf* and have one of your children lead it. Or you can teach your child beneficial knowledge about their religion, which they use to create a *waqf* that helps the poor and needy. Or if you don't have children of your own, you can create a *waqf* for orphans and these orphans become the children that pray for you, and they grow to become scholars and productive citizens of the *ummah*.

Start planning today - not for your personal legacy, but for your Barakah legacy. Start setting up projects, no matter how small, that are long-term, beneficial, and where you'll pick up the rewards and fruits in this life and the next.

PRACTICAL TIPS FOR ADOPTING A HEREAFTER PERSPECTIVE AND PLANTING SEEDS FOR GENERATIONS TO COME:

- **Begin a high-*himma* project:** Have a project that is high-*himma* that is linked to the Hereafter. It could be a project inspired by the Prophetic *hadith* above on the three things that will help you in your grave. Think of this project as a project that will last at least 1000 years. What would it look like? How will you set it up? How will you make sure it lasts?
- **Don't fall for the allure of personal legacy:** Avoid making your long-term projects about you (see chapter seven on intentions). Hereafter is not about your personal legacy, but about the Barakah legacy that you'll leave behind. Think about creative ways to leave a *sadaqa jariya* through the institution of *waqf*.
- **Perform annual reviews and quarterly reviews on your Hereafter projects:** Every Ramadan, spend some time thinking about your long-term Hereafter projects, and see what action you need to put in place from one Ramadan to the next so that you're constantly contributing towards your Hereafter investment portfolio. Perform quarterly reviews of these projects to make sure that you're on track.
- **Make *dua* for your high-*himma* projects:** We often make *dua* for issues and challenges we face in this world. What if we start making *dua* for our high-*himma* projects, asking Allah to accept them and benefit generations to come?

CHAPTER TWELVE

Pray and Persist for Your Goals, Until You Achieve Them or Are Guided to What's Better

Seek help with perseverance and prayer- though this is hard indeed for anyone but the humble.

(QURAN: 2:45)

In the vibrant district of Fatih in Istanbul, there stands a modest, yet deeply inspiring mosque called the Sanki Yedim Mosque. The mosque, whose name intriguingly translates to 'as if I have eaten', is a testament to the power of patience, persistence and prayer.

The story of its humble beginnings is that of a man named Khair Al-Din Efendi. He was a simple man, with poor means but a big dream to build a mosque in his city.

Khair Al-Din didn't have enough money to build a mosque, so he adopted an interesting saving strategy: whenever he would go about in Istanbul and find himself tempted to indulge in the delicious food served in the corner of every street, he would instead put his hand on his stomach and utter the words "Sanki Yedim", or "as if I have eaten", and move on. In doing so, he set aside the money he would have spent on the street food in a box, patiently and persistently accumulating it over the years.

After years of this practice, coupled with unwavering prayer, Khair Al-Din Efendi discovered that he had managed to save a good sum which he used to fund the construction of a small mosque. As word of his incredible journey spread, the people of Fatih began to affectionately refer to the mosque as Sanki Yedim Camii, or "as if I have eaten mosque." It still stands today, more than 270 years later.

Think back to the gardener's equation:

Free Will + Natural Laws + Allah's Will = Outcome

This chapter is about this last element of the equation: seeking Allah's permission and pursuing your goals even when the outcome is not according to plan (your plan, that is). This chapter is about the secret to all success: *sabr* and *salah*.

Let's start with *sabr*. Normally, we translate *sabr* as patience. However, I personally like to translate it as perseverance. Why? Because *sabr* is not passive. It's not about waiting and hoping for a miracle to happen. *Sabr* is about perseverance and persistence with full trust that the outcome is in Allah's hands.

An Arabic poet once said *"Al-Sabr Fallah"* - *sabr* is like a farmer because you work so hard on your land, and it'll be months before you see the result of your *sabr* (i.e. gardener mindset).

> **SABR FOR HIGH HIMMA INTENTIONS**
>
> Traditional Islamic texts describe three forms of *sabr*:
>
> 1. **Sabr for obeying God:** This type of patience helps you persevere in acts of worship, such as fasting, prayer, *hajj*, giving charity, and inner spiritual work.
> 2. **Sabr for avoiding sins:** This form of perseverance helps you resist your lower self and its desires, such as not looking at what's forbidden or resisting temptations like gambling, adultery or consuming alcohol.
> 3. **Sabr for life's trials and tribulations:** This kind of patience helps you navigate life's various challenges, whether they are minor inconveniences, personal losses or major calamities.

These three levels of patience empower you to endure life with grace and be the best version of yourself in any situation.

In addition to the above three types of *sabr*, there is **a fourth type** of *sabr* mentioned in the Quran that we need to emphasise. This form of patience arises from being steadfast on the path towards ambitious goals or aspirations, what we call high *himma* intentions. An example of this type of patience can be found in the biographies of the companions of Prophet Muhammad ﷺ, who went through immense trials to spread the message of Islam.

This type of *sabr* brings a special kind of Barakah – unexpected victory and support from Allah. During the battle of Badr, Prophet Muhammad ﷺ told the believers that angels were fighting alongside them. Allah reminded them that their support would be increased with patience and God-consciousness (QURAN 3:124-125).

> *[Remember] when you said to the believers, "Is it not sufficient for you that your Lord should reinforce you with three thousand angels sent down?*
>
> *Yes, if you remain patient and conscious of Allāh and they [i.e., the enemy] come upon you [attacking] in rage, your Lord will reinforce you with five thousand angels having marks [of distinction]."*
>
> (QURAN 3:124-125)

In the classic battle of Prophet Dawud against Jalut and his forces (David and Goliath), some of the believers panicked when they saw Jalut's large army against their small force, "but those who knew that they were going to meet their Lord said, 'How often a small force has defeated a large army with God's permission! God is with those who are steadfast'" (QURAN: 2:249). And that's exactly what happened due to the *sabr* of the believing force.

When you are trying to do something of significance and importance in life, there's a guarantee that you'll face some kind of set back or difficulty and that you'll need to persevere for long periods of time making small or large sacrifices until victory comes. This *sabr* is a way for Allah to test you and see how honest and truthful you are in pursuing the goal you want to achieve. In another verse, Allah makes this type of patience, a pre-requisite to being given leadership:

> *We raised from among them leaders, guiding by Our command, when they patiently endured and firmly believed in Our signs.* (QURAN 32:24)

Many people, unfortunately, falter and struggle with this type of *sabr*. Especially in our fast-paced, instant gratification world. We often lack the ability to withstand prolonged periods of hardship as we have not been conditioned to cope with adversity. However, if we stay the course and stay patient, not only will we be able to achieve unimaginable feats, but we'll receive rewards for our patience as promised by Allah:

> *Be steadfast: God does not let the rewards of those who do good go to waste.* (QURAN 11:115)

My point here is that we should not think that just because we subscribe to Barakah Culture that the road towards our high *himma* intentions will be rosy, or that God will make the path easy for us. This is simply not true, as exemplified by the life of Prophet Muhammad ﷺ - the best of creation. He had to deal with tough circumstances to spread his mission; he faced threats to his life, physical and verbal abuse, losing his beloved wife Khadijah, three of his daughters and two sons, and losing a lot of his companions and relatives:

> *Sa'd bin Abi Waqqas, said: "I said: 'O Messenger of Allah, which people are most severely tested?' He said: 'The Prophets, then the next best and the next best. A person is tested according to his religious commitment. If he is steadfast in his religious commitment, he will be tested more severely, and if he is frail in his religious commitment, his test will be according to his commitment. Trials will continue to afflict a person until they leave him walking on the earth with no sin on him.'"* (IBN MAJAH)

As you try to seek the Barakah of your intentions and goals in life, recognise that you'll need to have *sabr* to pursue those goals and persist in trying to achieve them, as well as patiently endure the challenges that come your way.

However, Allah knows that we have limited capacity of *sabr*, and we can get overwhelmed easily, hence why He prescribed *salah* as the second pillar of support to help us persevere and persist with goals. Let's explore this further.

Finding Strength Through Prayer

As a human being, you're weak and sometimes cannot deal with a situation with patience and endurance alone. You need external support to help you, hence Allah mentions *sabr* and *salah* together in the verse:

> *Seek help with steadfastness and prayer- though this is hard indeed for anyone but the humble.* (QURAN 2:45)

Salah is a way to recharge your batteries and reconnect your heart and soul to the Divine so that you build the spiritual capacity to have *sabr* and persist and endure for your goals. This explains why Allah commanded his Prophet to stay up the nights and pray; his mission was so difficult that he needed to pray at night to build his spiritual capacity to succeed with his mission:

> *O you who wraps himself [in clothing] Arise [to pray] the night, except for a little - Half of it - or subtract from it a little Or add to it, and recite the Qur'ān with measured recitation. Indeed, We will cast upon you a heavy word. Indeed, the hours of the night are more effective for concurrence [of heart and tongue] and more suitable for words. Indeed, for you by day is prolonged occupation. And remember the name of your Lord and devote yourself to Him with [complete] devotion. [He is] the Lord of the East and the West; there is no deity except Him, so take Him as*

Disposer of [your] affairs. And be patient over what they say and avoid them with gracious avoidance.

(QURAN 73: 1-10)

Scholars and caliphs of the past understood the power of prayer as spiritual fuel, and often engaged in extra prayers to develop the spiritual muscles necessary to fulfil their responsibilities.

Some of the early scholars and caliphs recognised the heavy burden and responsibility upon them, and used to pray extensively during the day. Caliph Harun Al-Rashid, for instance, would perform 100 *rak'ats* of prayer daily, while Imam Ahmad Bin Hanbal would offer between 100 to 300 *rak'ats*. Although these practices may seem excessive, they recognised the significance of relying on *salah* and *sabr* to effectively shoulder their responsibilities.

Contrastingly, followers of Hustle Culture focus only on perseverance and grit as the main ingredient for success, as if grit is a readily available resource that anyone can download and employ immediately in their lives. They don't recognise that our human capacity for grit and perseverance is limited and differs based on one's life circumstances and experiences. For example, a person growing up in a rough neighbourhood might have more grit and *sabr* than someone who grew up in a pampered environment where all their needs were met.

In Barakah Culture, even someone with a very limited threshold of perseverance and *sabr* can access the unlimited and divine source of *sabr* through the power of *salah*. One of Allah's 99 beautiful names and attributes is Al-Sabur - The Most Patient and Enduring - to remind us that we should draw unlimited *sabr* from Him. And the first step to tap into Divine *sabr* is through the five daily prayers.

The Barakah of *Salah* – the Five Daily Prayers

A few years back, I held a retreat on a remote island in Indonesia. Participants around the world joined me for a seven-day retreat living the 'Productive Muslim' lifestyle. One of the features of the retreat was praying the five daily prayers in congregation.

One of the participants admitted that she didn't regularly pray and found it hard to understand why we need to pray five times each day. I asked her if she was willing to join us for the five daily prayers at the retreat since she was with us anyway, and she agreed.

By the end of the week, she was in tears, recognising the power and importance of prayer. She said that all these years, she felt like she was floating in the ocean, but this week, by showing up and praying five times a day, she felt grounded. She understood how the five daily prayers are necessary anchors to navigate her life.

The Barakah of *salah* starts with accepting the moral responsibility of establishing the five daily obligatory prayers in one's life so that your day is structured and planned around *salah*. I have not met anyone who truly lived a life of Barakah without this strong connection to Allah through *salah*.

One of the leaders of our *ummah*, who I had the honour

to meet and serve for a short period of time, is Dr. Ahmed Mohammed Ali, President of the Islamic Development Bank. Dr. Ahmed embodied Barakah Culture, especially when it came to *salah*. Once he was giving a keynote address and the *adhan* went off in the nearby mosque. He immediately fell silent, waited for the *adhan* to finish and then continued his speech. The reverence he had for prayer brought such reverence to him. I've regularly attended meetings with him when he'd pause a meeting so that he could perform his prayers first and then resume the meeting afterwards. *Salah* was such an important aspect of his being that we could see its effect on his character and leadership.

Sadly, people like Dr. Ahmed Mohammed Ali are rare, especially amongst Muslim leaders. One Muslim entrepreneur once remarked how he found it odd that whenever he was at Islamic entrepreneurship or business conferences or gatherings, rarely will the participants pray together when it's prayer time. Everyone is so busy and rushing off in different directions that they forget or delay to answer the call of our Lord.

It's so disheartening to witness how as an *ummah*, we've reduced the value of *salah* in our lives, all in the name of Hustle Culture and keeping up with busyness of life. Many professionals complain that on most days, they find themselves either completely forgetting about *salah*, or delaying their prayers so much that they end up missing them or making up three to four prayers together at night.

How can we expect Barakah from our Lord if we don't have the basic courtesy to stand before Him when He asked us to?

In an article on ProductiveMuslim.com, I wrote how being chronically late for salah delays the Barakah in our lives[17]. *Hasan Al-Basri said: "When salah is the least of your concerns, then what is your most important concern? As much as you fix your salah, your life will be fixed. Did you not know that salah was equated with Success: 'Come to Prayer, Come to Success.' How can you ask Allah for success when you are not responding to His right upon you?"*

If we to want to live a life of Barakah, see the Barakah effect manifest itself in all aspects of our lives and see those intentions that we want to pursue come to fruition, we need to start by establishing *salah* and making it the backbone of our Barakah Culture lifestyle. We need to organise our lives around *salah*, and not the other way around.

After delving into the significance of *sabr* and *salah* in achieving Barakah whilst striving for our goals, the next question is: what goals are worth praying and persevering for and when do we know it's time to quit? We'll explore this in the next section.

What Goals Are Worth Praying and Preserving for?

To answer this question, we must first embrace the following paradox:

1. You need to **believe that Allah is the best of planners** in your life and that He'll guide you to work on projects and ideas that are for your good even if you can't make sense how they connect with your life purpose.

2. You need to **actively experiment** and have a **bias towards action** to try ideas or projects that you're interested in until you see an opening for where you can put in the long-term effort to grow and nurture your goal.

Sometimes, we think we must wait for inspiration to hit us or wait for the perfect moment to pursue a particular goal. But as the Arabic saying goes, *"fil harakah Barakah"* (in movement and action there's Barakah) i.e., we need to have a bias towards action when pursuing goals, even when we don't have complete knowledge of how things will turn out. I've found that those who consistently act on their intentions and goals were more likely to find a life's intention than those who sat on their hands and waited for inspiration to strike.

I call this bias towards action 'following the breadcrumbs'. Imagine you're a bird and Allah places a breadcrumb on your path. When you take a step and eat that first breadcrumb, another breadcrumb appears. You've no idea where the breadcrumb leads but you trust Allah and focus on taking the next action.

When people ask me about what my vision was for **ProductiveMuslim.com,** I share with them – much to their surprise - that I really had no vision; I was just following the breadcrumbs that Allah put in front of me:

- I woke up one morning and the term 'Productive Muslim' **popped in my head**, so I took that breadcrumb and registered the domain name and started blogging.
- I got invited to deliver **a workshop based on my blogs** - I took that breadcrumb and prepared some slides and delivered the workshop.
- I bumped into **a publisher at a conference in Dubai,** so I took that breadcrumb and decided to send him a proposal for my first book *The Productive Muslim: Where Faith Meets Productivity* and ended up publishing the book a few years later.
- An opportunity opened for me to take **a leave without pay from work,** move to the US, and focus on ProductiveMuslim.com - another breadcrumb I took.

If you had told me on that fateful day, when the term 'Productive Muslim' entered my mind, that this would be my full-time business in a few years, I would have laughed because I saw no clear path to it. However, we plan, and Allah plans and Allah is the best of planners.

Some might argue that if we follow all breadcrumbs on our path, we'll get distracted and pulled in too many different directions. How do we know which goals and life intentions to pursue and not just fall for the next shiny object?

It can be overwhelming trying to make decisions on which goals and life intentions you should focus on for two reasons:

1. You don't have perfect and complete knowledge of the impact this decision will have on your life.
2. Moreover, once you decide, you forgo other opportunities that may or may not be better for you.

The indecision we feel can be paralysing, especially when we have a lot of good choices in front of us.

This abundance of choice and accompanying indecision is exasperating in the modern era, compared to previous generations. In the past, we had a lot more limited choices based on our circumstances and where we lived. Nowadays, with a click of a button, you can search for endless options for projects and goals to pursue.

To help you weigh the different decisions and seek God's Barakah, we developed a framework that can be applied to every decision we make. You can use this framework to answer questions as significant as: what should my intention or goal be in life? Or even: who should I marry or hire? It's based on the Prophetic guidance of praying *istikhara* prayer, and it's made up of four steps. The Barakah of this framework is the knowledge that despite all the unknowns and potential outcomes of your decision, you can proceed without regret because you followed Prophetic guidance.

The Four-Step *Istikhara* Process to Decision Making

Step 1: Understand the Decision

i. Ask yourself, what decision do I need to make?

This simple question can help resolve a lot of indecision around a topic.

What is it exactly that you're deciding on? Be specific. For example, let's say you're considering starting a business and that's your life goal. What decision are you making? Is it whether to get into the business? Or what type of business you need to get into? Or the business model you should explore? Choose one of the above questions and be clear on the decision you need to make. This is the first step towards making effective decisions and reducing the uncertainty around a decision.

ii. What's my intention for this decision?

Once you understand what decision you need to make, ask yourself: *why am I making this decision*? What's the intention behind it?

For example, you might realise that you're considering getting into business because all your cousins got into business, and you feel bad to be the odd one out.

Understanding our intentions and trying to purify them so that they are for the sake of Allah helps ensure that you make spiritually intelligent decisions.

iii. When do I need to make this decision?

Making decisions isn't stressful; it is indecision that's stressful – not knowing which way to turn. Setting a deadline will keep you from ruminating – often unproductively – on the decision at hand and force you to trust in your instincts and in Allah.

iv. Which areas of my life will this decision affect the most?

Understanding which areas of your life will be affected by a decision helps you think through ways to mitigate the impact of a decision and/or have relevant conversations with those who'll be affected, so you can better agree on how best to manage the impact of a decision.

Knowing that an area of your life will be impacted should not hold you back from pursuing a goal or intention, but it should help you prepare for it. For example, if you want to start a business, you might realise that the most affected area is your finances. Knowing this, you need to make financial arrangements to ensure that you have a 6–12-month runway to cover your expenses, while you work on your business and craft a backup plan in case your business fails.

v. Which part of this decision is my nafs attached to and why?

This is perhaps the most challenging question to ask yourself because it requires deep introspection and self-accountability.

Your *nafs* has desires, likes, and dislikes, and particular inclinations based on pleasure and pain. As I discussed in a previous chapter, while the *nafs* is not bad in and of itself, it has the tendency to lead us away from Allah because it tends to be attached to this world. Our challenge – as spiritual beings – is to train and discipline the *nafs* to turn towards Allah and not be connected to this temporal world so that it can be successful in the Hereafter.

Therefore, when it comes to decision-making, we need to be careful. Think deeply and introspectively about what part of a decision your *nafs* is attached to and why. Perhaps, for example, you're attached to an idea or project because it was your idea, and even though objectively the idea may not work, your *nafs* narcissistically doesn't want to let go. Hence, you pursue the idea anyway at high costs. Or you pursue an idea because it allows you to go against your parents' wishes and establish your independence, even though deep down you know your parents are right when they are trying to advise you against a decision.

Again, the purpose of this question is not to judge what your *nafs* likes or dislikes, but simply to reflect and understand your *nafs* so you can make spiritually-intelligent decisions.

vi. How do I currently feel about this decision?

This is a quick gut reaction check about a decision. How do you feel about the decision? Don't overthink this. Write down the first three to five emotions that come to mind.

You might realise that fearing a decision is just excitement coupled with a sense of vulnerability. As you think about which intention and goal to pursue, let your intuition guide you.

vii. What are the worldly or Hereafter opportunities and challenges of this decision?

This question prompts you to think of potential opportunities and challenges you'll face in this world and the next because of the decision.

For example, consider the *dunya* and *Akhira* paradigms when deciding whether to accept a marriage proposal from someone wealthy but not religious.

PROS: From a *dunya* perspective, the decision opens the opportunity for you to move up the socio-economic ladder, afford more things, and generally be well-off. Moreover, from a Hereafter perspective, you now have access to wealth that you can use to give to charity, support your family, and fund community projects.

CONS: The challenges of this decision from a *dunya* perspective could be social pressure to keep up with people from a higher class; worrying that family and friends may try to take advantage of you; wasting your time at superficial, worldly events etc.

And from a Hereafter perspective, you may end up having to deal with family members who are averse to any form of religiosity because they feel Islam is backward and not compatible with the modern world. This new material wealth may also impact your spiritual and character development, and you may become more arrogant and treat people poorly as a result.

Every decision opens opportunities and challenges for us in this world and the next, so you must choose wisely.

Step 2: Seek Counsel from People

In Islam, we are encouraged to seek counsel or 'shura' from people on decisions we need to make, even if we think we know the answer or have adequate judgement.

Prophet Muhammad ﷺ sought advice and counsel from his companions, including before the battles of Badr and Uhud. Sometimes the advice was successful as in the battle of Badr, and sometimes it wasn't as successful like in the battle of Uhud, but that did not deter the Prophet ﷺ to seek counsel from the companions, as Allah asked him to do:

> *"By an act of mercy from God, you [Prophet] were gentle in your dealings with them- had you been harsh, or hard-hearted, they would have dispersed and left you- so pardon them and ask forgiveness for them. Consult with them about matters, then, when you have decided on a course of action, put your trust*

in God: God loves those who put their trust in Him."

(QURAN 3:159)

Allah says in the Quran – describing the believers:

> *"And those who respond to their Lord; keep up the prayer; conduct their affairs by mutual consultation; give to others out of what We have provided for them."*
>
> (QURAN 42:38)

When seeking advice, you need to identify people who have knowledge or experience and can give you practical advice to act on. The person should be known for their honesty and trustworthiness and set their personal feelings aside to provide you with objective and straightforward advice.

Step 3: Seek *Istikhara* (Goodness) from Allah Through the *Istikhara* Prayer

The *istikhara* prayer is a special prayer taught by Prophet Muhammad ﷺ that we can make when we have a decision to make. It's a powerful way to seek goodness and Barakah from Allah on any decision you're making.

HOW TO PRAY *ISTIKHARA* PRAYER

- **Step 1:** Perform two *rak'at* prayer
- **Step 2:** After the prayer, make the following supplication:

  "O Allah, I consult You through Your Knowledge, and I seek strength through Your Power, and ask of Your Great Bounty; for You are Capable whereas I am not and, You know, and I do not, and You are the Knower of hidden things. O Allah, if You know that this matter (and name it) is good for me in respect of my faith, my livelihood and the consequences of my affairs, (or he said), the sooner or, the later of my affairs then ordain it for me, make it easy for me, and bless it for me. But if You know this matter (and name it) to be bad for my faith, my livelihood or the consequences of my affairs, (or he said) the sooner or the later of my affairs then turn it away from me, and turn me away from it, and grant me power to do good whatever it may be, and cause me to be contented with it). And let the supplicant specify the object." (BUKHARI)

Although you can pray *istikhara* once, there's no harm in repeating your *istikhara* prayer two to three times, especially if new information and insight comes to you.

Step 4: Take Action Based on What Your Spiritual Heart is Inclined Towards

Many people are confused about *istikhara* prayer and not sure how it works.

After you pray your *istikhara* prayer, notice of the following signs:

- You feel very comfortable regarding a decision and have no hesitation or concern.
- You see a dream that supports a decision.
- A person of knowledge and experience gives you a clear direction of what path to follow.
- You feel optimistic about a particular decision.
- Allah opens insights in your heart of the actual cost/benefit of a decision, so you make the most beneficial route.

Regardless whether we see a sign or not, once we have prayed *istikhara*, we should have certainty that Allah will guide our affairs. Therefore, after taking all the above steps, the next step is to act in the direction our heart is inclined towards and have complete trust that Allah will take care of the rest.

Barakah Culture has this beautiful humble approach to goal setting: it starts with intention and *istikhara*, is fuelled by *sabr* and *salah* and ends with gratitude. In the Barakah Culture, if things go our way, we'll be grateful, and if things don't go our way, we'll have *sabr* and restart until we reach our goals or we're guided to what's better.

When to Quit and When to Persist

When a plan or goal fails, Allah is directing you towards another path. But how do you know if Allah is testing your perseverance and your ability to endure or telling you that it's time to move on?

Put another way: when is there Barakah in giving up instead of persisting and pushing ourselves towards our goals no matter what?

This is a tricky question and it's hard to answer because we don't have knowledge of the unseen.

> *"Say [Prophet], 'I have no control over benefit or harm, [even] to myself, except as God may please: if I had knowledge of what is hidden, I would have abundant good things, and no harm could touch me. I am no more than a bearer of warning and good news to those who believe."* (QURAN 7:188)

For example, you're working on a busines and the business is not as growing as fast as you want - it's up and down. It's not great, but it's not bad either, and you're wondering if you should continue working on it or give up. My advice is to pray and persist for your business even if you're struggling, whilst at the same time asking Allah to show you either success and Barakah in your business or guide you to an alternative path. Only if the door is completely shut for you and you see no path forward do you quit and look for alternatives. In this case, that would be the business going completely bankrupt and there's no path back to solvency.

The Prophet Muhammad ﷺ prayed and persisted with his mission of spreading Islam even though he faced multiple setbacks, especially during his time in Mecca. Allah wanted to encourage the Prophet ﷺ to not give up with his mission and revealed to him the following verses in the early days of his mission:

> *"Then be patient for the decision of your Lord, [O Muhammad], and be not like the companion of the fish [i.e., Jonah] when he called out while he was distressed."* (QURAN: 68:48)

What's the significance of Allah mentioning Prophet Yunus? Prophet Yunus gave up on his mission because his people didn't believe him, and he left his town before seeking permission from God. He left the town on a ship and eventually was thrown into the sea and into the belly of the whale where he spent 40 days and 40 nights seeking forgiveness for giving up early.

Allah is telling Prophet Muhammad ﷺ to not give up until a decision comes from Him. It's a powerful reminder of the Master-slave relationship we spoke about in chapter eight. If something isn't working for you, don't give up until Allah shows you what's better or moves you from your current situation.

THE GARDENER EQUATION

Another way to determine when to quit and when not to quit, is by analysing the three elements in the gardener equation:

1. Free Will: What's the intention behind what you're pursuing? If the intention is God-centred, Hereafter-focused, purpose and impact driven, then you should pray and persist for your goal no matter what. If the intention is purely worldly and achieving that worldly goal would not help you get closer to God or improve your chances in the Hereafter, then you have a choice here of whether you should persist or not.
2. Natural Laws: If the natural laws aren't aligned with your goals, then you should probably quit. For example, if you have a health condition that makes it extremely risky to climb Mount Everest, you need to recognise that the natural laws are stacked against you.
3. Allah's Will: If Allah removes all the means for you to achieve that goal and there's simply no way for you to achieve what you want to achieve, then you must accept Allah's decree and ask to be guided to what's better. If, however, there's a chance that by Allah's Will and Power, something may come through, then keep praying and persisting.

In general, I've found the Barakah effect in giving up things that are ego-centred, and purely for my worldly pleasure (with no Hereafter benefit) and in sticking to things that are God-centred and Hereafter focused.

PRACTICAL TIPS TO PRAY AND PERSIST FOR YOUR GOALS

1. **Follow the *istikhara* process.** Before making any decision or pursuing any goal, follow the four steps shared earlier on making decisions that are God-centred and in line with Prophetic guidance. Check out our *istikhara* notepad on our online store that can help you follow these steps with every decision[18]
2. **Revisit your intentions.** When you have important goals that you're pursuing, renew your intentions for them and check if the processes are working for you or if you need to update them. Seek God's help constantly and pray for Barakah and *tawfiq* in your goals.
3. **Prioritise prayer.** Build your *sabr* capacity by establishing the five daily prayers and any additional prayers you can commit to consistently, especially night prayer.
4. **Follow the breadcrumbs.** Learn to read the spiritual signs and follow the breadcrumbs that Allah places in front of you and let go of the results. Upon you is the intention and effort, and Allah will take care of the outcome for you as He is the best Planner.

CHAPTER THIRTEEN

Remember Death to Stay Focused on What Matters

'Frequently remember the destroyer of pleasures (death)." – Prophet Muhammad ﷺ

In the summer of 2022, I travelled to Istanbul to attend a conference for Muslim entrepreneurs. Little did I know that within hours of arriving, I would receive devastating news that would remind me of the fragility of life. My mother-in-law, Tahira Khala, had passed away suddenly while visiting her family in India.

The next few hours felt like a daze, between trying to console my grieving wife and her family, to frantically trying to find the next available flight back to Dallas so I could be with my children whilst my wife travelled to India to visit her father and close relatives.

Tahira Khala's passing was deeply felt by all who knew her and even those who met her only once. For days after her death, we received countless messages from people near and far reflecting on her selfless and generous spirit, always eager to help those in need, especially the less fortunate.

Her last act of kindness was an invitation to an orphan

named Shahnavaz, whom she had helped and nurtured since he was a child. She had arranged to have his favourite meal prepared for him the next day, but tragically, she never lived to see it. Shahnavaz came that same evening after hearing of her passing and read the Quran for her the whole night.

Even to this day, as we recall her memory, we are reminded of the significance of making others feel appreciated and the crucial need to be ready for the inevitability of death.

The modern world has an uneasy relationship with death. We sanitise and hide death in hospitals and nursing homes. We treat death like an embarrassing failure of our technologically advanced healthcare system, instead of recognising it as a normal part of life. We see death as an enemy that must be fought at all costs rather than a decree that will take place at the appointed time - a window to our everlasting abode.

We've tried to deny, distance, and fight death so vehemently, that death now seems like a far-fetched nightmare rather than a day-to-day reality. Thus, we're often caught unprepared for it when it appears.

Islam encourages a healthy relationship with death. It is treated as part of life, like marriage and the birth of a child. We're commanded to remember death often because it helps us stay focused on what matters and not get distracted by Hustle Culture.

The Prophet Muhammad ﷺ said: "Remember the destroyer of pleasures (i.e. death)." (IBN MAJAH)

The above *hadith* might sound morbid, but it's a reminder that we all need a healthy dose of reality. Hustle Culture tries to convince us that life is a perpetual carnival (for those who work hard for it, of course) and conveniently tries to erase the memory of death from our lives. Islam reminds us that our time is limited, and when we die, our window of opportunity to do good deeds and earn God's pleasure will be closed. Therefore, death in Islam is seen as a motivating factor to do the best you can to prepare for the Hereafter.

This chapter will illustrate how embracing death and remembering death unlocks the Barakah effect in your life.

Our Fear of Death

The caliph Suleiman Ibn Abd al-Malik asked a scholar in his court, "Why do we hate death?" The scholar replied, "Because you've built this world and you've destroyed the Hereafter, so you hate to move from a place of comfort to a barren and desolate place."

If you operate from a Hustle Culture perspective, you'll fear death (or at least feel unprepared for death) for several reasons, including:

- Feeling like you haven't found your true purpose in life.
- A belief that you have unfinished business in this world that you must accomplish before you 'kick the bucket'.
- A desire to right your wrongs or address your regrets before it's too late.

However, if you subscribe to Barakah Culture, your perspective on death shifts:

- You understand your true purpose in life, and you see death as a gateway towards your ultimate purpose.
- You value your time on this earth - not from the perspective of time is money but time is your capital that you need to spend well to seek God's Mercy.
- You recognise that you'll only die at your appointed time, and no one can change that for you. Thus, you become fearless in pursuing opportunities and not giving up until your time is up.

"Why should I fear death? Either it's written for me to die today and there's nothing I can change about it, or it's not written for me to die today so what fear do I have?"

ALI IBN ABI TALEB

This is not to say that people who operate from within Barakah Culture don't fear death - they do. However, their fear stems from missed opportunities to do good and avoid sin, rather than missing out on this world.

In general, most people fall into the category of outright denial of death and don't often think about it, leading to a lack of focus and intentionality in how they live their lives. In their book, *The Time Paradox*, psychologists Phillip Zimbardo and John Boyd talk about how the denial of death impacts how we spend our days:

> *"Death is the end of a lifetime. Denial of death is a denial that time will end. If you deny that time will end you are likely to treat time much differently than you would if you felt time to be scarce and of limited duration. If you imagine your life as infinite, you are unlikely to value time as more precious than gold and more likely to treat it as ordinary grains of sand on a beach. Ironically, denying death relieves anxiety and psychological stress, but it may also lead you to devalue life, so you may live less fully."*

I briefly touched on the term Terror Management Theory (TMR) in Chapter Two of this book. TMR argues that most people make their life decisions from a place of fearing death, meaning that death plays a central role in defining human behaviour. According to TMR, "death anxiety drives people to adopt worldviews that protect their self-esteem, worthiness, and sustainability, and allows them to believe that they play an important role in a meaningful world."[19] Is this the reason we're so attached to Hustle Culture? We see our self-esteem, worthiness, and life sustainability through our jobs and work, rather than life after death, which is rarely thought of and discussed?

The truth is that none of us like to remember death - it's too hard of a truth for us to swallow. Our *nafs* doesn't like it because it realises that it'll leave this temporary abode, where it had free will to do what it pleases, and face the consequences of its action. Also, our *nafs*, like a child who walks into a candy store, wants to stay in this *dunya* because it doesn't want to face the reality of the outside world - the Hereafter.

Moreover, *shaytan* recognises our aversion to death and helps our *nafs* stay distracted and forgetful of death by keeping us busy with Hustle Culture and throwing every form of entertainment at us (the halal and haram) to keep us away from contemplating death.

In this way, forcing yourself to recognise, reckon, and always remember death, is the greatest antidote against Hustle Culture and challenge to *shaytan*.

Remember Death to Combat Hustle Culture

When you remember death, you'll have the courage to break free from Hustle Culture and refuse to be a slave to its tyranny. You'll remember your true purpose in life, and you won't be distracted by the glitters of this world. And you'll free yourself from four of the five pillars of Hustle Culture mentioned in chapter two in the following ways:

1. Materialism: You realise that you can't take much with you after you die and all that you amass in this world won't benefit you if not used or spent properly. You're reminded to give up some of your materialistic wealth to God before it's too late.

> *"Give out of what We have provided for you, before death comes to one of you and he says, 'My Lord, if You would only reprieve me for a little while, I would give in charity and become one of the righteous."*
>
> (QURAN 63:10)

2. Individualism: Death is the greatest equaliser. You realise that no matter how smart, powerful, beautiful, wealthy or famous you are, you'll die and be resurrected naked. All the differentiators and labels you had in life won't mean much. Remembering death humbles you to take off the cloak of individualism and see yourself as a human being seeking salvation from a Merciful God.

I recently came across an article about how billionaires are investing billions of dollars in biotechnology that supposedly will help prevent death. The following verse came to mind as I was reading the article:

> *You will surely find them clinging to life more eagerly than any other people, even more than polytheists. Each one of them wishes to live a thousand years. But even if they were to live that long, it would not save them from the punishment. And Allah is All-Seeing of what they do.* (QURAN 2:96)

Instead of accepting death as the great equaliser, the billionaires try to buy their way out of death, not aware of God's plan for them.

3. Consumerism: Remembering death curbs our consumerist instinct and takes away the pleasure of shopping for the sake of shopping. We become more frugal and spend our wealth not on consumables but on long-term investments, especially *waqf* projects.

> Once upon a time, there was a wealthy merchant who wanted to surprise his family with a sweet gift of grapes. He sent his servant to deliver the grapes with a request to save some for him to enjoy upon his return from work. But when the merchant arrived home and asked for the grapes, his family informed him that they had devoured all the grapes. The merchant was dismayed and left his home.

He went and searched for a piece of land for sale and, upon finding one, bought it without hesitation. He then hired a skilled contractor to build a mosque on the land.

Upon his return home, the merchant's family asked where he had been. He shared with them what he did, stating, "Now I can die in peace. You did not remember me with some grapes that I asked you to keep for me, how will you remember me after I die with charity?"

4. Capitalism: Death motivates you to share your wealth through *zakat* and *sadaqa*. Instead of trying to cut corners and reduce your *zakat* bill, remembering death encourages you to give more, adding more Barakah to your wealth.

When you finally free yourself from Hustle Culture, you'll find Barakah in your life.

Why Remembering Death Brings Barakah

If we want the Barakah effect in our lives, we need to remember death often because it'll be the driver that will make us seek Barakah in all we do.

Prophet Muhammad ﷺ said: "The Hour will not be established until time passes rapidly, such that a year is like a month, a month is like a week, a week is like a day, a day is like an hour, and an hour is like the flicker of a flame." (TIRMIDHI)

Many of us experience this *hadith* in our lives. Time passes by so rapidly that last year seems like last month, and last month seems like last week, and yesterday seems like an hour ago.

Combine the speed at which time is moving with our imminent death, and we feel a panicked sense of urgency that time is moving too fast to get anything done.

For me, this *hadith* is a call to action to make every moment count and fuse every breath with Barakah so that even as time flies by so quickly, we make each hour, each day, each week, each month, and each year full of Barakah and goodness.

This *hadith* is **a reminder that we should not waste our time in frivolous matters** that add little value to our lives, and that seeking Barakah is not 'a nice thing to do' but essential if we want to live a meaningful life.

- Think of the **businessperson who remembers death** often- will they try to cheat their customers, cut corners, not pay their suppliers or will they recognise that if they want to die as a martyr, they need to be an honest trader? 'The trustworthy, honest Muslim merchant will be with the martyrs on the Day of Resurrection." (IBN MAJAH)

- Think of the **parent who considers death often** - will they waste their child's upbringing in frivolous matters, or will they focus on nurturing a child that remembers God?

> *Or were you witnesses when death approached Jacob, when he said to his sons, "What will you worship*

after me?" They said, "We will worship your God and the God of your fathers, Abraham and Ishmael and Isaac - one God. And we are Muslims [in submission] to Him." (QURAN 2: 133)

- Think of the **scholar who remembers death often** - will they give fatwas (religious edicts) that suit their desire or a ruler's preference, or will they stay true to the message of Islam and inheritance of the Prophets?

From the moment we wake up and until we sleep, remembering death helps us remain focused on the ultimate goal of living a God-centred, Hereafter-focused, and purpose-driven life, all in service of Allah.

HOW REMEMBERING DEATH HELPS US ADOPT BARAKAH CULTURE

As you delve deeper into the teachings of this book, it's essential to understand how remembering death can have a significant impact on adopting the Barakah Culture. **Here are four ways in which this practice can help transform your life:**

1. Purifying your intentions: Reflecting on the inevitability of death enables you to focus on higher levels of intention. You won't be obsessed with 'what's in it for me?' and instead think more about 'how can I please Allah?'

2. **Adopting a gardener mindset:** Realising that you can die at any moment in time helps you focus on achieving intentions rather than outcomes. When you liberate yourself from the outcomes and results in your life and focus on the long-term sustainability of your goals even after you die, the doors of Barakah open for you.
3. **Planning for your legacy:** The prospect of death motivates you to plan for your good deeds and establish a *waqf* that can continue for generations after you're gone.
4. **Prioritising meaningful relationships:** Remembering death makes you prioritise important relationships in your life, such as your relationship with Allah, your parents, and your family. You'll focus on cultivating meaningful connections with those who matter most and invest less time in superficial relationships.

By keeping the inevitability of death at the forefront of your mind, you can embrace a Barakah Culture that will enable you to live a more fulfilling and impactful life.

PRACTICAL TIPS FOR REMEMBERING DEATH OFTEN

Remembering death is the 'shock therapy' one needs to snap out of Hustle Culture and embrace Barakah Culture.

The question is: how can we infuse the remembrance of death in our lives more consistently, instead of waiting for us to lose a loved one or a near death experience to remind us?

A few practical tips:

1. **Attend funeral prayers regularly:** Make it a habit to attend any funeral prayer that you hear about, whether you know the person or not. Simply attending a funeral prayer at the mosque and seeing the body carried in front of you is a powerful reminder of death.
2. **Attend burials:** Make it a habit to witness a burial at least once a month. Get involved in the burial if you can, from washing the body, to carrying the body to its grave, to helping position the body inside the grave. That physical experience of washing, carrying, and positioning a body will be a visceral reminder of death that will keep you grounded.
3. **Make it a habit to contemplate death often:** Once a week, either after Friday prayers or some time when you're alone in remembrance of God, sit with yourself and imagine yourself going through the detailed description of what happens to a person after they die as described by Prophet Muhammad ﷺ. Imagine yourself being one of the good souls and what that means. Im-

agine yourself being one of the bad souls and what that means. After your contemplation session, start reflecting on what actions and choices you need to make in your day or week to ensure that your soul departs as a good soul.

4. **Speak about death often with your family, friends, colleagues, and employees:** Make it a natural part of your conversations rather than a taboo subject that should never be mentioned. Talk about your will, how you want your burial to take place, and where you prefer to die.
5. **Be prepared for your own death:** Develop an 'in case I die' file that contains all your important information, passwords, will, and any special instructions you want to leave behind. It's best if you have an appointed lawyer or estate planner who can act on your behalf away from the emotions of family. Prepare for your death so at least your family knows what to do after you die, instead of adding confusion to their grief

.

CHAPTER FOURTEEN

Send Abundant Salawat Upon Prophet Muhammad

"Whoever prays for Allah's blessings upon me once, will be blessed for it by Allah ten times."

PROPHET MUHAMMAD ﷺ

This is the chapter that I looked forward to writing the most, yet I was most nervous about.

Whenever I asked a scholar or righteous person to tell me about the Barakah of Prophet Muhammad ﷺ, they'd normally be speechless and say something along the lines of: "this is beyond me".

So here I am, in my far inferior knowledge, trying to write a chapter on the Barakah of Prophet Muhammad ﷺ. All I can rely on is assistance from God and His Barakah to make this chapter a blessing to everyone who reads it and acts upon it. *Ameen*.

Let's start with our opening story:

A man found himself drowning in debt, with creditors hounding him for their money. Desperate for relief, he borrowed 500 dinars from a wealthy merchant, promising to repay the loan on a specific date. Despite his best efforts, the man's financial situation worsened, and the deadline for repayment arrived with no way for him to fulfil his promise.

The merchant, seeking justice, brought the man to the local judge to resolve the matter. The judge ordered the man imprisoned until he could pay his debt. However, the man pleaded for one day to bid farewell to his family. The judge asked: "Who'll be your guarantor and guarantee to us that you'll come back tomorrow and not run off instead?" The poor man went quiet for a bit and then said, "My guarantor is Prophet Muhammad ﷺ. If I don't come back tomorrow, then be my witness O judge, that I'm not from the *ummah* of Prophet Muhammad ﷺ". The judge was moved by such a powerful claim of guarantee, and he let the man go to his family for one night.

The man went to his wife and told her that the judge had sentenced him to prison. She asked how was he allowed to go home? He said, "I was let go by making Prophet Muhammad ﷺ my guarantor." The wife said: "Since Prophet Muhammad ﷺ is your guarantor, then let us send abundant *salawat* and prayers upon Prophet Muhammad ﷺ tonight and may Allah open something for you."

Together they prayed and sent abundant blessings upon the Prophet Muhammad ﷺ until they fell asleep.

That night, as the man slept, he was visited by the Prophet Muhammad ﷺ in a dream. The Prophet ﷺ spoke to him, saying, "O man, when morning arrives, go to the governor and ask him to pay your debts. Offer my *salams* and let him know that Prophet Muhammad ﷺ asked him to do so. If he doubts you, present him with proof". Curious, the man inquired, "What is the proof, O Prophet of Allah?" The Prophet ﷺ replied, "Tell him that the Prophet Muhammad said, 'O governor, you usually send 1000 *salawat* upon me each night. Last night, you miscounted, but your *salawat* still reached me in full.'"

Awakening with joy in his heart, the man quickly dressed and hurried to the governor's office. Upon arrival, he relayed the Prophet's message to the stunned governor, who asked for his proof of the dream. The man provided the proof shared by the Prophet ﷺ. Overwhelmed with emotion, the governor not only supplied the funds to repay the debt but also gifted the man an additional 2500 dinars as a gesture of gratitude.

The man then went to the courthouse to settle his debt, finding the judge eagerly awaiting his arrival. Before he could speak, the judge revealed that he too had dreamt of the Prophet Muhammad ﷺ and offered the man another 500 dinars to repay his debt.

Soon after, the wealthy merchant entered the court, embracing the man and sharing his own dream of the Prophet Muhammad ﷺ. He forgave the man's debt, insisting he keep the original 500 dinars.

Once burdened by a 500 dinar debt, the man now found himself with 4000 dinars, all due to the Barakah of sending abundant *salawat* upon the Prophet Muhammad ﷺ.

This story is not unique to this poor man or the people involved - rather, it's a story that talks about a culture that deeply revered and loved Prophet Muhammad ﷺ, and made it part of their daily practice to send abundant *salawat* upon him day and night, wishing to see a glimpse of him before meeting him on the Day of Judgement.

Unfortunately, we've lost this deep love and reverence for the Prophet ﷺ, and barely send *salawat* upon him.

Some Muslims might ask: why all this reverence for the Prophet Muhammad ﷺ? Isn't he just a man whom we respect? Why must we go to extremes to express our love and reverence?

This question reveals a deep ignorance of the status of Prophet Muhammad ﷺ and a lack of appreciation for the immense amount of Barakah he brought to the world.

Firstly, we should revere and send blessings upon the Prophet ﷺ because we were commanded to do so in the Quran:

> *Indeed, Allah showers His blessings upon the Prophet, and His angels pray for him. O believers! Invoke Allah's blessings upon him, and salute him with worthy greetings of peace.* (QURAN 33:56)

The above command is so unique because Allah starts with Himself and His angels sending blessings upon the Prophet and then commands us to follow suit. We need to trust there are deep, spiritual reasons for Allah, His angels, and us – as believers- to continuously send blessings upon Prophet Muhammad ﷺ.

Secondly, if Prophet Muhammad ﷺ wasn't sent to mankind, how lost would humanity be by now? The Prophet came 500 years after the last messenger (Esa/Jesus) and the world was in disarray. His message gave hope, mercy, and a direction for humanity.

Currently, we feel humanity is lost, because the *ummah* of Prophet Muhammad ﷺ have abandoned their leadership position in the world. They have let the West and East take over and plunder us deep into darkness and confusion.

Prophet Muhammad ﷺ was born into a similar darkness and confusion, and in just 23 years, he managed to eradicate the darkness of ignorance, idolatry, and tribalism, and bring us into the light of Islam.

When we recognise that Prophet Muhammad ﷺ spent his entire life after receiving the first revelation in service of his mission so that you and I could understand what *la ilaha illa Allah* (No god but Allah) means; what Barakah is; and understand what happens to us after we die, how can we not revere him and send abundant *salawat* upon him?

When we recognise the beautiful character of Prophet Muhammad ﷺ – his family and companions relayed every little detail about his exemplary life, both public and private– it's impossible not to fall in love with him.

And when you recognise that you belong to the *ummah* of the man whom Allah honoured in so many occasions and whom the angels look forward to honour on the Day of Judgement – how could you not send abundant *salawat* upon him?

<u>**Here's the thing:**</u> sending abundant *salawat* upon Prophet Muhammad ﷺ nurtures the love for the Prophet that perhaps you're missing today, and this love will make you emulate him and follow him, which will lead you to God:

> *Say, 'If you love God, follow me, and God will love you and forgive you your sins; God is most forgiving, most merciful.'* (QURAN 3:31)

Maybe you're struggling to truly revere and love the Prophet as he should be revered and loved. If that's true, start by sending abundant *salawat* and notice that love grow inside you.

One unique characteristic of Barakah Culture is how much it reveres, loves, and respects Prophet Muhammad ﷺ. So much so that any attack, rebuking, or making fun of Prophet Muhammad garners such strong reaction from the Islamic *ummah* that it makes people wonder who this person is that's loved by 1.8 billion people globally for centuries after his death.

This love for Prophet Muhammad ﷺ is inherited by generations of Muslims and is revived through abundant *salawat* upon Prophet Muhammad ﷺ.

The Barakah of the Prophet Muhammad

When we study the *sirah* (biography) of Prophet Muhammad ﷺ we can't help but notice the Barakah of his life - peace be upon him.

There are three levels of Barakah we can explore in his life:

1. Barakah in his <u>being</u>
2. Barakah in his <u>life</u>
3. Barakah in his <u>daily routine</u>

Let's start with the first one: **Barakah in his being.**

1. Barakah in his being

We mentioned in the introductory chapters that the definition of Barakah is that Allah attaches Divine Goodness to a thing, tangible or non-tangible.

We can all agree that perhaps Allah placed the most Barakah in the being of Prophet Muhammad ﷺ and everything associated with him.

When he was picked up as an orphan by the family of Halima Al-Sa'diyya, they noticed Barakah in their land, food, and cattle. And when Khadija hired the Prophet to lead her caravan for trade, she noticed the Barakah in the profits that the Prophet ﷺ brought back.

This Barakah continued and flourished during his Prophethood so that everything he touched and was part of became full of Barakah. The city of Medina has twice the Barakah of that in Mecca as per the *hadith* of Prophet Muhammad ﷺ. The book that was revealed to him - the Quran- is full of Barakah and is incorruptible till the Day of Judgement. As his *ummah*, we have the highest share of Jannah and we're the first *ummah* to enter Jannah.

There's Barakah in anything physical or symbolic linked to him - whether it's books, poems, relics, or teaching programmes. A poet who writes poetry praising the Prophet ﷺ would say: I did not honour Muhammad with my poem, but my poem was honoured by the mentioning of Muhammad.

The companions witnessed first-hand the Barakah of the

Prophet Muhammad ﷺ through physical miracles. They saw a miraculous increase in food or drink, so that food that was enough for two people sufficed an entire army, or water that would hardly be enough to quench the thirst of one person quenched the thirst of a caravan. It explains why the companions would almost fight for water that dripped from the Prophet ﷺ when he made *wudhu*, or collected his sweat when he napped, or felt honoured with one strand of his hair.

The Prophet ﷺ simply radiated the immense amount of Barakah that Allah placed in his being.

2. Barakah in his life

If you were someone who takes a dry approach to studying the *sirah* and simply state the facts of Prophet Muhammad's ﷺ life, you might wonder where's the Barakah?

Where's the Barakah in someone who lost both his parents before the age of six, lost his guardian grandfather before the age of eight, lived as a poor child and shepherd in Mecca until his teens, lost two sons when they were young and three daughters when they were old, and lost his beloved wife Khadijah. He was then persecuted, attacked, ridiculed, and called names. Many of his friends and followers were killed, tortured, and exiled because of his message.

Where's the Barakah in all of this?

Despite everything that happened to Prophet Muhammad ﷺ, he was the greatest messenger, the most successful messenger, with an impeccable character that is revered to this day – herein lies the Barakah.

> *"My choice of Muhammad to lead the list of the world's most influential persons may surprise some readers and may be questioned by others, but he was the only man in history who was supremely successful on both the religious and secular levels."*
>
> MICHAEL H. HART, 'THE 100, A RANKING OF THE MOST INFLUENTIAL PERSONS IN HISTORY'.

We see his perfect character in poverty and wealth; as an orphan and as a widower; through sadness and fear; happiness and victory; divorce; the loss of loved ones, including his children and a friend; and dealing with enemies and allies. From how he spoke to the kings of his time, to how he sat on the floor and ate with the poor. From which foot he used to enter the mosque, to how he entered a city as a conqueror with his head bowed down in humility. From how he sought retribution for treachery, to how he forgave.

We literally see the full spectrum of human life in his biography. As a nation, we can refer to his life as a model and guide in private matters as well as public matters.

Think about that: what other story of a person can you refer to when dealing with any situation in your life? Whether you're struggling at work or with your family? Struggling as a child or as a parent? As a community leader or as a community follower? In the story of his life, we find blueprints, wisdoms, and words of advice that are timeless and applicable to this day. That's Barakah.

There's Barakah in how his life was woven together through Divine Love and Protection:

- Yes, he was born an orphan but **Allah sent the right people to care for him** at his most vulnerable time. "Did He not find you an orphan and shelter you?" (QURAN 93:6)
- Yes, he grew up poor with his uncle, taking care of sheep but that **taught him leadership skills** that would be priceless later. The Prophet ﷺ said, "Allah did not send any prophet but shepherded sheep." (Bukhari)
- Yes, he lost all his sons when they were toddlers and infants, but that **saved the Islamic message** from becoming a heredity practice.
- Yes, he buried all his children except one, but that taught us how to **grieve as parents without losing faith** in Allah.
- Yes, he was ridiculed, mocked, attacked and persecuted, but each of those incidences became **life lessons on how to survive** and thrive as a Muslim community when we are persecuted.

Every event in his life was not in vain. It was a not coincidence or random. Every event, every moment, every breath was full of Barakah, with impacts, echoes, and lessons we're still learning and benefitting from today.

Allah mentions in the Quran, “And We raised your reputation high” (QURAN 94:4). It’s amazing how one man is remembered by billions around the world for centuries. One man whose story is passed from generation to generation.

This reverence is not typical for a great man of history. This is the embodiment of Barakah in the life and being of a man whom Allah chose to be the final messenger to mankind.

If you want Barakah in your life, you need to be attached to him through his story, through sending blessings upon him, and through living his example, from how he slept to how he dealt with the major issues in his lifetime.

3.Barakah in his routine

Prophet Muhammad ﷺ is one of the most revered and influential people in history. He was a man whose life was recorded in minute detail, and for centuries people would follow in his footsteps in the way they dressed, ate and slept. Yet, his life lessons are rarely applied to our modern-day challenges, and his routines are rarely emulated as they used to. We’re quick to inquire about the routines of billionaires, celebrities and tech moguls, but we question why we should follow the routine of a man who lived 1400 years ago.

One of the ironies of modern life is, although we’ve progressed with our technologies, we’ve regressed in our humanity. As Dr. Martin Luther King Jr. said, “Our scientific power has outrun our spiritual power, we’ve created guided missiles but misguided humanity”. We think that because we live in the 21st century, in modern buildings with modern amenities and technologies a touch away, we're somehow a different breed or a separate human species from people who came before us, and therefore their lifestyle does not apply to ours, and their habits and routines are beneath us.

Meanwhile, we're obsessed with the routines of successful entrepreneurs and CEOs. Just Google the term 'habits of successful people', and you'll see millions of search results with articles and books on how successful people approach their lives. **But there are three issues with this approach:**

1. **Pseudo-Truth:** We only see the parts of their routine that they allow us to see. And we don't know the person as a whole. (i.e. what are their habits and routines when they are lazy and are having a bad day?)
2. **One Dimensional:** Most of the habits and routines highlighted are work-related routines, and we rarely see spiritual, physical or social routines highlighted.
3. **The 1%:** Most modern-day successful people have had a leg-up on the social ladder. They typically have a solid socio-economic base or live in centres of civilisation that allow them opportunities to prosper. Think of all the successful Silicon Valley entrepreneurs. It's hard to imagine some of them succeeding at the scale they did if they started from the slums of an impoverished nation.

Contrary to the above, Prophet Muhammad ﷺ was:

- A successful person across all areas of his life. Not by my account, but by the statement of many historians and biographers throughout history (Muslim and non-Muslim).
- His life was recorded in minute detail by his family, friends, and even enemies. We see him during his most intimate moments as well as his public moments.
- He was successful despite being born in the "uncivilised" deserts of Arabia (away from the centres of culture and civilisation of his time)
- An orphan whose father died before he was born, and mother died when he was only six. He lived in poverty for most of his life.
- He was successful with his mission despite the odds stacked against him and losing many of his family members and friends due to his message.
- He is loved and revered by over two billion people today and his message survived over 1400 years.

When we look closely at the lives of those who came before us, we notice that they faced the same challenges we face. The challenge of finding meaning and purpose in life, balancing various roles, becoming successful in our endeavours, maintaining relationships, and leaving a legacy to be remembered. They loved, bled, cried, laughed, and lived their humanity, and left us examples to follow. And what better story to follow and learn from then the story of a man who, according to his wife, was a walking breathing Quran (the last divine message to mankind)?

"Fine, but he was a Prophet! Someone special, I'm not special." Yes, he was special, but he was also sent as a role model for you to follow:

> *"The Messenger of God is an excellent model for those of you who put your hope in God and the Last Day and remember Him often."* (QURAN 33: 21)

The Daily Routine of Prophet Muhammad

A few years ago, I attempted to translate the daily routine of Prophet Muhammad ﷺ into a practical guide that we can adopt in our lives so we too can taste Barakah. But before I share it here, a few points:

- Using the word routine might not be the best description of a typical day in Prophet Muhammad's life. As you'll read below, he used to adapt each day to the needs of his family and community and did not follow a strict 9-5 routine. Having said that, you'll see a clear structure for his days (mostly surrounding prayer times) and never was a moment wasted or not utilised at its best.
- The foundation of understanding the Prophet's routine is his famous saying, "I was sent to perfect good character" (*Al Adab al Mufrad*). Every decision and choice he made regarding how he spent his time, who he spent it with, and what he did on a day-to-day basis, comes back to this foundation.

- The Prophet's primary mission in life was to save humanity by inviting them to the way of God. That was his full-time occupation. He was also a father, grandfather, husband, father-in-law, brother-in-law, and leader of his community. Again, keep this in mind as you read about his day-to-day routines and habits.

"And indeed, you are of a great moral character."

(QURAN 68: 4)

Below, we describe the Prophet's daily routine based on a typical day during the latter part of his life, in the city of Medina, when things started to settle down. This is after most of his enemies had embraced Islam, and he was in a position of strength in the Arabian peninsula.

The Prophetic Morning

Close your eyes and imagine for a moment that you're zooming into the humble dwelling of Prophet Muhammad ﷺ. It's almost time for *fajr* prayers, and Prophet Muhammad ﷺ is either awake praying and remembering God or taking a brief nap after a long night in prayers.

Bilal, his companion and African *muethin* (caller of prayer), calls the Medinan community to worship with his beautiful voice and the Prophet ﷺ rubs his eyes, picks up his *siwak* (a natural toothbrush made from the Salvadora persica tree - known as arak in Arabic) and upon completing purifying his breath, utters the words, "All praise is for Allah who gave us life after having taken it from us and unto Him is the Resurrection". He sits up, listening intently to the call to prayer, repeating the words of the *muethin*, and then gets up to prepare himself for prayer.

He prays a couple of *rak'ats* in his home and lies on his right side waiting to be called to lead the prayers. If his wife is awake, he might spend these calm, precious moments speaking to her lovingly, staying present, and nurturing his relationship with her. Perhaps during these moments, he might reflect on what he told his companions: "Whoever among you wakes up physically healthy, feeling safe and secure within himself, with food for the day, it is as if he acquired the whole world." (IBN MAJAH)

When Bilal sees that the people have gathered for prayer, he comes close to the Prophet's house and says: "Prayer, O Prophet of God".

The Prophet ﷺ comes out of his house, looks up to the sky, then says: "In the name of Allah, I place my trust in Allah, and there is no might nor power except with Allah. O Allah, I take refuge with You lest I should stray or be led astray, or slip or be tripped, or oppress or be oppressed, or behave foolishly or be treated foolishly".

Then he enters the mosque with his right foot and supplicates: "In the name of Allah, and prayers and peace be upon the Messenger of Allah. O Allah, open the gates of Your mercy for me. I take refuge with Allah, The Supreme and with His Noble Face, and His eternal authority from the accursed devil".

When Bilal sees him entering the mosque, he calls the iqama (a call signifying the start of prayer) and the companions stand in neat straight rows behind the Prophet ﷺ who then leads them in long, serene dawn prayers.

After the prayers, the Prophet ﷺ spends time remembering God with special early morning supplications, and then turns to face his congregation behind him.

During these early moments, when people are fresh from their sleep and refreshed with prayers, he converses with them. Sometimes he shares moving teachings that make them cry. Sometimes, he asks questions to provoke curiosity and creativity. Sometimes, he shares a dream he had or asks if any of them saw a dream so he might interpret it for them. And sometimes he just sits and listens to his companions as they discuss life matters among themselves. He stays present in their company until the sun rises.

After sunrise, the Prophet ﷺ goes back to his home. He enters his home with his right foot saying: "In the name of Allah we enter and in the name of Allah we leave, and upon our Lord, we place our trust". As soon as he enters, he uses the *siwak* again, and greets his whole family, asking how they are and praying for them. During his visits, he might ask if there's any food available that day; if there is, he eats, and if there's none, he says, "Then, I'm fasting".

He begins his day with gratitude, recognising what a gift it is to live another day and reminding himself (and us) that there's life after death, which gives him drive and purpose to live the best version of himself that day.

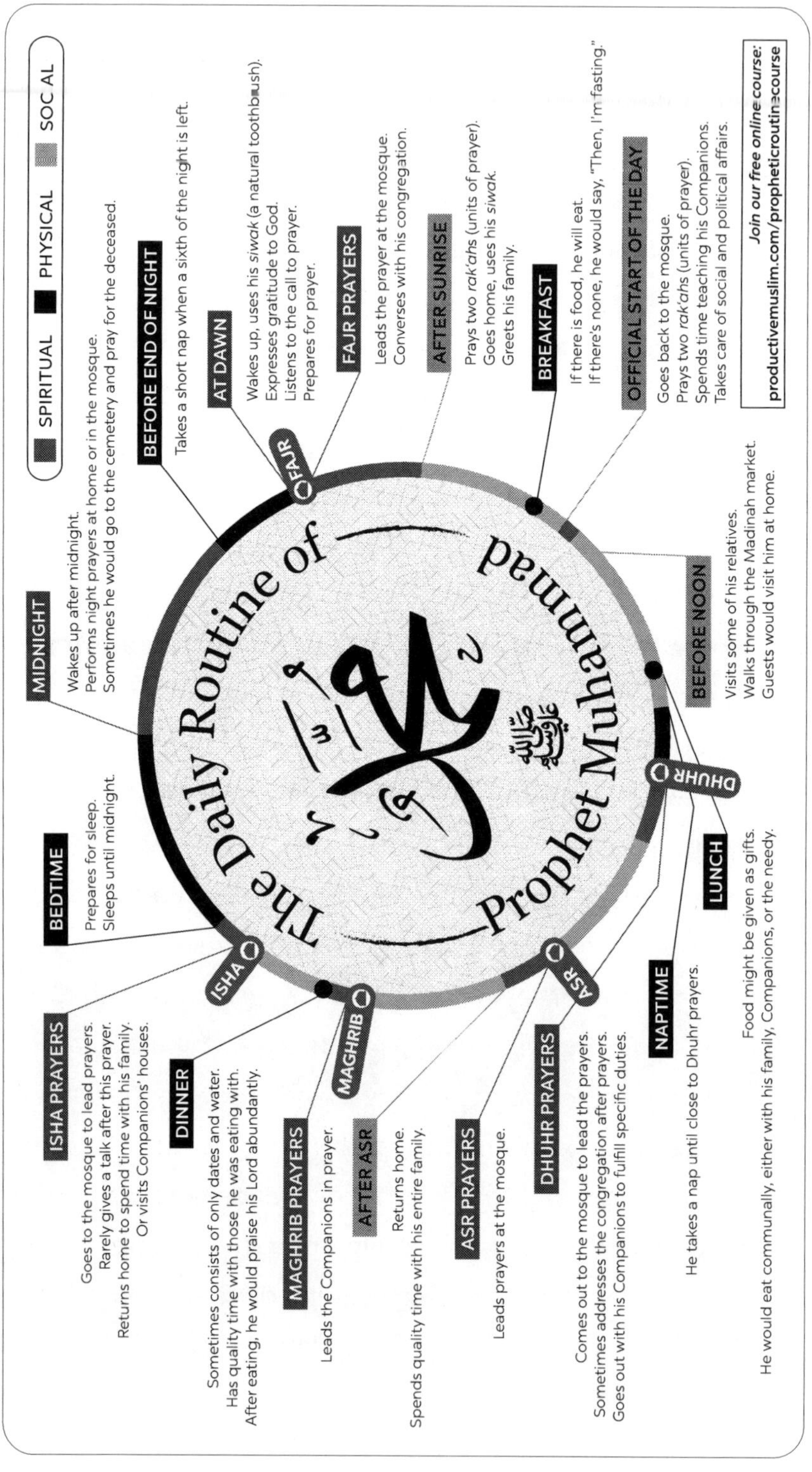
SPIRITUAL
PHYSICAL
SOCIAL
The Daily Routine of Prophet Muhammad
MIDNIGHT
Wakes up after midnight.
Performs night prayers at home or in the mosque.
Sometimes he would go to the cemetery and pray for the deceased.
BEFORE END OF NIGHT
Takes a short nap when a sixth of the night is left.
FAJR
AT DAWN
Wakes up, uses his siwak (a natural toothbrush).
Expresses gratitude to God.
Listens to the call to prayer.
Prepares for prayer.
FAJR PRAYERS
Leads the prayer at the mosque.
Converses with his congregation.
AFTER SUNRISE
Prays two rak'ahs (units of prayer).
Goes home, uses his siwak.
Greets his family.
BREAKFAST
If there is food, he will eat.
If there's none, he would say, "Then, I'm fasting."
OFFICIAL START OF THE DAY
Goes back to the mosque.
Prays two rak'ahs (units of prayer).
Spends time teaching his Companions.
Takes care of social and political affairs.
Join our free online course:
productivemuslim.com/propheticroutinecourse
BEFORE NOON
Visits some of his relatives.
Walks through the Madinah market.
Guests would visit him at home.
DHUHR
LUNCH
Food might be given as gifts.
He would eat communally, either with his family, Companions, or the needy.
NAPTIME
He takes a nap until close to Dhuhr prayers.
DHUHR PRAYERS
Comes out to the mosque to lead the prayers.
Sometimes addresses the congregation after prayers.
Goes out with his Companions to fulfill specific duties.
ASR
ASR PRAYERS
Leads prayers at the mosque.
AFTER ASR
Returns home.
Spends quality time with his entire family.
MAGHRIB
MAGHRIB PRAYERS
Leads the Companions in prayer.
DINNER
Sometimes consists of only dates and water.
Has quality time with those he was eating with.
After eating, he would praise his Lord abundantly.
ISHA
ISHA PRAYERS
Goes to the mosque to lead prayers.
Rarely gives a talk after this prayer.
Returns home to spend time with his family.
Or visits Companions' houses.
BEDTIME
Prepares for sleep.
Sleeps until midnight.

REFLECTIONS ON THE PROPHETIC MORNING ROUTINE:

Think about these first few steps. How do they compare with our first actions when we wake up?

- **He wakes up at dawn (before sunrise) for the morning prayers.** Every successful person will tell you that the secret to productivity and success is to wake up early. In fact, one of Prophet Muhammad's famous sayings is, "The early hours are blessed for my nation" (TIRMIDHI), meaning there are blessings and goodness in these early hours.
- **He's mindful and present during these first few moments of waking up,** conscious of his first few actions by cleansing his mouth, expressing gratitude to God, and intently listening to the call to prayer. Compare this with our addiction to checking our phones as soon as we wake up and the impact it has on our focus and mindset.
- **He begins his day with gratitude,** recognising what a gift it is to be alive for another day and reminding himself (and us) that there's life after death. This gives him drive and purpose to live the best version of himself that day.
- **He's mindful in every step:** entering the mosque with his right foot, leaving with his left, entering his home with his right, and blesses every transition with a supplication or prayer. There are numerous recorded supplications of the Prophet for practically every transition or action a person might go through in a day; from supplications for entering and leaving one's home, to supplications for putting on

clothes and taking them off, to supplications for entering and leaving the bathroom. These supplications serve the purpose of keeping someone spiritually conscious and aware throughout their day.

- **His primary task is the morning prayers and remembering his purpose of life.** What is our first major task? Responding to emails? Rushing to get kids to school because we woke up late?
- **He nurtures his relationships before sunrise,** asking about his family and companions, engaging with them in meaningful conversations (and not act too busy to be involved in their lives).
- **He is easy going.** If there's food, he has breakfast. If there's no food, he fasts. Compare this with the obsession most of us have for our morning cup of coffee or some other breakfast item that we simply can't start our day without.

The Prophetic Morning till Afternoon

After he visits his family, he goes back to the mosque and prays two *rak'ats*. Then, he sits in the mosque, and the companions gather around him.

This is a known time for everyone in Medina to visit the Prophet ﷺ if they want to spend time with him, ask him anything, or need anything from him.

The Prophet ﷺ spends this time teaching. He shares the knowledge that Allah has given him, as well as takes care of the political and social affairs of his community.

This is the time that the Prophet ﷺ also receives delegations from nearby and far lands. Either newly converted tribes to his faith or friendly tribes that do not embrace his faith but nevertheless come to pay their respects. He greets his guests, honours them, and asks about their news and how he can help them.

At these gatherings, the Prophet ﷺ never has a particular seat or clearly marked symbol, to the point that when strangers come to the gathering, they have to ask who among them is the Prophet. Only later in his life did the companions insist on making a special raised area for him, to which the Prophet agreed.

Sometimes food is given as a gift at this gathering, and the Prophet ﷺ and everyone around him eats together communally. Even if the food is little, there's enough for everybody - a sign the companions take to be the Barakah (blessing) of having the Prophet amongst them.

During these morning hours between sunrise and just before noon, the Prophet ﷺ also goes to visit some of his relatives and companions. He visits his daughter Fatimah and spends time with his grandsons, playing with them as their playful granddad or he visits his friends who were sick or those who lost a loved one.

Also during these hours, he walks through the Medina market, greeting the passers-by with his beautiful smile, talking with young children and asking about them. If a person stops him (whether male or female, young or old), he stops and listens to them and sees how he can help them. Sometimes he walks alone, other times with his companions.

Before noon, the Prophet ﷺ goes to his house, and as soon as he enters, he first uses the *siwak*, says *salam* to his family, and prays some *rak'ats* of an optional (forenoon) prayer called *duha*. Then, sometimes if there's food he eats, and if there isn't, he continues his fast if he started fasting that morning.

Usually, at this time, the women of Medina come and visit the Prophet ﷺ and ask questions about faith and rituals, which they might be embarrassed to ask in a crowded mosque.

This is the time when he also helps his family, serving them by repairing shoes and clothes, milking the sheep or goat, and completing daily chores. He also spends quality time with his family, talking, smiling, and laughing with them.

Sometimes, while at home, his close companions visit him at this hour, such as Abu Bakr, Umar and Uthman.

Then he takes a nap until close to the *dhuhr* prayer.

When noon time comes, and Bilal calls for prayer, the Prophet ﷺ wakes up from his nap if he's still asleep, performs *wudhu* (ablution), and then prays in his home four units of prayers before the main *dhuhr* prayer. He waits for the *salah* in his house, then he comes out to the mosque, and Bilal calls for the prayer to start.

After the *dhuhr* prayer, he sometimes uses this opportunity to address his congregation about an important spiritual or social matter. Afterward, he returns home and prays two units of voluntary prayers after the noon prayer. Then, he goes out with his companions to fulfil specific duties needed in the city, or he stays in the mosque until *asr* prayer.

Once he returns from the mosque after *asr* prayer, he

spends quality time with his entire family in a relaxed, joyful atmosphere; he asks his family questions, or they ask him questions, and the Prophetic house learns and grows in understanding of the Divine revelation.

REFLECTIONS ON THE PROPHETIC AFTERNOON ROUTINE:

This part of the Prophet's day might be difficult to draw specific routines from, but consider the following:

- **He has designated 'office hours' in the morning** so people know where to find him and they can ask their questions. If you're a leader and executive, being available and present for your team is extremely important.
- **He naps! The most influential man in history,** the man whose task was to save humanity, and the man who has over two billion followers today, takes time to nap. Let this sink in for a bit. Don't tell me you're too busy or too important to nap.
- **His day is interjected with prayers and more prayers.** Barely a few hours pass in his day before he prays. It's as if he's recharging his batteries and taking a break from the world with prayers.
- **He visits his family and community and doesn't expect people to visit him.** This is the leader of his community, the most beloved and respected person in town. You probably expect people to come and visit him all the time. Yet he takes time out of his day to go in the market, visit the sick,

spend time with the poor. A powerful lesson in servant leadership.

- **Whenever he's home, he spends quality time with his family.** One of most powerful testimonies to his character was that we never hear any family member, friend, or community member complaining to the Prophet saying, "You're always busy! You never give me enough time". How many of us can honestly say they haven't heard that complaint in their life at least once? When Aisha (the wife of the Prophet Muhammad ﷺ) was asked "What did the Prophet ﷺ do in his house?" She replied, "He used to keep himself busy serving his family and when it was the time for prayer, he would go for it." (BUKHARI)

The Prophetic Evening

When the *maghrib* (sunset) call to prayer is made, he goes to the mosque and leads his companions in a short prayer.

This is dinner time in Medina, so he doesn't give a talk or sermon after this prayer. Everyone is hurrying home to cook and eat their meals before the last prayer of the day.

He comes home and prays two optional *rak'ats* of prayer after *maghrib*, then he has his dinner. Sometimes, if there's food, he invites some of his friends over for dinner. Other times, he comes home and finds nothing except dates and water. Sometimes, days pass without any food being cooked in the house of the Prophet ﷺ.

When there is food, his food is placed on the floor for him. He never eats on a table. When the food is brought to him, he says, "*Bismillah*" (In the name of Allah) and eats what's next to him. He eats with three fingers (thumb, index finger, and middle finger) of his right hand. He never complains about whatever is presented to him: he either eats it or leaves the food if he doesn't like it.

If he eats with one of his wives, he makes this quality time for her. He may feed her, eat from the same spot as her or drink from the same place in the cup as her.

If he sits with his friends, the dinner meal always involves a pleasing talk, teaching manners or spreading knowledge.

After he finishes eating, the Prophet licks his fingers and praises his Lord abundantly for the food, no matter how little. He then washes his mouth.

The Prophet ﷺ remains in his home until the call to prayer for *isha* (night) is called. He does not hasten this last prayer of the night. If the companions gather early, he starts the prayer; if the companions are delayed, he delays the prayer.

He would rarely speak or give a talk after this prayer because the people are tired and need their sleep.

Then the Prophet ﷺ returns to his home and prays two optional *rak'ats* (units) of prayer after *isha* (night) prayer. He then spends some time talking to his family and enjoying their company. Sometimes he goes to his close companions' houses and spends time with them.

Sometimes on his way back from one of his friend's houses, he passes by someone reciting Quran beautifully, and he stands there and listens. Or he enters the mosque and talks to whoever is there, as the poor always spend their nights there.

When he enters his home, he prepares himself for sleep, hangs his clothes and comes into bed with his wife, sharing a blanket and a pillow together. His bed is made of animal skin stuffed with fibre, and his pillow is made of similar material – needless to say, these leave some marks on his skin as he sleeps but that doesn't bother him. He places his *siwak* close to his head so that he uses it as soon as he wakes up.

He sleeps on his right side and places his hand under his right cheek, and then recites some supplications before sleeping.

He then sleeps, and if he turns during sleep, you hear him remembering God - as his heart is always connected to Him. He continues sleeping until midnight.

When the night reaches midnight, Prophet Muhammad ﷺ wakes up and sits, wiping the sleep from his face. He takes his *siwak* and brushes his teeth with it. Then, he looks up to the sky and recites the last 10 verses of chapter three in the Quran. He gets up and makes *wudhu* (ablution), puts his clothes on, and starts his night prayer either at home or in the mosque.

If you were to observe the Prophet ﷺ praying at night, you'd feel that he's genuinely immersed in another world and he's in no haste to finish. He gathers all his emotions, feelings, and callings, and pours them into his prayers and calling upon his Lord. He may recite hundreds of verses or spend a whole night on one verse and keep repeating it. If he recites a verse that has mercy in it, he asks Allah for His forgiveness. If he recites a verse that has punishment in it, he seeks Allah's refuge from the punishment. And if he recites a verse that glorifies his Lord, he praises his Lord.

Not only are his recitations lengthy, but his bows and prostrations are almost as long. One day, one of his companions decides to join him for the night prayer. The prayer is so physically demanding that the companion almost quit, unable to continue.

The Prophet ﷺ remains in this state of praying, supplicating, glorifying, reciting, bowing, and prostrating from midnight until there is nothing left of the night except a sixth of it. He then wakes his wife to join him for the final three units of prayer (known as *witr* prayer), and they pray together.

Sometimes during the hours between midnight and dawn, the Prophet ﷺ goes to the nearby cemetery and prays for his deceased family, friends, and followers.

When the night is about to end, and the last sixth remains, the Prophet ﷺ takes a short nap and rests his body until *fajr* prayer, before the beginning of a new day.

REFLECTIONS ON THE PROPHETIC EVENING ROUTINE:

- **The Prophet winds down:** praying, spending time with his family, and getting to bed early. His humanity comes through in these moments. He is tired and needs sleep like all of us.
- **However, he wakes for the night prayer, which is his spiritual way of recharging for his mission.** These prayers aren't a chore or burden on him. He genuinely enjoys them

and finds solace and peace in them. It's as if the Prophet finds his 'me time' and 'self-care' time in these night prayers, away from the demands of his family and community.

- **He is loyal to his family and friends even after they passed away.** How many of us would sincerely remember our deceased loved ones in the middle of the night, and perhaps also go to the cemetery to pay our respects at that hour? If you're a leader, to what extent will you go to show loyalty to those who follow you?

His routine brings Barakah

I've taught the above routine to thousands of people - online and in-person - and every time I share his routine, I get the same reaction: how did a man who changed the face of the earth have such a simple, balanced routine?

A few thoughts:

- He structured his day around prayer times and that brought Barakah to his life.
- He was grateful and praised His Lord abundantly and that placed Barakah in his time.
- He spent the night in prayer and worship, a huge source of Barakah that is known to those who practice *tahajjud* and *qiyam* regularly.
- He was God-centred, Hereafter focused, and present, purpose, and impact driven. Every interaction with him radiated with Barakah.

The Barakah of Sending Abundant Salawat Upon the Prophet

> *Indeed, Allah confers blessing upon the Prophet, and His angels [ask Him to do so]. O you who have believed, ask [Allah to confer] blessing upon him and ask [Allah to grant him] peace.* (QURAN: 33:56)

Now that I've shared the reason for the Barakah of Prophet Muhammad ﷺ, I hope we find it in our heart to send abundant *salawat* upon him for the Barakah.

Sending peace and blessings upon Prophet Muhammad ﷺ is a beautiful way to establish love and reverence in the heart of a believer towards the Prophet ﷺ. Moreover, it is the quickest way to attract Barakah in one's life:

> *The Prophet ﷺ said: "Whoever prays for Allah's blessings upon me once, will be blessed for it by Allah ten times."* (MUSLIM)

Whenever I feel that I'm stuck in a situation, stressed out, or need abundant Barakah or blessing in my life, I put extra effort to send *salawat* upon Prophet Muhammad ﷺ, and I always feel the Barakah of those *salawat* on my life and situation.

Ubayy bin Ka'b said: "I said: 'O Messenger of Allah! Indeed I say very much salah for you. How much of my salah should I make for you?' He said: 'As you wish.'" [He said:] "I said: 'A fourth?' He said: 'As you wish. But if you add more it would be better for you.' I said: 'Then half?' He said: 'As you wish. And if you add more it would be better [for you].'" [He said:] "I said: 'Then two-thirds? 'He said: 'As you wish, but if you add more it would be better for you.' I said: 'Should I make all of my salah for you?' He said: 'Then your worries would be solved and your sins would be forgiven.'" (TIRMIDHI)

What more can a person want from this life than all their worries to be solved? And what more can a person want from the Hereafter than all their sins to be forgiven?

Imam Ibn Al-Qayyim mentions 40 benefits of sending salawat upon Prophet Muhammad ﷺ including:

1. It provides us ten blessings from God
2. It opens the doors for answering our prayers
3. It is a means for forgiveness of our sins
4. It can lead to fulfilment of our needs
5. It is a form of purification of the heart
6. It is a means to repel poverty
7. It's a source of Barakah

I cannot emphasise enough the importance of this practice in our daily lives. If daily practice is difficult, then at least make a point to send *salawat* abundantly on Fridays:

The Messenger of Allah ﷺ said: "Send a great deal of blessing upon me on Fridays, for it is witnessed by the angels. No one sends blessing upon me but his blessing will be presented to me, until he finishes them." A man said: "Even after death?" He said: "Even after death, for Allah has forbidden the earth to consume the bodies of the Prophets, so the Prophet of Allah is alive and receives provision.'" (IBN MAJAH)

Don't be of those whom the prophet described as the miser when he said: "The miser is the one in whose presence I am mentioned yet does not pray for Allah's blessings upon me." (TIRMIDHI)

O Allah, let Your Blessings come upon Muhammad ﷺ and the family of Muhammad ﷺ, as you have blessed Ibrahim and his family. Truly, You are Praiseworthy and Glorious. Allah, bless Muhammad and the family of Muhammad, as you have blessed Ibrahim and his family. Truly, You are Praiseworthy and Glorious.

اللهم صل على سيدنا محمد وسلم

ACKNOWLEDGEMENTS

Alhamdulillah

Their prayer in them will be, 'Glory be to You, God!' their greeting, 'Peace,' and the last part of their prayer, 'Praise be to God, Lord of the Worlds.' (QURAN 10:10)

The final word of the 100-word Barakah Culture manifesto I penned in the city of Barakah, the city of our beloved Prophet Muhammad ﷺ, is "*alhamdulillah*".

More than just "Praise be to Allah," for me, it represents a profound sense of gratitude and recognition of Allah's countless blessings upon me.

Alhamdulillah - I am immensely grateful to Allah for allowing me to complete this book and for you, dear reader, for reaching its conclusion.

Alhamdulillah - I thank Him for His guidance in selecting this topic, maintaining my interest in the concept of Barakah, and providing me with invaluable resources and ideas that have given birth to this work.

Alhamdulillah - I am indebted to the wonderful individuals who have helped me bring this book to life. My publisher,

Sharif H. Banna, and the team at Claritas, who worked tirelessly to review, edit, and publish this book with *ihsan*. My editor, Kimberly Meilun, who expertly transformed my first draft into a reader-friendly version, offering encouragement that this book would resonate with many, *inshaAllah*.

Alhamdulillah - I am grateful for my insightful book reviewers, including Sharif H. Banna, Omar Usman, Dina Basiony, Dr. Khalil Abdur-Rasheed, Dr. Abdallah Rothman, and Ibrahim Anwar, whose unique perspectives and honest advice shaped the book's final form.

Alhamdulillah - for the scholars, authors, and thinkers I interviewed for this book—Dr. Samir Mahmoud, Sh. Tamara Gray, Dr. Khalil Abdur-Rasheed, Dr. Abdallah Rothman, Dr. Meraj Mohiuddin — thank you.

Alhamdulillah – for the amazing Productive Muslim Company community, who shared their experiences with the book's models and frameworks, enriching its content.

Alhamdulillah - for those close to me for their unwavering support. My mastermind circle, Peter Gould and Chris Blauvelt; the dedicated team at the Productive Muslim Company; my parents, siblings, and in-laws, who have always supported my dreams.

Last but not least – *alhamdulillah* - for my wonderful wife, Farah, and children, Umair, Maryam, and Eesa – thank you for being the motivation for me to write and share these ideas with the world. I pray that you benefit from these words long after I'm gone.

Alhamdulillah, without Allah's permission and *tawfiq*, none of this would be possible. I pray that He enables us to embody the teachings in this book and accept our collective efforts to make Barakah Culture a reality. *Ameen*!

ENDNOTES

1 If you want to learn more about 21 sources of Barakah that are referred to in the Quran and Sunnah, see Appendix A for 21 Sources of Barakah.

2 Learn more about the importance of the Islamic calendar here: https://productivemuslim.com/the-islamic-calendar-letsgohijri/

3 Quoted in T. Burckhardt, Fez: City of Islam, Islamic Texts Society, Cambridge, 1992. pp.152-154.

4 Name changed to protect her identity.

5 Gümüsay, A. A. 2019. Embracing religions in moral theorie]s of leadership. Academy of Management Perspectives. 33:3, pp. 292-30

6 If you'd like a detailed description of what each mindset, value, or ritual means, see Appendix B.

7 For more on *istikhara*, including a practical too to help you make *istikhara*, check out: https://productivemuslim.com/istikharahnotepad/

8 One of the tools we developed at The Productive Muslim Company to help individuals and teams practice these Barakah Culture mindsets, values, and rituals regularly, is the Barakah Journal that you can find on our online store at BarakahJournal.com

9 The term "slavery to God" may unsettle some individuals, especially considering the dark history of human slavery. Nevertheless, it's crucial to recognise that Allah refers to us in the Quran as *abd* (meaning slave) rather than *khadim* (meaning servant), and within the Islamic framework, being a slave of God is considered the highest spiritual

position one can reach.

10 See my Chapter 2 of The Productive Muslim Book

11 https://www.youtube.com/watch?v=kireaaq7ip8

12 The terms "gardener mindset" and "carpenter mindset" are used as metaphors to illustrate the contrasting mindsets found in Barakah Culture and Hustle Culture, respectively. Please note that the use of the term "carpenter mindset" is not intended to diminish the value or importance of real-life carpenters or make a generalisation that all real-life gardeners/carpenters adopt these mindsets in their personal lives.

13 You can read the article here: https://productivemuslim.com/how-satan-impacts-workplace-productivity/

14 barakahjournal.com

15 [Article: https://www.bbc.com/worklife/article/20211201-family-estrangement-why-adults-are-cutting-off-their-parents?utm_source=pocket_mylist\

16 Abdurrashid, K., Dr. (2020). Financing Kindness as a Society: The Rise & Fall of Islamic Philanthropic Institutions (Waqfs). Yaqeen Institute for Islamic Research. https://yaqeeninstitute.org/read/paper/financing-kindness-as-a-society-the-rise-fall-of-islamic-philanthropic-institutions-waqfs

17 Faris, M. (2017, December 12). How being chronically late for salah affects your productivity & what to do about it. ProductiveMuslim.Com. https://productivemuslim.com/chronically-late-for-salah/

18 shop.productivemuslim.com

19 Psychology Today https://www.psychologytoday.com/us/basics/terror-management-theory

REFERENCES

Abdurrashid, K., Dr. (2020). Financing Kindness as a Society: The Rise & Fall of Islamic Philanthropic Institutions *(Waqfs)*. Yaqeen Institute for Islamic Research. https://yaqeeninstitute.org/read/paper/financing-kindness-as-a-society-the-rise-fall-of-islamic-philanthropic-institutions-waqfs

Adham, H. (2022, February 4). How Inferiority Complex is Hurting you and the Ummah (and How we can Fix This). *ProductiveMuslim.Com*. https://productivemuslim.com/inferioritycomplex/

Al-Attas, S. M. N. (2014). *Islam and Secularism*. Ta'dib International.

Al-Azami, N. (2022). *Muhammad (s): 11 Leadership Qualities that Changed the World*. Claritas Books .

Al-Badawi, Mostafa. (2016). *Higher Reality: Manifestations of the Unseen*. Islamic Village.

ALBAIK. (n.d.). *AlBaik Story* . ALBAIK. Retrieved January 1, 2019, from https://www.albaik.com/en/section/albaik-talk/how-we-started

Al-Bayhaqi, I. (2018). *The Blessings of Specific Time: Fadail Al Awqat* (A. Ahmed, Trans.). Bardiy.

Al-Haddad, A. I. A. (1989). *The Book of Assistance*. Fons Vitae.

Al-Jawziyah, I. Q. (1972). *Bada'i al-Fawa'id* (2nd ed., pp. 186–187). Maktabat al-Qahirah.

Allah, A. ibn M. I. Ata', & Kugle, S. A. (2005). *Book of Illumination*. Fons Vitae.

Auda, J. (2012). *A Journey to God*. Claritas Books .

Bradford, J. (2019, August 21). 3 Powerful Ways to Secure Your Children's Future (If You Die & Leave Them Behind). *ProductiveMuslim.Com*. https://productivemuslim.com/secure-childrens-future/

Brooks, D. (2020a, February 10). David Brooks: The Nuclear Family was a Mistake. *The Atlantic*. https://www.theatlantic.com/magazine/archive/2020/03/the-nuclear-family-was-a-mistake/605536/

Brooks, D. (2020b, February 10). David Brooks: The Nuclear Family was a Mistake. *The Atlantic*. https://www.theatlantic.com/magazine/archive/2020/03/the-nuclear-family-was-a-mistake/605536/

Burkeman, O. (2016, December 22). Why Time Management is Ruining our Lives. *The Guardian*. https://www.theguardian.com/technology/2016/dec/22/why-time-management-is-ruining-our-lives

Er, M. E. (2008). *The Soul of Islam: Essential Doctrines and Beliefs*. Al-Medina Institute.

Faris, M. (2011, January 18). 18 Sources of Barakah. *ProductiveMuslim.Com*. https://productivemuslim.com/18-sources-of-barakah/

Faris, M. (2017, December 12). How Being Chronically Late for Salah Affects your Productivity & What to do About It. ProductiveMuslim.Com. https://productivemuslim.com/chronically-late-for-salah/

Faris, M. (2018, December 6). Barakah Culture vs. Hustle Culture: How to Win More Days Without Losing Your Soul. *ProductiveMuslim.Com*. https://productivemuslim.com/barakah-vs-hustle-culture/

Faris, M. (2019). *The Productive Muslim*. Claritas Books .

Faris, M. (2020, July 27). Why the Islamic Calendar Matters More than you Think. *ProductiveMuslim.Com*. https://productivemuslim.com/the-islamic-calendar-letsgohijri/

Faris, M. (2021, September 20). How Satan Impacts Workplace Productivity. ProductiveMuslim.Com. https://productivemuslim.com/how-satan-impacts-workplace-productivity/

Gopnik, A. (2016a). *The Gardener and the Carpenter: What the New Science of Child Development Tells us about the Relationship between Parents and Children*. Macmillan.

Gopnik, A. (2016b). *The Gardener and the Carpenter: What the New Science of Child Development Tells us about the Relationship between Parents and Children*. Farrar, Straus and Giroux.

Gümüsay, A. A. (2019). Embracing Religions in Moral Theories of Leadership. *Academy of Management Perspectives*, *33*(3), 292–306. https://doi.org/10.5465/amp.2017.0130

Hafez, M. (2021). *Inventing Laziness: The Culture of Productivity in Late Ottoman Society*. Cambridge University Press.

Attas, Abd Allah ibn Alawi, Al-Haddad, I. 'Abdallah I. A., & al-Badawi, M. (2003). *The Book of Assistance*

Ibn Ata'illah, A. ibn M. (2016). *The Book of Wisdoms: Kitab Al-hikam, A collection of Sufi Aphorisms* (V. Danner, Trans.). White Thread Press.

Levinson, D. J. (1986). *The Seasons of a Man's Life*. Ballantine Books.

Lovering, C. (2022, October 10). Do Words Have the Power to Change Your Brain? *Psych Central*. https://psychcentral.com/blog/words-can-change-your-brain-2#1

Mahmoud, S., Dr. (2019, May 28). The Purification of the Self (Tazkiyat al-Nafs) — samirmahmoud.com. *Samirmahmoud.Com*. https://www.samirmahmoud.com/article/the-purification-of-the-self

Muhammad, G. (2017). *A Thinking Person's Guide to Islam: The Essence of Islam in 12 verses from the Qur'an*. White Thread Press.

Newberg, A., & Waldman, M. R. (2013). *Words Can Change Your Brain: 12 Conversation Strategies to Build Trust, Resolve Conflict, and Increase Intimacy*. Penguin.

Nursi, S. (1993). *From the Risale-i Nur Collection: The Words*. www.nurpublishers.com.

Nursi, S. (2005). *Islam and the World: The Rise and Decline of Muslims and its Effect on Mankind*. Https://risaleinur.com/.

Rothman, A. (2021). *Developing a Model of Islamic Psychology and Psychotherapy: Islamic Theology and Contemporary Understandings of Psychology*. Routledge.

Savage, M. (2021, December 1). Family Estrangement: Why Adults are Cutting off their Parents. *BBC*. https://www.bbc.com/worklife/article/20211201-family-estrangement-why-adults-are-cutting-off-their-parents

Siddiqui, A. R. (2015). *Tazkiyah: The Islamic Path of Self-Development*. Kube Publishing Ltd.

The Atlantic. (2019). Work Is the New God [Video]. In *YouTube*. https://www.youtube.com/watch?v=HAPQnCBnOLc

The Productive Muslim Company. (2017). WDS 2017 - Keynote Address: "Barakah: The Missing Soul of Productivity" [Video]. In *YouTube*. https://www.youtube.com/watch?v=x8mVbLirw3w

Thompson, D. (2019, February 24). The Religion of Workism Is Making Americans Miserable. *The Atlantic*. https://www.theatlantic.com/ideas/archive/2019/02/religion-workism-making-americans-miserable/583441/

Today, P. (2011, August 23). Terror Management Theory. Psychology Today. https://www.psychologytoday.com/us/basics/terror-management-theory

Tsiaras, A. (2011). Conception to Birth -- visualized [Video]. In *TED Talks*. https://www.ted.com/talks/alexander_tsiaras_conception_to_birth_visualized

Zahl, D. (2019). *Seculosity: How Career, Parenting, Technology, Food, Politics, and Romance Became our New Religion and what to do About It*. Fortress Press.

Zimbardo, P., & Boyd, J. (2009). *The Time Paradox: The New Psychology of Time that will Change your Life*. Atria Books.

الجوزية, ا. ق. (2002). التفسير القيم تفسير ابن قيم الجوزية. دار الكتب العلمية.

العمري, أ. خ. (2006). القردوس المستعار والفردوس المستعاد:

.أحمد خيري العمري .*Forged Paradise and Regained Paradise*

الكافي، ع. ع. (2017). قصة ابي حنيفة بركة المال الحلال - عمر عبد الكافي
[Video]. In *YouTube*. https://www.youtube.com/watch?v=kireaaq7ip8

محمد بن عبد الرحمن الحبيشي, م. ب. ع. ا. (2012). كتاب البركة في فضل السعي والحركة.
مطبعة الفجالة الجديدة.

APPENDIX A

21 Sources of Barakah

In our attempt to learn more about Barakah and how to attract Barakah in our lives, we studied the Quran and *hadith* and came across these 21 sources of Barakah.

Our focus has been on passages that mention 'Barakah' (blessings) or those that suggest its themes, such as Abundance and Sustenance.

The list below isn't exhaustive. Therefore, if you find more sources of Barakah from the Quran and Sunnah that we haven't captured below, please email us at contactus@productivemuslim.com. Thank you for your help!

	Source of Barakah		Evidence from the Quran/Sunnah
	Main Category	**Sub-category**	
1	**Good Intentions and Right-eousness**		"And I did not create the jinn and mankind except to worship Me. I do not want from them any provision, nor do I want them to feed Me. Indeed, it is Allah who is the [continual] Provider, the firm possessor of strength." (QURAN 51:56-58)
2	**Piety and Belief in Allah**		"And if only the people of the cities had believed and feared Allah, We would have opened upon them blessings from the heaven and the earth; but they denied [the messengers], so We seized them for what they were earning." (QURAN: 7:96)

Practical Tips to Implement this Source of Barakah

1. Using the **Barakah Journal** (BarakahJournal.com), write down your intentions for your day or week.
2. **Review your intentions** often and ask yourself: what is my intention? Whether it's behind a task, project, or plan for the day.
3. **If you're stuck on a project** or have an important decision to make, revisit your intentions and choose the path that's more righteous.
4. If you find that your intentions are not pure, take a moment to sit with yourself to renew your intentions. **Don't let bad intentions creep in!**

---

1. Always seek ways to **improve your piety,** asking yourself at decision points: is it more pious for me to follow this path or not? The Prophet ﷺ said, "Piety is good manner, and sin is that which creates doubt and you do not like people to know of it". [Muslim]
2. **Find a mentor/teacher/scholar** who can alert you when you seem to slip in your piety and help you make more pious decisions.
3. **Find good companions** who can remind you of the pious path to Allah ﷻ.

3	**Putting Your Trust in Allah (Tawakkul)**		"... And whoever fears Allah - He will make for him a way out. And will provide for him from where he does not expect. And whoever relies upon Allah - then He is sufficient for him. Indeed, Allah will accomplish His purpose. Allah has already set for everything a [decreed] extent." (QURAN 65:2-3) Prophet Muhammad ﷺ said: "If only you relied on Allah ﷻ a true reliance, He would provide sustenance for you just as He does the birds: They fly out in the morning empty and return in the afternoon with full stomachs." (IBN MAJAH)

1. **Constantly say the *dua*** (supplication) of leaving the house since it reminds you to have trust in Allah as you go about to seek His bounties. The *dua* in Arabic: *Bismillaah, tawakkaltu 'alallaah, wa laa hawla wa laa quwwata ' illaa billaah.* Translation: In the Name of Allah, I have placed my trust in Allah, there is no might and no power except by Allah." (TIRMIDHI)

   The Prophet Muhammad ﷺ said: "Whoever says – upon going out of his home (the above *dua*) it is said to him: You have been sufficed, protected, and guided, and the *shaytan* would move aside from him, then say to another *shaytan*: What access do you have to a man that has been guided, sufficed, and protected?" (TIRMIDHI)

2. **When faced with a challenging task**/action/meeting/assignment, do your best to overcome the challenge and remind yourself of your *tawakkul* and trust in Allah ﷻ.

4	**Connecting with the Quran**	**The Quran itself is Barakah**	"And this is a Book which We have sent down, bringing blessings, and confirming (the revelations) which came before it..." (QURAN 6:92)
		Reciting Surah Al-Baqarah	"Recite Surah Al-Baqarah, for using it produces blessing and abandoning it produces regret, and the slothful are unable to recite it." (MUSLIM) "Whoever recites the last two verses of Surah Al-Baqarah at night, that will be sufficient for him." (IBN MAJAH)

1. **Have an appointment with the Quran** every day at a certain time. Respect that appointment just like you respect an appointment with a prominent personality.
2. Allocate at least **30 minutes of Quran recitation** each day, not five pages, or one page or 20 minutes, but a full 30 minutes at a minimum. You want to experience connecting with the Quran in abundance. Uthman Bin Affan said: "If our hearts were pure, we'd never be bored from reciting the Quran".
3. **Commit to memorising the Quran,** even if you tried and failed in the past to memorise it. Simply starting and sticking to a memorisation journey will help develop your connection with the Quran.

1. Make it a habit to **recite the entire Surah Al-Baqarah** in your home or office at least once a month.
2. I personally like to recite Surah Al-Baqarah **when I start a journey** – seeking the Barakah of Allah on that journey.
3. **Listen to Surah Al-Baqarah often** - while travelling, before sleeping etc. The more you familiarise yourself with the *Surah*, the easier it will be for you to recite and potentially memorise.
4. **Recite Ayat al-Kursi** (verse 255 of Surah Al-Baqarah) after every prayer, in the morning/evening, and before sleeping.
5. Recite the **last two verses of Surah Al-Baqarah** before sleeping.

		Applying the Quran	"And if only they upheld [the law of] the Torah, the Gospel, and what has been revealed to them from their Lord, they would have consumed [provision] from above them and from beneath their feet. Among them are a moderate community, but many of them - evil is that which they do." (QURAN 5:66)
5	**Remembrance of Allah**	**Saying Bismillah**	"The Messenger of Allah ﷺ was eating food with six of his Companions when a Bedouin came and ate it all in two bites. The Messenger of Allah ﷺ said: 'If he had said *Bismillah*, it would have sufficed you (all). When any one of you eats food, let him say *Bismillah*, and if he forgets to say *Bismillah* at the beginning, let him say *Bismillah fi awwalihi wa akhirih* (In the Name of Allah at the beginning and at the end).'" (IBN MAJAH)

1. **Use a Quran with translation** for understanding the meaning of *ayahs* along with reciting them.
2. **Create a Quran study group** with your family and friends and spend time contemplating on one verse each day/week.
3. **Make a list of verses which you connect deeply with.** Think about why these in particular affect you. Look up their meanings and interpretations then write down your own thoughts.

1. **Remember to say Bismillah** before the start of any activity, e.g. eating, drinking, opening your laptop, sending an email, signing a deal, etc.
2. **Say Bismillah consciously** – and remember you're invoking Allah's name on the task/activity you are about to begin.

		Istighfaar	Prophet ﷺ said: "If anyone continually asks forgiveness from Allah, Allah will appoint for him a way out of every distress, and a relief from every anxiety, and will provide for him from where he did not reckon." "'And said, 'Ask forgiveness from your Lord; Verily, He is Oft-Forgiving. He will send rain to you in abundance. And give you increase in wealth and children, and bestow on you gardens and bestow on you rivers'." (QURAN 71:10-12)
		Sending *salawat* upon the Prophet	Prophet Muhammad ﷺ said, "He who sends blessings on me once, Allah ﷻ sends him blessings ten times." (NASA'I)

1. **When you have sinned:**
    a. Stop sinning.
    b. Regret deeply and truly for the sin you committed.
    c. Seek forgiveness from Allah ﷻ.
    d. Make a strong intention never to return to that same sin again.
    e. Perform a good deed to compensate the sin.
2. After each *salah*, seek **forgiveness**.
3. Make it a habit to **seek the forgiveness of Allah** ﷻ whenever you receive a blessing or something good happens to you:
4. Make it a habit to **pray *tahajjud*** and seek His forgiveness before *fajr* prayer.
5. Whenever you feel blue, seek Allah's ﷻ forgiveness.

---

1. Have a daily *wird* of **reciting *salawat* upon Prophet Muhammad** ﷺ. For example, aim for 100 *salawat* per day in the morning and evening (increase this *wird* over time)
2. **On Fridays,** increase your *salawat* abundantly, above and beyond your daily *wird*.
3. When you supplicate to Allah, start and end end your *duas* **with *salawat***.

6	**Eating**	**Eating with people**	"The Companions of the Prophet said: Messenger of Allah we eat but we are not satisfied. He said: Perhaps you eat separately. They replied: Yes. He said: If you gather together at your food and mention Allah's name, you will be blessed in it." (IBN DAWUD)
		Eat without wasting	Messenger of Allah said, "*Shaytan* appears at everything done by you; he appears even at one's dinner. When a morsel of any of you falls, he should pick it up and remove any dirt on it, and then eat it. He should not leave it for *shaytan*, nor should he wipe his hand with the towel until he has licked his fingers, for he does not know in what portion of the food the blessing lies." (MUSLIM)
		Eating from the sides and bottom of dish	The Prophet said: "When one of you eats, he must not eat from the top of the dish, but should eat from the bottom; for the blessing descends from the top of it." (IBN DAWUD)

1. Encourage your family to have at least **one meal together daily.**
2. Get into the habit of **inviting people for lunch and dinner** – and try to make it simple so inviting guests doesn't feel overwhelming.
3. Develop the habit of **inviting people you know** or don't know at least once a week.

1. Train yourself to **eat less** and take small servings of food.
2. Truly **contemplate and appreciate** the blessing of food.
3. **Slice fruits or vegetables** rather than consuming whole.

1. **Eat from a corner or small portions** so that leftovers can be taken home/stored fresh and consumed for the next meal or transformed to another food or to serve animals.

			The Messenger of Allah ﷺ said: "When food is served, take from the sides and leave the middle, for the blessing descends in the middle." (IBN MAJAH)
		Breaking fast with date fruit	The Prophet ﷺ said, "When you break fast, you should do it with a date-fruit for there is blessing in it, and if you do not find a date- fruit, break it with water for it is pure." The Messenger of Allah ﷺ added: "Charity towards a poor person is charity, and towards a relation is both charity and maintaining the ties (of kinship)". (TIRMIDHI)
		Suhoor	The Prophet ﷺ said, "Take *suhoor* as there is a blessing in it." (BUKHARI)
		Zamzam	About Zamzam, the Prophet ﷺ said, "It is blessed (water) and it also serves as food." (MUSLIM) The Prophet ﷺ said: "The water of Zamzam is for whatever it is drunk for."

1. Whenever you plan to fast, **check that you have dates** and add them to the grocery list if you don't.
2. Try not to have other items so it **ensures you start with dates and water.**
3. **Carry dates in a small packet** if you are going to break your fast at the office or on the go.

1. **Delay your *suhoor*** as much as possible (ideally before *fajr*).
2. Even if you don't feel like eating before *fajr*, **have a sip of water** for the Barakah in *suhoor*.

1. **If you go for *umrah*** or family and friends are going for *umrah*, get some Zamzam water and make it a habit to drink it every now and then.

Dua		"Anas Bin Malik reported: My mother Umm Anas came to Prophet Muhammad ﷺ and she prepared my lower garment out of the half of her headdress and (with the other half) she covered my upper body and said: 'Allah's Messenger, here is my son Unais; I have brought him to you for serving you. Invoke blessings of Allah upon him'. Thereupon he (Prophet Muhammad) said: 'O Allah, make an increase in his wealth, and progeny'. Anas said years later when he was old: "By Allah, my fortune is huge and my children, and grand-children are now more than one hundred." (MUSLIM)

1. **When you ask someone to make *dua* for you,** especially your parents, ask them to make *dua* that Allah grants you Barakah in your life. It's the best *dua* you could ask for! Don't ask for a job, spouse or children but ask for Barakah in those requests.
2. **Stick to the *sunnah* supplications** during the day and night, pick up *Fortress of a Muslim* (or visit makedua.com) and learn the *duas* that are to be made during different times of the day and during different activities.
3. **In your daily *duas*** at different times, ask Allah ﷻ for Barakah and make it one of your priority *duas* for the rest of your life.

8	**Earning Halal & Contentment of Wealth**	**Honesty in trade**	The Messenger of Allah ﷺ said: "Both parties in a business transaction have a right to annul it so long as they have not separated; and if they tell the truth and make everything clear to each other (i.e., the seller and the buyer speak the truth, the seller with regard to what is purchased, and the buyer with regard to the money) they will be blessed in their transaction, but if they conceal anything and lie, the blessing on their transaction will be eliminated." (BUKHARI AND MUSLIM)

1. **Keep a file in your house** with invoices/receipts of all major items you bought for yourself, your home or business, as well as a file with all invoices/receipts for maintenance you've performed on these items. This will help you give an accurate history of the items when you are about to sell them.
2. For major items such as a car/house, **it's best to get an independent, third opinion** on the condition of the item before attempting to sell it. These professionals may have more insight into the condition of the item more than you do and will provide a more accurate description to the potential buyer.
3. **For items you want to sell online,** take as many photos as possible of the item and be as detailed as you can in your description. This is also part of honesty.

		Earning *halal* income	Messenger of Allah ﷺ said: "O you people! Indeed Allah is *Tayyib* (good) and He does not accept but what is good. And indeed Allah ordered the believers with what He ordered the Messengers. He said: 'O you Messengers! Eat of the good things and do righteous deeds. Verily I am well acquainted with what you do'." (QURAN 23:51).' And He said: 'O you who believe! Eat from the good things We have provided you (QURAN 2:172).' He said: "And he mentioned a man: 'Who is undertaking a long journey, whose hair is disheveled and he is covered with dust. He raises his hands to the heavens and says: "O Lord! O Lord!" Yet his food is from the unlawful, his drink is from the unlawful, his clothing is from the unlawful, and he was nourished by the unlawful. So how can that be accepted?'" (TIRMIDHI)

1. **Before you accept a new post/job,** check how *halal* it is. Ensure that you understand exactly what you'll be doing and ask a scholar to ensure that your role is *halal*.
2. **Remember that if you leave something for Allah** ﷻ, e.g. a *haram* job, the Prophet Muhammad ﷺ promised that Allah will replace it for you for something better. The Prophet ﷺ said: "Whoever gives up something for the sake of Allah, Allah will compensate him with something better than it." (SAHIH)

		Being content with *halal* income	"I asked the Prophet (for some money) and he gave me, and then again I asked him and he gave me, and then again I asked him and he gave me and he then said, "This wealth is (like) green and sweet (fruit), and whoever takes it without greed, Allah will bless it for him, but whoever takes it with greed, Allah will not bless it for him, and he will be like the one who eats but is never satisfied. And the upper (giving) hand is better than the lower (taking) hand." (BUKHARI)

1. **Remind yourself often your *rizq* (sustenance)** is not just how much money you have in your bank. Be grateful for the *rizq* in your health, family, and wellbeing.
2. **Truly understand what your financial needs** are and see the income that covers those needs. If Allah blesses you with more, be grateful. If Allah tests you with less, readjust your budget accordingly and ask Allah for Barakah.
3. **Look at the people suffering in worldly matters** to realise how blessed you are. The Messenger ﷺ said: "Whoever looks to one above him for his religion, and follows him in it, and whoever looks to one who is below him in worldly matters, and praises Allah for the blessings He has favoured the one who is above him with, then Allah writes him down as grateful and patient." (TIRMIDHI)

9	**Gratitude to Allah**		"And [remember] when your Lord proclaimed, 'If you are grateful, I will surely increase you [in favour]; but if you deny, indeed, My punishment is severe'." (QURAN 14:7)

1. **Count your blessings:** although one can never count all his/her blessings, even the futile attempt to count one's blessings will bring overwhelming gratitude to someone's heart and overwhelming humility to thank His Lord who provided to him. Allah ﷻ says in the Quran: ""And if you would count Allah's favours, you will not be able to number them; most surely Allah is Forgiving, Merciful."" [QURAN 16:18)

2. **Stop complaining** and reflect upon difficult situations. Complaining makes us feel the situation is worse. Instead, try to analyse the situation with an intention to see the positive side. Take a pen and paper and write a letter to Allah. Think about your current situation and what you want. The exercise should help you gain greater perspective on your situation, opening up an opportunity for reflection and understand that wasn't there before. Recite this whenever you encounter a difficult situation: '*Al hamdu lillah wa ala kulli haal*', praise and thanks to Allah in all kinds of situations.

3. **Sujood Al-Shukr:** Abu Bakrah ؓ narrates that when the Prophet ﷺ heard any news that made him glad, he would fall down prostrating to Allah.

4. **Allow others to be a part of your blessing.** Do not share the blessings boastfully but share them moderately with others, mostly in a way that will benefit others too. While getting a bonus unexpectedly, buy a meal for a homeless person. If you have knowledge about something that will be beneficial for others, share it with them.

5. **Acknowledge help given to you by others** and truly mean it when you appreciate someone for their support. This helps you realise that Allah has placed good people around you.

10	**Charity**		Allah's Messenger ﷺ said, "Allah ﷻ said, 'O son of Adam! Spend, and I shall spend on you." (BUKHARI)
11	**Hajj/ Umrah**		The Prophet ﷺ said: "Perform *hajj* and *umrah*, one after the other, for performing them one after the other removes poverty and sin as the bellows removes impurity from iron." (IBN MAJAH)

1. Look hard and close at **how you spend your time and money** (your two most precious resources) and ask yourself how you can give some of these resources in charity.
2. Try to find **charity acts that can be done regularly.** The Prophet Muhammad ﷺ said: "The best loved deeds to Allah are the ones that are continuous even if they are not very many." (BUKHARI)
3. Give in charity **what you love and good,** not what cannot be put into use.
4. Try to **ensure that your charities have a human connection.** Yes, you should give to charity organisations. However, make an effort to go out of your way and visit poor people in your neighbourhood and aim to sponsor/help a specific family, taking care of their children's education, or their medication, or their rents.
5. **Forgive your needy debtors** and waive their debts with the intention that it's *sadaqah* for them.

---

1. Make an intention to **perform *hajj/umrah*** every year (even if you can't make it, you'll be rewarded for that intention).
2. Setup a ***umrah/hajj* fund** where you save money for this endeavour only.

12	**Family**	**Maintaining ties of kinship**	The Messenger of Allah ﷺ said: "Learn enough about your lineage to facilitate keeping your ties of kinship. For indeed keeping the ties of kinship encourages affection among the relatives, increases the wealth, and increases the lifespan." (TIRMIDHI)

1. **Find out who your relatives are.** This is an obvious first step, but many people skip it out of embarrassment of admitting that they don't know all their relatives. Have a sit-down with your parents and ask them about their brothers/sisters/uncles/aunts, etc. Draw a family tree and keep a digital copy.
2. **Find out their contact details.** Whether it's a phone number, an e-mail address, Facebook profile, Skype or Twitter ID! You'll probably find it easier to get this information through your parents, but you can also try with cousins, uncles, and aunts.
3. **Get in touch.** If your relatives are using social media, get in touch with a simple *salam*. They will likely be pleasantly surprised to hear from you. If a phone call is the only way to get in touch with them and if you don't know them very well, rather than making a cold phone call, start breaking the ice by sending them regular text messages ending with your name and perhaps a "son/daughter of so and so" so they can recognise you. After a while, give them a call (with your parents around to ease the introduction).
4. **Interview the grandparents.** I'll never forget an interview my sister had with my grandfather a few years before he passed away. It was a moving interview about his life story and one that our entire family cherishes. There's so much wisdom, experience, and lessons that can be learned from our elders. Just sit with them, ask them some questions and press record. No need to make it formal, just sit and listen.
5. **Visit/invite relatives for *iftar*.** If your relatives are in the same city, you should invite each other to *iftar*. If parents aren't keen because of issues between relatives, try to do it amongst the 'youngsters' or the 'cousins'. Then at the *iftar* you can discuss various ways to resolve family feuds and stay in touch with the family.

12	**Family**	**Maintain-ing ties of kinship**	

6. **Set up internet/video chat.** Next time you visit your ancestral home, the family village, or your grandparents house, take a laptop or a tablet and Skype. Find out how you can set up internet for your family there and teach them the steps of making Skype calls/video calls. Once they figure it out, it will likely be the next big thing in the village!

7. **Spend charity/*zakat* on relatives.** Unfortunately, these days a lot of Muslims have forgotten about spending charity/*zakat* on their poor relatives. We have clear instructions from Allah that our charities/*zakat* should be for our relatives as well as the poor and needy in other parts of the world. In fact, scholars emphasise that we should prioritise our charities so it goes to those closest to us first, then to the wider Muslim community. There are ways of doing this practically, including giving through another member of the family who's more senior, or you could sponsor one of their significant expenses, e.g. their child's education or a medical operation etc.

8. **Be the focal point for your family.** If you implement some of the advice above, you'll soon be the focal point for family ties/meetings for your family. Happily take this responsibility and try to arrange various activities e.g. arranging family trips, draw family tree day, family fundraising for an Islamic project, e.g. mosque/orphanage, etc.

9. **Resolve old issues once and for all.** Once things start 'warming up' between relatives and you can see an opportunity to resolve old issues, try to resolve them formally, ideally through a senior member. Try to do it this Ramadan! People will be happy to forget/forgive during Ramadan/Eid and hopefully restart their relationships once again on the basis of love, mercy and *Ihsan inshaAllah*.

		Saying *salam* to family	The Messenger ﷺ said: "Dear son, when you enter your house, say *Assalamualaikum* to your family, for it will be a blessing both to you and to your family." (AT-TIRMIDHI).
		Elders	The Messenger of Allah said: "No young person honours an elder due to his age, except that Allah appoints for him one who will honour him at that age." (TIRMIDHI) "The blessing (Barakah) is with the elders among you." [IBN HEBBAN & HAKIM]

1. a) Whenever you enter your house, make it a habit to **say *salam* loud and clear,** even if no one is there.
2. Paste a **sticker on the entrance** of your house reminding yourself to say *salam*.

---

1. **Listen to them.** Make time and listen to what elders have to say, their stories etc.
2. Make time and **accompany them** for their routine checkup.
3. Decide a **'grand' time** and ask the children to spend some time with their grandparents.
4. Train the children of the house to **accompany them for a walk.**
5. Ask for **advice** or share your worries.
6. Choose a day to **pay a visit** to them or to spend time with them.
7. Volunteering at the **local retirement home** if you are away from the elderly of your family.

13	**Waking Up Early**		The Messenger of Allah ﷺ said: "O Allah, bless my nation in their early mornings (i.e., what they do early in the morning)." (IBN MAJAH)

Spiritual tools: waking up for *tahajjud* and *fajr*.

1. **Know who Allah is.** This is the key and number one tool to waking up for *fajr*. If you know who you're worshipping, and you know that He requests that you get up and pray to Him, you'll wake up.
2. **Sincerity.** Be sincere about waking up for *fajr*, don't just say to yourself: '*InshaAllah*, it'll be nice if I wake up for *fajr*' but be sincere about it, and say: 'I will wake up for *fajr* by Allah's Permission'.
3. **Perform *wudhu* before sleep.** Allah's Messenger ﷺ said: "Purify these bodies and Allah will purify you, for there is no slave who goes to sleep in a state of purity but an Angel spends the night with him, and every time he turns over, [the Angel] says, 'O Allah! Forgive Your slave, for he went to bed in a state of purity." Do you think that such a person would be left to oversleep and miss *fajr*?
4. ***Witr* prayer and *dua*.** Make sure you don't sleep before performing your *witr* prayer, and supplicate to Allah during your *witr* prayer to help you wake up for *fajr*. Remember: "You Alone we Worship, and You Alone we Seek help from".
5. **Read some Quran.** Ending the day with verses of the Noble Quran will sure put your focus straight on waking up for *salah*. The Prophet Muhammad ﷺ used to recommend that we recite Surah Al-Sajdah, and Surah Al-Mulk (chapters 32 and 67) before going to sleep.
6. **Remember Allah before you go to Sleep.** This is part of the first point I made, and you can find all the supplications you need to recite before going to sleep in daily remembrance books like Fortress of a Muslim. You might need to read these duas from a book at first, but within a week or two you should be able to memorise them fully and just recite them before dozing off.
7. **Remember the rewards attached to *tahajjud* and *fajr* salah.** From being safe from being a hypocrite, to having light on the Day of Judgement, to being under Allah's protection the whole day, to having laziness removed from us that day and being productive.

I cover more practical tools to wake up in my previous book, *The Productive Muslim: Where Faith Meets Productivity.*

14	**Marriage**		"And marry the unmarried among you and the righteous among your male slaves and female slaves. If they should be poor, Allah will enrich them from His bounty, and Allah is all-Encompassing and Knowing." (QURAN 24:32)
15	**Salah**	**Praying regular prayers**	"And enjoin prayer upon your family [and people] and be steadfast therein. We ask you not for provision; We provide for you, and the [best] outcome is for [those of] righteousness." (QURAN 20:132)
		Praying *Istikhara*	See chapter 12 for details on the *istikhara* prayer and how it can help you attract Barakah to your decision-making process.
		Praying voluntary prayers – especially *duha* and *tahajjud*	"And rise at 'the last' part of the night, offering additional prayers, so your Lord may raise you to a station of praise." (QURAN 17:79)

1. If you're looking to get married, **take all the means to prepare your personal and financial affairs** to prepare for marriage and ask Allah for His bounty.
2. **Always seek ways to improve your marriage** and make it healthier and happier. Learn about marriage and read about it. Not just before marriage, but even after you get married.
3. **If things do go bad in your marriage,** seek ways to resolve it in the best possible manner. Don't let the emotionally charged situations lead you to inflict harm against each other that'll bear scars for years to come. Remember that *shaytan* is trying to destroy your marriage, don't give him the opportunity.

---

1. **Learn about *salah*,** how to perform it properly and understand that it's a connection between you and your Lord.
2. **Prepare for *salah* early,** as soon as the *adhan* (call to prayer) goes off, and don't neglect it or worse, forget about it.
3. **Carry with you a portable prayer mat,** and always be conscious of your next prayer (especially during a busy day).

---

1. Whenever you feel **you're losing Barakah** in your day, time, wealth, make *wudhu* and pray extra voluntary prayers such as *duha*, *qiyam* and *tahajjud*. This will add Barakah in your day.

16	**Places with Barakah**	**Mecca/ Medina/ Al-Aqsa**	"Indeed, the first House [of worship] established for mankind was that at Mecca - blessed and a guidance for the worlds." (QURAN 3:96) The Prophet ﷺ said, "O Allah! Bestow on Medina twice the blessings You bestowed on Mecca." (BUKHARI) "Exalted is He who took His Servant by night from al-Masjid al-Haram to al-Masjid al- Aqsa, whose surroundings We have blessed, to show him of Our signs. Indeed, He is the Hearing, the Seeing." (QURAN 17:1)
		Quba and mosques in general	The Messenger of Allah ﷺ said: 'Whoever purifies himself in his house, then comes to the Quba' Mosque and offers one prayer therein, will have a reward like that for *umrah*." (IBN MAJAH)

1. Make it a priority to **pay a visit** to these places.
2. Learn and **watch videos** about them to motivate you to visit them.
3. When planning vacations or business trips, see if these **blessed places are enroute** and try to include them on your itinerary.

17	**Times with Barakah**	**Ramadan**	"Indeed, We sent it down during a blessed night..." (QURAN 44:3) The Messenger of Allah ﷺ said: "There has come to you Ramadan, a blessed month, which Allah, the Mighty and Sublime, has enjoined you to fast. In it the gates of heavens are opened and the gates of Hell are closed, and every devil is chained up. In it Allah has a night which is better than a thousand months; whoever is deprived of its goodness is indeed deprived."
		Day of Arafah	A'isha ؓ reported Allah's Messenger ﷺ as saying: "There is no day when God sets free more servants from Hell than the Day of Arafa." (MUSLIM)

1. Prepare **a schedule** for Ramadan.
2. Learn how to be the **best version of yourself in Ramadan** with our Ramadan resources: www.productivemuslim.com/ramadan
3. If you really can't make the most of the whole of Ramadan, **focus your efforts on the last 10 nights**.

It is a day of immense Barakah for those who are not performing *hajj* too. So maximise the Barakah by:

1. Fasting on the day of Arafa.
2. Make a lot of supplications.
3. Recite a lot of *takbeer* (Allahu Akbar), *tahmeed* (alhamdulillah), *tahleel* (la ilaha illa-Allah) and *tasbeeh* (subhan-Allah)
4. Seeking forgiveness of Allah ﷻ.

		Last third of every night	Allah's Messenger ﷺ said, "Our Lord, the Blessed, the Superior, comes every night down on the nearest Heaven to us when the last third of the night remains, saying: "Is there anyone to invoke Me, so that I may respond to invocation? Is there anyone to ask Me, so that I may grant him his request? Is there anyone seeking My forgiveness, so that I may forgive him?" (BUKHARI)
		Morning of Thursday	Messenger of Allah ﷺ said: "O Allah, bless my nation early in the morning of Thursday." (IBN MAJAH)
		Day of Ashura	Ibn Abbas ؓ, when he was asked about the fast of Ashura' said: "I do not know that the Prophet ﷺ fasted any day because of its virtue, except this day" meaning the month of Ramadan and the day of Ashura.' (NASA'I)

1. If waking up for *tahajjud* daily is difficult, make it **a habit once a week** or once a month.
2. If that's difficult, **pray your voluntary prayer** and *witr* after *isha* and ask Allah to bless you with *tahajjud*.
3. One of the **mental blocks you need to overcome** is that waking up for *tahajjud* will make you feel tired during the day. Believing that *tahajjud* brings Barakah to your day would encourage you to wake up and experience the Barakah Effect throughout the day.

1. Create a special Thursday **morning routine.**
2. Aim to **fast** on Thursday.
3. Schedule an i**mportant task** on Thursday morning.

1. Fast on the day of **Ashura**.
2. Fast the **previous or the next** day of Ashura.

		Time between *adhan* and *iqama*	"The supplication made between the *adhan* and the *iqama* is not rejected. (IBN DAWUD)
		Rain	The Prophet ﷺ said: "Two (prayers) are not rejected, or seldom rejected: Prayer at the time of the call to prayer, and (the prayer) at the time of fighting, when the people grapple with each other." Musa ﷺ said: Rizq ibn Sa'id ibn AbdurRahman reported from AbuHazim on the authority of Sahl ibn Sa'd ﷺ from the Prophet ﷺ as saying: And while it is raining. (IBN DAWUD)
18	**Avoiding Sins**		Messenger of Allah ﷺ said: "Nothing increases one's life span except righteousness and nothing repels the Divine decree except supplication, and a man may be deprived of provision by a sin that he commits." (IBN MAJAH)

1. Say the ***dua*** after the call to prayer.
2. Send ***salawat*** to Prophet Muhammad peace be upon him.
3. **Recite:** *Rabbana aathina fidunya hasanathan, wa fil akhirathi hasanathan, waqina adhaban naar.*
4. Dedicate this time for **supplication**.

---

1. Narrated Aisha رضي الله عنها: Whenever Allah's Messenger ﷺ saw the rain, he used to say, "O Allah! Let it be a strong fruitful rain." (BUKHARI)
2. Seek forgiveness of Allah سبحانه وتعالى.
3. Ask Allah سبحانه وتعالى for what you want.

---

1. **Seek forgiveness** of Allah سبحانه وتعالى often.
2. **Stop blaming others** or your circumstances for committing sins and take responsibility of your wrongdoings.
3. **Don't 'normalise' sin** in your life and accept it as a part of modern life. Acknowledge it as a sin and work towards avoiding it.
4. **Identify the sins that you often commit.** Understand the temptations and the personal trait/situation which lead to those sins.
5. **Seek help from Allah** سبحانه وتعالى to protect you from your sins and if you do commit, to give you the courage and sincerity to seek His forgiveness.

19	**Seeking Beneficial Knowledge**	**Seeking Knowl-edge**	"... Allah will raise those who have believed among you and those who were given knowledge, by degrees..." (QURAN 58:11)
		Knowl-edge of religion	"If Allah ﷻ wants to do good to a person, He makes him comprehend the religion..." (BUKHARI)
		Sup-porting/ spending time with persons seeking knowl-edge	"There were two broth-ers (that lived) at the time of the Prophet ﷺ. One of them would come to Prophet, whereas the other one would seek his sustenance (by working). So the one who used to seek his sustenance complained to the Proph-et about his brother. The Prophet replied, 'It is pos-sible that you are provid-ed your *rizq* because of him'." (TIRMIDHI)

1. **Recite this dua often:** *Rabbi zidni ilma* (O my Lord, increase me in knowledge) (QURAN 20:114)
2. Find **areas you're struggling with** and seek knowledge in those areas.
3. Listen to the old and young, the rich and poor. **Everyone can teach you something.**
4. Develop **a habit of reading.**
5. **Share your knowledge** with others.

1. Develop **a life-long relationship with a scholar/ sheikh** who can be your spiritual mentor and guide to seeking Islamic knowledge.
2. In the absence of a scholar/sheikh, create **a small *halaqa* in your locality** where you seek knowledge of religion together and cover books, lectures, or discuss religious concepts.

1. **Sponsor a student** with their tuition fees.
2. Purchase school **supplies** for students.
3. Volunteer to **tutor/mentor** students.
4. Work as a **teaching assistant.**

20	**Plants/ Trees**	**Date Palm Tree**	"While we were sitting with the Prophet ﷺ, fresh dates were brought to him. The Prophet said, 'There is a tree among the trees which is as blessed as a Muslim'. I thought that it was the date palm tree and intended to say, 'It is the date-palm tree, O Allah's Messenger!' But I looked behind to see that I was the tenth and youngest of ten men present there, so I kept quiet. Then the Prophet said, 'It is the date palm tree'." (BUKHARI)

1. **Plant date trees** in your garden so it reminds you of a believer.
2. If date trees don't grow normally in your area, you can **plant a small indoor or outdoor palm tree.**

21	**Helping People**	**Help others**	The Messenger of Allah ﷺ "Whoever relieves the hardship of a believer in this world, Allah will relieve his hardship on the Day of Resurrection. Whoever helps ease someone in difficulty, Allah will make it easy for him in this world and in the Hereafter. Whoever covers the faults of a Muslim, Allah will cover his faults in this world and in the Hereafter. Allah helps the servant as long as he helps his brother. Whoever travels a path in search of knowledge, Allah will make easy for him a path to Paradise, for a people do not gather together in the houses of Allah, reciting the Book of Allah and studying together, except that tranquility will descend upon them, mercy will cover them, angels will surround them, and Allah will mention them to those with Him. Whoever is slow to good deeds will not be hastened by his lineage." (MUSLIM)

1. If someone sought you for help while you're busy, **do not turn them down.** When you help them, Allah will in turn facilitate your affairs for you.
2. Be **attentive to the needs** of the people around you and offer help whenever possible.
3. **Volunteer in support groups/NGOs/charities** that introduce you to cases of people who need help and be engaged in helping other with whatever is within in your capacity.
4. Participate in **fundraising efforts,** even with a little money.
5. Register your name at a **blood bank** and donate blood.
6. **Talk to the homeless people** you find on your travels and provide moral support. Just smiling and asking 'how are you?' can make someone's day.
7. **Give away gently used clothes,** toys, and furniture to those in need.
8. **Conduct collection drives for food,** clothes, books etc. and donate it to community centers, countries hit by disasters and wars etc.
9. Pay a visit to the nearest **community centre or shelter home** and spend time with them.
10. **Visit an elderly centre** and help the elderly in their daily chores.
11. When you cook dinner, make it a plan to make extra so you **can donate it to a homeless person.**

21	**Helping People**	**Help others**	Allah's Messenger ﷺ said, "A Muslim is a brother of another Muslim. So he should neither oppress him nor hand him over to an oppressor. And whoever fulfilled the needs of his brother, Allah will fulfill his needs." (BUKHARI)
		Helping the weak in society	Messenger of Allah ﷺ said: "Bring me the weak, for you only receive provision and Divine support by virtue of your weak ones." (NASA'I)

APPENDIX B

Barakah Culture Values, Mindsets, and Rituals

	Value	Arabic	Description
1	Mercy & Compassion	الرحمة	To be merciful and compassionate towards yourself and others.
2	Peace	السلام	To have inner peace and be a source of peace - not fear/stress - for others.
3	Truthfulness	الصدق/ السعي للحق	To be truthful with yourself, and in your intentions, words, and actions. To avoid lying to yourself or others.
4	Family	الأهل/ الأرحام	To prioritise and give due time, attention, and support to family: parents, spouse, children, and next of kin.
5	Modesty & Concealment	الحَيَاء والسِتر	To embody modesty and cover the faults and flaws of others.

6	Beauty	الجمال	To beautify your thoughts, heart, words, actions, and relationships.
7	Justice	القسط والعدل	To speak and act justly even if against yourself.
8	Generosity	الكرم	To give others from your time, wealth, knowledge, and experience (and expect nothing in return).
9	Excellence	الإحسان	To seek excellence in thoughts, words, and actions by recognising that Allah sees you even if you don't see Him.
10	Strength	القوة	To seek spiritual, physical, intellectual, and all forms of strength and use that for the sake of Allah, not to harm/oppress others.
11	Uprightness	الرشد	To do what's right morally, ethically, and honestly in all situations.
12	Trustworthiness	الأمانة	To consistently fulfill your promises, contracts, and trusts on time and to the best of your ability.
13	Easiness	السهولة واللين	To be easy, down-to-earth, and approachable.

14	Moderation	الاعتدال/ الاقتصاد	To avoid excessiveness in all matters and seek the middle path.
15	Gentleness	الرِفق	To be gentle in words and actions.
16	Teamwork & Cooperation	التعاون	To help and work well with others for the sake of a greater good.
17	Responsibility	المسؤولية	To take responsibility for your actions and not blame others.

	Mindset	Arabic	Description
18	Forbearance & Forgiveness	الحِلم والمغفرة	To exercise patience especially when others do wrong or are difficult to deal with.
19	God-Consciousness	التقوى	To be conscious of Allah, and act accordingly.
20	Humbleness to Allah	التواضع لله	To realise that your skills/talents are gifts from Allah, so you tame your ego when successes are achieved.
21	Contentment	الرضا	To be pleased with what you already have and the decree of Allah when it occurs (whether good or bad).

22	Beautiful Patience & Perseverance	صبر جميل	To persevere in challenging situations and turn them into positive experiences.
23	Reliance upon Allah	التوكل على الله	To trust Allah and rely upon Him in all matters.
24	Consistency	المداومة	To commit to doing consistent actions and habits - even if they're small.
25	Hereafter-focused	السعي للآخرة	To always work for the eternal afterlife and consider the *akhirah* - outcome of actions
26	Gratefulness	الشكر	To be mindfully grateful to Allah for the seen and hidden blessings, favours and opportunities, and grateful to people around you.
27	Steadfast-ness upon the Truth	الثبات على الحق	To not fear the truth and its outcomes. To stand firm for the values you believe in.
28	Love for the Sake of Allah	الحب في الله	To see the good in people and love them purely for the sake of Allah.
29	Purpose & Impact-Driven	التركيز على الغاية والأثر	To be driven by higher purpose and impact, not solely for short-term results.

30	Abundance	السعة	To recognise that blessings and bounties are from Allah, and His Kingdom and blessings are infinite and limitless.
31	Introspection and Self-accountability	التفكر والمحاسبة	To regularly reflect on your words and actions and how they could be better.
32	Presence	الحضور	To be present mindfully in order to connect deeply with others.
33	Intentionality	استحضار وتجديد النية	To remember the intentions behind your actions and renew your intentions often.
34	Taking Initiative	الإقدام والسبق في الخير	To take initiative in what is beneficial for you in this life and the next, and not hesitate or delay good words or actions.

	Ritual	Arabic	Description
35	Consult Allah & Others	استشارة واستخارة	To consult Allah through the *istikhara* prayer, and seek counsel from relevant people.
36	Seek Beneficial Knowledge	طلب العلم	To commit to lifelong learning, seeking beneficial knowledge as an act of worship.

37	**Making *Dua***	دعاء	To make *dua* and ask Allah for help in your daily affairs (big or small).
38	**Keeping Ties of Kinship**	صلة الرحم	To exert sincere effort to remain in touch with your relatives.
39	**Eating with People**	مشاركة الطعام مع الناس	To seek the blessing of eating and sharing your meals with people, and to never eat alone.
40	**Remembrance of Allah**	ذكر الله	To remember Allah daily and in all prescribed timings/situations.
41	**Reconciliation**	الإصلاح	To work on making things right between people who are in disagreement.
42	***Tawbah* & Constant Returning to Allah**	التوبة والإنابة	To come back humbly to Allah and repent regularly for our sins.
43	**Praiseworthy Planning**	التخطيط المحمود	To link good intentions to your plans and have complete trust in Allah in the results.
44	**Charity**	الصدقة	To be charitable and give abundantly, generously, and consistently without fear of loss.

45	Salah	الصلاة	To prioritise *salah* (obligatory/voluntary) with calmness, tranquility, and presence throughout the day.
46	Reciting Quran	قراءة القرآن	To spend quality time with the Quran despite a busy schedule and overwhelming responsibilities.
47	Waking up Early	الاستيقاظ مبكرًا	To seize the Barakah in the early hours by starting the day early.
48	Lowering the Gaze	غض البصر	To protect your heart by mastering your gaze and not directing it at anything which is unlawful.
49	Controlling the Tongue	إمساك اللسان	To think before speaking and speak only when speech is better than silence.
50	Helping People	مساعدة الناس	To be conscious of people's needs and hasten to lend a helping hand before you are asked.
51	Sending Blessings upon Proph-et Muham-mad ﷺ	الصلاة على النبي صلى الله عليه وسلم	To send abundant *salawat* upon the Prophet ﷺ daily.

Made in the USA
Las Vegas, NV
27 September 2024

4434a66a-201a-4c1c-8597-1a4cee586ad5R01